EAT YOUR GREENS

EAT YOUR GREENS

FACT-BASED THINKING TO IMPROVE YOUR BRAND'S HEALTH

Edited by

Wiemer Snijders

Matador
9 Priory Business Park,
Wistow Road, Kibworth Beauchamp,
Leicestershire. LE8 0RX

Tel: 0116 279 2299
Email: books@troubador.co.uk
Web: www.troubador.co.uk/matador
Twitter: @matadorbooks

ISBN 978 1789016 758

British Library Cataloguing in Publication Data.
A catalogue record for this book is available from the British Library.

Printed and bound by CPI Group (UK) Ltd, Croydon, CR0 4YY
Typeset in 10pt Gill Sans by 4word, Bristol, UK

Matador is an imprint of Troubador Publishing Ltd

MIX
Paper from
responsible sources
FSC® C013604

CONTENTS

FOREWORD

Stimulating better thinking

Eat Your Greens is an eclectically excellent collection of papers by some of the best thinkers and practitioners in marketing and communications. But the apparently eclectic nature of the contributions belies the seriousness of the endeavour, which is to bring together a body of evidence-based thinking in one useful and inspiring reference book.

The original idea for the book is Wiemer Snijders'. The APG got involved part of the way through the project because we were keen to support the idea of bringing evidence-based thinking closer to the heart of creative strategy. While the world we occupy is apparently awash with data and facts, it is as hard as ever to find rigorous analysis combined with practical prescription, and in a form that is usable and stimulates better thinking.

Encouraging creative thinking and fuelling effective creativity are a fundamental part of the APG's purpose. The last few years have seen a number of real advances in thinking about how creativity works, and how to plan for successful communications. These ideas have taken root precisely because they are based on thoughtful interpretation of data collected carefully, and applied with understanding and flair.

The contributors cover a broad and diverse selection of subjects, but they are united by passionate personal interest and great intelligence, and cover many of the things that are uppermost in our minds as strategists: long versus short-term thinking; the fallacies of an obsession with communications and digital toys; brand equity; a female future, and so much more.

We'd like to thank all the contributors for their 'greens'. We find the analogy rather delightful, and I should say that it's the very best of freshly prepared and high quality intellectual produce that appears in the book. We'd also like to thank Wiemer for his unfathomable wells of energy, and all of you for embracing the idea that fact-based thinking has the power to create change and nurture the best of creativity.

Sarah Newman
Director, APG

INTRODUCTION

There is an abundance of data and technology available to better understand the people to whom we are selling our products and services. However, it is useless if we don't know how to use it effectively.

Progressively, this industry relies on short-term metrics, as they produce instant feedback. But we seem to have forgotten that the business of building brands is also a long game. It is one thing to measure whether someone has clicked on your ad, but the true effect of advertising is something you might have to wait several years for to effectuate. As marketing analyst Daniel Yankelovich described, disregarding what cannot be easily measured in favour of measures that do is artificial and misleading. But the ultimate step is to say that what can't easily be measured really doesn't exist – which he considered suicide.

We also seem infatuated with metrics and tactics that have little relation to our actual buying behaviour. Things like tweets, buyer personas, NPS ('Net Promoter Scores') and engagement rates. We convince ourselves that, with enough multivariate analyses (emphasising small differences over similarities) and significance tests (flagging differences where there aren't any), we will get a better grip on people's purchasing behaviour. Unfortunately, these things are mostly figments; cast on our office walls by projectors, flip charts and sticky notes.

So, if marketing is out of touch with reality, how can we fix it?

Thankfully, there exists a large body of knowledge that provides a more realistic view on how we can effectively sell more, to more people, and for more money. Dr Archie Cochrane introduced the concept of evidence-based medicine to the world, from which many benefited. It is Andrew Ehrenberg who did the same for the marketing industry. And its effects are starting to take hold, in part thanks to the continuous efforts made by Byron Sharp and his colleagues. But even amongst those who know and read such academics, the question of how to apply these learnings remains the subject of much debate.

And herein lies the objective of this book: not only to counter some of the hype and what we believe to be nonsense in the industry, but also to provide perspectives on how marketing can better itself, inspired (not contrived) by the advances in marketing science.

Some of the papers (or, for the purposes of this book, 'chapters') are written by some of the best-known thinkers and practitioners in the industry; others are written by people you might never have heard of, but from whom, nonetheless, you will no doubt find inspiration. The brief to all of the contributors was simple: tell us how you apply or find inspiration from marketing science in a short, easy-to-digest paper (some provided more than one paper). I did not ask them to write to a particular topic; this was intended as a bag of nutritious 'mixed greens', but as it happens, the papers did fall naturally into loose categories. The book starts with a contemporary view of the marketing industry (chapters 1–17), before moving on to specific topics within it (chapters 18–34), and concluding with a more forward-looking view (chapters 35–42). The chapters offer a mix of perspectives, and varying styles: some are more academic in approach, others less formal. All are interspersed with some lively cartoons from Tom Fishburne.

These writers, these people 'from the trenches', don't have all the answers, and at times can be found a little at odds with each other, but they have all been willing to share their unfiltered views on how to make marketing much more effective and simpler. After all, eating your greens is meant to be good for you…

After digesting this knowledge, you might experience the uncomfortable tension we feel when we encounter conflicting thoughts or beliefs. But if we want to fix our collective disconnect, the challenge also lies in our ability and willingness to reduce this so-called 'cognitive dissonance'. If we can bring ourselves to notice and accept it, and be more open to the message it brings, we can get a clearer sense of what needs to change – and our role in that process.

Finally, an anecdote from John Scriven, who worked closely with Andrew Ehrenberg for years. After listening to a presentation from Ehrenberg in the early 1990s, the then CMO of a global consumer packaged goods (CPG) company asked, 'Does anyone else know about this? It will give significant competitive advantage.' Ehrenberg drily replied that the results had been published some time before. The CMO then asked what he needed to do about these findings. To which Ehrenberg answered, 'That's for you to work out!'

If you like what you've read thus far, please read on. But don't stop there. Explore the evidence, don't assume too quickly, and find out what you think for yourself.

Wiemer Snijders

MAJORITY REPORT

Written by **Wiemer Snijders** and **Charles Graham**

This chapter discusses the most fundamental patterns in buyer behaviour. Simple, almost universal rules with far-reaching implications for everything we do in marketing. The evidence presented here is the result of almost six decades of scientific research investigating the repeat buying of thousands of brands in hundreds of categories and in many countries. It includes recent results from two loyalty studies revealing the role that vast numbers of light buyers play in building sales over time. The aim of this chapter is to focus attention on this forgotten majority. Without them, you wouldn't have a brand.

That doesn't look normal...

I was holding a jar of pesto: 'Best before 19 March 2012.' After unscrewing the cap, it took only one look to realise this stuff would end up in the bin. I shouldn't have bothered to look. After all, it was already 24 March... 2018.

Hundreds of products must have passed through that fridge. Yet over the last six years, this little jar had spent its time safely tucked away in the corner, blocked by other, more frequently used products. I had completely forgotten about it. What other purchases could I remember making from six years ago? Not many; and I suspect few other people could either. If I asked how often you had bought a particular brand or category, you would probably overestimate your recent purchases and underestimate those from longer ago. Most shopping, especially in consumer-packaged goods, can be characterised as routine and habitual. This might lead us to think that many people frequently buy the same brand. Let's put that assumption to the test.

What does normal look like?

Below is an example from my work in a non-alcoholic beverages category to illustrate what a typical customer base looks like for a popular brand. About 1.5 million people bought this brand over the course of a year, although, it turns out, at very different rates: some buying far more frequently than others. Figure 1 presents the data in the familiar reporting splits of light, medium and heavy buyers.

Here, the biggest bar immediately grabs our attention. First, because it represents sales, our primary interest, and secondly because it supports the

Figure 1: Heavy buyers contribute most to sales

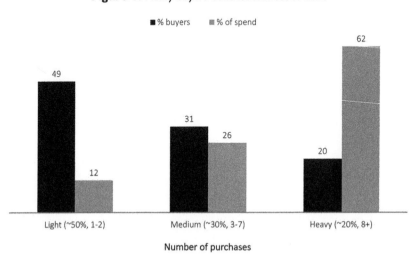

Source: The Commercial Works client data, beverages, 2016, 52 weeks' buying

familiar story that the heaviest 20% of buyers contribute by far the highest proportion of them. They are the brand's most valuable and important customers, and therefore an obvious market target. For many, the 'Pareto share' narrative may be the only take-out from the figure because this type of reporting split encourages 'confirmation bias' – seeing only what we expect to see – by focusing attention on the heaviest buyers, the loyalty success story.

Let's look more carefully at two other take-outs from the same chart. First, the top 20% of customers have a less extreme Pareto share than business school has taught us. It is not 80:20 but 60:20. This may not in itself be a danger sign (*help*, our heaviest buyers are not loyal enough!), since a less extreme ratio is well supported by evidence. Importantly, it almost certainly *does not* mean that we should invest precious marketing resource in purchase frequency (at least, not yet).

Secondly, at the left side of the graph, we see a far less appealing picture: half the annual customer base bought this brand just once or twice, to deliver only 12% of total sales – the smallest bar on the chart, and a lot of effort for a very small return. This group appears to warrant little of our attention.

Except that it is quite usual for half of the customer base to buy just once in a year, and although we might be tempted to disregard these light buyers by slicing up the numbers in this way, it is a mistake that could cost the brand dearly.

Figure 2 shows the same data in a more granular form, with the proportion of buyers and their relative sales contributions grouped by purchase frequencies. Now, a different picture emerges.

This distribution gives a far clearer picture of loyalty. The brand is well known, yet almost three quarters of its buyers bought it five times or less, together realising nearly 30% of annual sales. This seems surprising (it was for our client), yet marketing science says that it is quite normal. The pattern is closely predicted by a statistical curve, the 'Negative Binomial Distribution' or NBD, and every brand's customer base is like this, as Ehrenberg (inter alia) has pointed out. The main implication is simple: light buyers matter a lot.

Marketers may be tempted to focus on the people who buy often because they engage frequently and account individually for important sales volume. This is the 'heavy buyer fallacy': the tendency to overlook the fact that most

Figure 2: Light buyers matter a lot

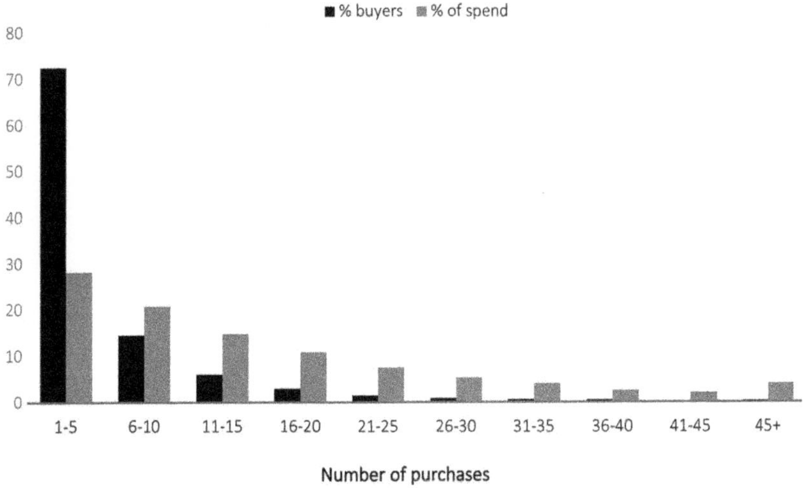

■ % buyers   ■ % of spend

Number of purchases

Source: The Commercial Works client data, beverages, 2016, 52 weeks' buying

customers are lighter buyers who together buy enough to matter a lot, as Figure 2 clearly shows, and Figure 1 does not. Since every customer base follows the NBD, brand share must depend on attracting light buyers. Sure, the heaviest buyers are important, but every brand must also reach out a long way to nudge in its lightest buyers from competitors.

One further evidence-based finding is that individual households don't buy at the same rate from period to period. Roughly half of the heaviest buyers will be lighter the following year, but lighter buyers will then become heavier. This is known as 'buyer moderation', or 'regression to the mean'. The main implication is not to think of your individual buyers as being fixed in their frequency of weight or purchase. They largely aren't, and so it is unhelpful to target this year's heavy buyers – it is better to target all category buyers instead, as we will show.

Special brands

Some might wonder whether the NBD applies to 'special' or niche brands with high loyalty in their DNA. The answer is clear from Figure 3. We looked at more brands in the same beverage category, analysing 12 in four sub-categories: 1) big/high share; 2) premium; 3) functional – often with digestive benefits (eg tomato juice); and 4) smallest, or niche. Each bar represents the average proportion of the customer base at each purchase frequency for three competing brands in the sub-category.

Figure 3: All brands have a very similar customer base

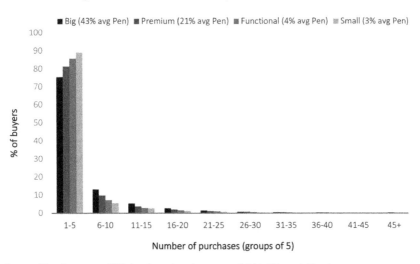

Source: The Commercial Works client data, beverages, 2016, 52 weeks' buying

The figure shows that the brands in each sub-category (and hence each part of the market) attract the same type of loyalty – the shape is very much the same. No matter what sort of beverage you are selling, or how you position it, by far the largest part of the customer base bought five times or less that year. So, if buying your favourite beverage brand about once a month seems quite restrained, it actually makes you a heavy buyer.

Big brands are proportionally less dependent on very light buyers. The leftmost, black bar shows that roughly three quarters of the biggest brand's buyers bought five times or less, where for the smallest, this percentage reached 90%. It is exactly the other way around for the other bars in the chart. There, big brands have the largest proportion of buyers in each other group.

The one rule that rules them all

And this is the robust, law-like pattern in buyer behaviour known as the 'Law of Double Jeopardy'. Small brands suffer twice, just because they are small. They have fewer buyers than big brands, and those buyers are on average a little less loyal. The sets of four bars in the chart describe four sub-categories, each with very different numbers of buyers – from high share through differentiated to low share – but because loyalty is always distributed in this way over whatever buyers the brand does have, the bars can be seen as a blueprint for brand growth or decline.

This is the one rule that rules them all. Or, as the late Andrew Ehrenberg wrote in the final pages of his book *Repeat Buying*:

> *Of the thousand and one variables which might affect buyer behaviour, it is found that nine hundred and ninety-nine usually do not matter. Many aspects of buyer behaviour can be predicted simply from the penetration and the average purchase frequency of the item, and even these two variables are interrelated.*

The relationships and patterns in buying behaviour are so regular that they can be successfully modelled, and the predicted values used to understand and benchmark actual or future brand performance measures. The patterns underpin much of the evidence presented in Byron Sharp's 2010 book *How Brands Grow*, and are incorporated in the underlying theory of the NBD-Dirichlet model, labelled as one of marketing science's greatest achievements. This chapter will not dive into the details of the model, but one of its most intriguing and counterintuitive assumptions is that markets are stationary. In the next section, we will see what the patterns we have discussed can tell us when we look at multiple years of buying, and investigate a well-known brand that grew substantially.

Multiple years of buying

If buying is so predictable, what does it say about people like me, who perhaps only buy pesto once in six years? Or indeed people who use pesto quite regularly, but only bought that cheaper brand once in six years because the other one was out of stock? How unusual is that? And how valuable or important can it be to that brand?

Not easy questions, as most panel data is reported on a yearly or quarterly basis, although panels now do monitor purchasing behaviour over quite long periods. Charles Graham has been looking at loyalty where the outcomes matter most – over the long term – and has made three important findings about light buyers in two separate studies spanning six and five years.

1. Light buyers have an important cumulative effect on brand penetration

Penetration just keeps on growing as ever-lighter buyers keep joining the brand for the first time. For stationary brands in stationary markets, penetration can often double between a quarter and a year, and double again between one year and three to five years, even though, from year to year, market share and most other brand performance metrics remain stable. That might sound like an anomaly, but your user base must keep on growing just to maintain share.

Figure 4 explains penetration growth effects over time. The grey curve represents the rate at which the category picks up buyers: very fast at first, soon reaching near saturation. By contrast, the black, brand penetration curve moves more slowly, and is still growing even at year five. This brand is a leading detergent, it reaches a third of UK households in a year. We see its curve crossing the 35% line at year one, and the flat dotted line represents its stable annual penetration. This shows that every year the brand reached about a third of the population, although its annual penetration was made up of different households each year – many drop out to come back later, and many come back in from earlier years, or for the first time. The obvious implication here is that it makes no sense to target on the basis of one year's sales. Typically, you haven't even met half of your eventual customer base.

Figure 4: Essential brand building and headroom for growth

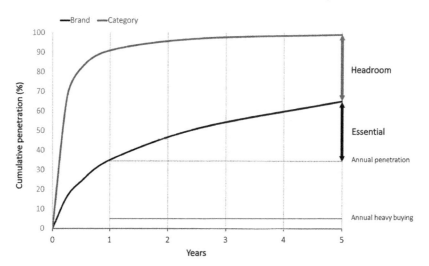

Source: Kantar Worldpanel, UK detergent, 2009–2014, continuous buyers only

Of course, some heavy buyers are heavy every year, but even they do not account for all the buyers under the lower dotted line, the households buying 5+ times in a year (horizontal, solid line). Even this proportion will be a different household mix each year.

So, the figure demonstrates two important jobs to be done: first, essential brand building means maintaining the trajectory of penetration growth; secondly, in order to grow, that trajectory must be accelerated into the headroom to attract even more category buyers, a bit faster each year. The continuous addition of so many lighter buyers also says quite a lot about loyalty, leading us to the second finding.

2. Even over time, light buyers are an important part of the buyer mix

The study looked at 220 brands in 22 categories over five years – it found the same story in every one. Even though over five years there is ample opportunity to make a second purchase, across all the brands, 45% of the average customer base still consisted of buyers who had bought that brand just once.

Table 1 illustrates the importance of ultra-light buyers: those buying between once and five times in five years. It turned out that they account for almost 80% of the total customer base, with the biggest difference (as before) in the class who bought just once. The NBD and Double Jeopardy still apply.

Table 1: Ultra-light buying

220 brands in 22 categories	Percentage of households buying (n) times in five years					Ultra-light buyers
	Once	Twice	Three	Four	Five	(%)
Category buying	17	9	6	5	4	41
First brand	32	14	9	6	5	66
Fifth brand	45	16	8	5	4	78
Tenth brand	53	15	8	5	3	84
Average (ten largest brands)	45	15	8	5	4	77
Sales importance (%)	15	9	6	5	4	39

Source: Kantar Worldpanel, 2009–14, continuous buyers only

3. Heavy buyers are less important to sales than we may think

The Pareto share we discussed earlier never reaches 80:20. In the long run, loyalty is important – repeat buyers contribute disproportionately to sales, of course, but even in this cumulative data they didn't deliver much more than 60% of purchases. This means that the lightest 80% of buyers account for about 40% of stationary brand sales, and the implications are clear: light and super-light buyers matter a lot to brand performance – maintaining share depends on accumulating light buyers to build penetration.

So, what happens to loyalty if a brand accelerates into the headroom, and grows?

Staying ahead of the curve

Take a brand like Dove, for example, shown in Figure 5 (which stems from Graham's first long-term buying study spanning six years of continuous buying). During the period analysed, this brand grew its share by 50% and ran its famous and numerously awarded 'Dove for Real Beauty' campaign; yet Graham's data shows that a little over one-third of Dove's buyers still only bought it once.

Only once. In six years.

Figure 5: Ultra-light buying for Dove

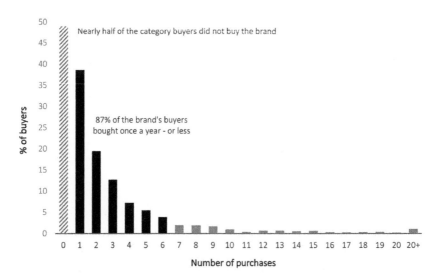

Source: Kantar Worldpanel, continuous buying only

And over 80% of Dove's buyers bought the brand at the rate of once a year or less. This group turned in more than half of their sales! So, despite being highly differentiated, the shape of loyalty in Dove's customer base remained normal, and the brand grew not by developing exceptional repeat buying from existing customers, but mostly by attracting new, but largely very light buyers.

In Figure 5 we have added an extra bar – the tallest of them all. It shows category buyers who didn't buy the brand during the period. Many will buy the brand in the future, but the rate at which they are attracted in determines whether the brand will grow, decline or maintain its share. The size and nature of this target is a golden opportunity for marketers. The potential to grow is as tall as the bar. There is no need to educate the market at great expense either. These households already know the benefits of the product because they use it, and most buy it regularly from an established repertoire of brands. They have probably seen *this* brand advertised and on store shelves, so it may be quite familiar, but they just have not tried it yet. How can they be encouraged to, even just once? This has big implications for the margin you should be willing to give up for that first purchase.

Ever since Ehrenberg first published about it in 1959 – when Elvis topped the charts with *Jailhouse Rock* – the importance of light buyers has been known to those who cared to look. However, these new findings reveal that the case was actually understated. Brand owners will need to come to terms with this 'unbearable lightness of buying', and realise that they should first and foremost be concerned with reaching and nudging all those potential buyers. Not surprisingly, one of our clients asked, 'But from whom will we steal all those buyers?' I will answer that question next.

Stealing (light) buyers

The big idea behind segmentation, targeting and positioning is that it helps drive more sales through the exceptional loyalty of a subset of buyers in the market. You essentially signal 'I understand you, look what I've made just for you' in the hope that these buyers will be so delighted that they choose never to switch to a competing brand again. They will become your buyers.

Unfortunately, the evidence clearly says that this is not what happens. It tells us instead that your customers are mostly other brands' customers who occasionally buy you. So, does it matter if you sell a functional or a premium brand? Or both? Take the beverages category again: most brands shared buyers during that analysis period. The extent to which they did so can be measured in a 'Duplication of Purchase' analysis.

First, here's the assumption: in a perfectly competitive market, brands should share buyers in proportion to their size, not their attributes. There are no segments in which buyers choose only certain brands and absolutely no others. Figure 6 illustrates the concept, and how to check this.

Figure 6: How brands share buyers in proportion to their penetration

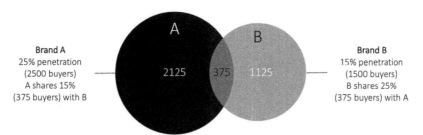

Brand A
25% penetration
(2500 buyers)
A shares 15%
(375 buyers) with B

2125   375   1125

Brand B
15% penetration
(1500 buyers)
B shares 25%
(375 buyers) with A

Although the number of shared customers is the same, the proportion of the customer base being shared differs according to the size of the brand – so small brand B is sharing a larger proportion (25%) of its buyers with the bigger brand A, which is sharing a smaller proportion (15%) the other way. Markets consist of many brands, but even so the assumption is that brand size must determine the sharing relationship consistently for every pair if they are true (competing) substitutes.

A manager who is unaware of this pattern might look to her budget, her objectives and the current market, and assuming it to be segmented, choose to:

- target the buyers of smaller brands (maybe on the basis that they will be easier to steal);
- target bigger brands (they have more buyers to steal);

- target the buyers of brands with a similar offering or positioning; or
- target existing customers in order to prevent all that sharing in the first place.

So, let's have a look to see where brands found their additional buyers over five years of marketing investment. Table 2 (below) shows, along each row, the proportion of the five-year brand customer base shared with every other brand. Making up the matrix in this way (ie in brand size order) reveals the sharing between each brand pair. A five-year duplication table like Table 2 has seldom been seen before, and the picture is instructive.

The first thing to notice is that there are numbers in each cell: all brands share their customers with all other brands. Furthermore, the sharing reveals nearly perfect competition because it is mostly in line with brand size. At the bottom of the table (last row) the predicted values (there is a model) can be compared to the column average and to specific cells. Deviations are small, and so there is a strong relationship between actual and predicted values (for the statistically minded, the correlation is 98%).

Table 2: Duplication of Purchase in deodorants

% buyers of ↓ who also bought →	Sure	Dove	Soft & Gentle	Nivea	Vaseline	Dove Go Fresh	Tesco	Right Guard	MUM	Mitchum
Sure		51	49	39	26	23	18	18	10	10
Dove	63		47	38	27	28	16	15	10	10
Soft & Gentle	69	53		43	29	25	20	20	12	9
Nivea	73	57	57		34	29	20	22	12	12
Vaseline	71	58	55	49		29	18	22	11	11
Dove Go Fresh	70	69	54	48	33		19	20	12	9
Tesco	66	49	52	39	26	23		19	12	10
Right Guard	80	53	62	52	36	28	22		8	12
MUM	60	45	48	38	25	23	19	11		11
Mitchum	63	49	41	39	26	19	16	18	11	
Average	68	53	51	42	28	25	19	18	11	10
Predicted values	69	56	49	37	26	22	19	16	12	11
Deviations from predicted values	-2	-3	2	5	3	2	0	2	-1	-1

Source: Kantar WorldPanel: Continuous UK buyers 2009–14
(The table lists the 10 largest brands; the calculation of averages and predicted values was based on a more comprehensive set)

This means that, despite the competitive brand positionings, no distinct groupings that might represent customer segments emerged. Brands shared category buyers across the market. One of the biggest deviations in the table is for Dove Go Fresh – it shared 69% of its buyers with its parent brand against an expected value of 56%; in other words, it was cannibalising brand sales, by not competing across the market. The table shows that there is little evidence that over the five years brands have done anything but build their customer base from the pool of all category buyers to maintain or grow share.

Who is loyal to grocery brands anyhow? Services are very different

A frequently heard comment is that these laws are helpful, but of course they only describe markets with a lot of repeat purchasing. The evidence does indeed show that buying differs between markets, polarising them into either repertoire (CPG categories categorised by switching within a brand portfolio) or subscription (buyers subscribed to one supplier over time until a switch, eg in financial services or utilities). In subscription markets, the patterns (NBD, Double Jeopardy and Duplication of Purchase) still hold, although they apply in rather slow motion. Figure 7 provides an example from my work in car insurance showing the close relationship between average duplication, ie sharing and its predicted values; loyalty to car insurance providers is no different.

The correlation analysis tells us that 80% of sharing is in line with what we would expect; so, competition is defined more by brand size than by any special brand positioning. The relationship is less strong than in the five-year duplication table (Table 2), but this is more due to the relatively small sample (1,500 people) and the fact that car insurance is a market where certain brands apply very stringent rules about who they will or will not accept. Because car insurance brands therefore also largely appear to be constrained by the established patterns, this type of analysis provides powerful and useful benchmarks to evaluate acquisition and retention efforts, even in subscription markets. So, for all brands, the main implication of this pattern is to target the market.

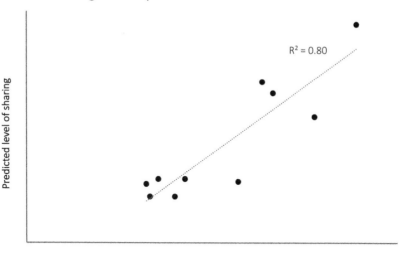

Figure 7: Duplication of Purchase in car insurance

Source: The Commercial Works client data, car insurance, 2016

How to use these norms and patterns

The law-like patterns I have described are empirical generalisations, developed by marketing scientists such as Andrew Ehrenberg and Byron Sharp into usable benchmarks and rules that help decision making. They are not prescriptive: they don't tell managers what to do. Instead they are descriptive: they describe what normally happens (and what doesn't), so knowledge of them helps to make marketing simpler and more effective.

For example, why plan to change the shape of the NBD? In 60 years of research, no brands – from global market leaders to start up challengers – have been found with anything other than NBD loyalty. The scientists are still looking – that was the motivation for the long-term studies, but the findings together with everything that went before suggests that long-term brand building succeeds by working with (rather than against) the grain of the evidence. And that evidence still shows that all brands have some easy-to-reach heavy users, but that large numbers of light buyers are critical for brand maintenance and growth – for most of its customer base a brand will be rather like that jar of pesto: rarely bought and easily forgotten.

Making sense of it all

In 2014, *Marketing Week* reported that CMOs' average tenure of four years is the shortest in the C-suite; a period during which most customers will have bought their brand four times, but probably less. Who will take responsibility and manage the long game? Peter Field and Les Binet have for years advocated the need for a more long-term view on brand building. In this book, Field describes how the 'short-termism' in our industry is increasingly killing effectiveness. The findings presented here provide further support for that notion.

The patterns described in this chapter relate to many of the other stories you will find in this book. Now that you are aware of them, you will probably see why some are critical of short-term (ROI) metrics associated with heavier purchase behaviours. The difference in scale between that and the critical, continuous task of accumulating so many light buyers who think very little about the brand should now be in much sharper focus. If you are a great brand, attracting this majority of buyers into your customer base requires a creative, single-minded approach to the task of maintaining your rightful place in their minds and on store shelves. Be noticed, and be there when you are needed – welcome old friends and reach out to new ones. Don't just talk to your best friends.

Finally, it is of course completely up to you whether you choose to swim against or with the current of marketing science. Either way, it's tough out there. You might still drown, but one option requires a lot less effort. So, take a deep breath and dive into the rest of this book!

References

Aaker, DA. *Strategic Market Management* (6th edition). John Wiley, 2001

Anscombe, FJ. 'Sampling theory of the negative binomial and logarithmic distribution'. *Biometrika*, 37 (3/4), 1950

Bevelin, B. *Seeking Wisdom: From Darwin to Munger* (3rd edition). PCA Publications, 2007

Bhattacharya, CB. 'Is your brand's loyalty too much, too little, or just right? Explaining deviations in loyalty from the Dirichlet norm'. *International Journal of Research in Marketing*, 14 (5), 1997

Binet, L, and Field, P. 'Empirical generalisations about advertising campaign success'. *Journal of Advertising Research*, 49 (2), 2009

Binet, L, and Field, P. *Marketing in the Era of Accountability: Identifying the marketing practices and metrics that truly increase profitability.* WARC, 2007

Binet, L, and Field, P. *Media in Focus: Marketing effectiveness in a digital era.* IPA, 2017

Binet, L, and Field, P. *The Long and the Short of It: Balancing short and long-term marketing strategies.* IPA, 2013

Carpenter, GS, Glazer, R, and Nakamoto K. 'Meaningful brands from meaningless differentiation: the dependence on irrelevant attributes'. *Journal of Marketing Research* 31 (3), 1994

Dawes, JG, and Trinh, G. 'Category and brand purchase rates (still) follow the NBD distribution'. Working paper, 2017

Ehrenberg, A. 'Repeat-buying: facts, theory and applications'. *Journal of Empirical Generalisations in Marketing Science*, 5, 2000

Ehrenberg, A. 'The pattern of consumer purchases'. *Applied Statistics* 8 (1), 1959

Ehrenberg, A, Barnard, N, Kennedy, R, and Bloom, H. 'Brand advertising as creative publicity'. *Journal of Advertising Research*, 42 (4), 2002

Ehrenberg, A, Goodhardt, GJ, and Barwise, P. 'Double Jeopardy revisited'. *Journal of Marketing*, 54 (3), 1990

Ehrenberg, A, Uncles, MD, and Goodhardt, GJ. 'Understanding brand performance measures: using Dirichlet benchmarks'. *Journal of Business Research*, 57 (12), 2004

Goodhardt, GJ, Ehrenberg, A, and Chatfield, C. 'The Dirichlet: a comprehensive model of buying behaviour'. *Journal of the Royal Statistical Society*, 147 (5), 1984

Graham, C. 'The patterns of long-term repeat buying in Dirichlet markets'. PhD thesis, 2013

Graham, C, Scriven, J, and Bennett, D. 'Brand loyalty. Plus ça change..?' Using the NBD-Dirichlet parameters to interpret long-term purchase incidence and brand choice'. Proceedings of the International Marketing Trends Congress, 2012

Graham, C, Sharp, B, Trinh, G, and Dawes, J. 'The unbearable lightness of buying'. Report 73 for corporate sponsors, Ehrenberg-Bass Institute for Marketing Science, 2017

http://adage.com/article/news/ten-years-dove-s-real-beauty-aging/291216/

https://www.linkedin.com/pulse/do-heavy-buyers-account-80-your-sales-volume-jan-benedict-steenkamp/

https://www.linkedin.com/pulse/what-most-effective-way-organic-brand-growth-mass-target-steenkamp/

https://www.marketingweek.com/2017/02/16/cmos-shortest-tenure-c-suite/

Jung, S-U, Gruca, T, and Rego, L. 'Excess loyalty in CPG markets: a comprehensive examination.' *Journal of Empirical Generalisations in Marketing Science*, 13 (1), 2010

Kahneman, D. *Thinking, Fast and Slow*. Farrar, Straus and Giroux, 2011

Kotler, P. *Marketing Management: Analysis, planning, implementation, and control* (8th edition). Prentice Hall, 1993

McDonald, C, and Ehrenberg, A. 'What happens when brands gain or lose share? Customer acquisition or increased loyalty?' Report 31 for corporate members, Ehrenberg-Bass Institute for Marketing Science

McPhee, W. *Formal Theories of Mass Behavior*. Free Press, 1963

Reeves, R. *Reality in Advertising*. Alfred Knopf, 1961

Ries, A, and Trout, J. *Positioning: The battle for your mind*. Warner Books, 1986

Romaniuk, J. 'Are you blinded by the heavy (buyer)... or are you seeing the light?' *Journal of Advertising Research*, 51 (4), 2011

Romaniuk, J, and Sharp, B. *How Brands Grow: Part 2*. OUP, 2015

Schmittlein, DC, Cooper, LG, and Morrison, DG. 'Truth in concentration in the land of (80/20) laws'. *Marketing Science*, 12 (2), 1993

Sharp, B. *How Brands Grow: What marketers don't know*. OUP, 2010

Sharp, B, and Romaniuk, J. 'There is a Pareto Law – but not as you know it.'

Report 42 for corporate sponsors, Ehrenberg-Bass Institute for Marketing Science

Sharp, B, et al. 'It's a Dirichlet world: modeling individuals' loyalties reveals how brands compete, grow, and decline'. *Journal of Advertising Research*, 52 (2), 2012

Sharp B, Wright, M, and Goodhardt, G. 'Purchase loyalty is polarised into either repertoire or subscription patterns'. *Australasian Marketing Journal*, 10 (3), 2002

Sudman, S, and Bradburn, N. 'Effects of time and memory factors on response in surveys'. *Journal of the American Statistical Association*, 68, (344), 1973

Uncles, M, Ehrenberg, A, and Hammond, K. 'Patterns of buyer behavior: regularities, models, and extensions.' *Marketing Science*, 14 (3–2), 1995

2

PEOPLE WHO PREDICT THE DEATH OF BRANDS DON'T UNDERSTAND WHY THEY EXIST

Written by **Shann Biglione**

There is little marketing pundits like more than proclaiming the death of 'old systems'. In recent years, it has increasingly been argued that brands themselves might be dying, whether as a result of customer indifference or because new technology is weakening the role of branding in purchase decisions. This chapter argues that such predictions are probably overblown, and at odds with shopper behaviours linked less to societal trends than to basic human needs.

Some marketers are, deep down, serial killers. It wasn't enough to call the death of TV (still doing pretty well). Then it wasn't enough to call the death of advertising (still growing – and flash news – most of Google's *and* Facebook's revenues). No, harbingers are now chanting the death of brands themselves.

The usual suspects normally include four trends: e-commerce; consumer reviews; the decline of mass advertising; and Artifical Intelligence (AI). At the risk of trivialising some of the arguments, here's how they usually go.

> *'E-commerce is making all products available at once, meaning we have greater choice and thus reducing the value of the branded options'.*

Here's the thing, though – hyper-availability is not something new. Mega-supermarkets and massive shopping malls have been around for long enough to hint at the fact brands are not suffering from hyper-availability. If anything, it shows that brands thrive in hyper-availability markets, precisely because their primary purpose is to help in easing the decision-making process. Besides, the second argument for e-commerce disrupting brands is that it takes away the power of negotiation for shelf space. Maybe, but from the interactions we've seen with e-retailers, those negotiations are still very much common practice. You'd be crazy to think Amazon won't be monetising access to first page and promotions. So, who knows, maybe e-commerce will actually *increase* the value of having a strong brand with high salience.

> *'Consumer empowerment is allowing consumers to filter through the bullshit of marketing and get only the best products'.*

This argument is usually linked to e-commerce. And sure, when your category is objectively comparable, maybe. But not only aren't there too many of these, we know that consumers' decisions are not always driven by rational arguments. Besides, anyone who's spent time on e-commerce reviews can tell you that competing brands tend to have pretty close ratings to one another (thanks to the 'endowment effect'), and that it's easy to revert to your choice for the most familiar brands against all evidence (which is why there isn't a big correlation between movie reviews and box office). That side of the argument is oftentimes a 'halo effect' for something we've known all along: brands cannot overcome a shitty or inferior product. But that is less a function of the brand itself failing than just recognising that we often confuse the word 'brand' with the whole entity of the business. As a matter of fact, I'm pretty certain any suffering or failed brand with equity can be revived by a good product (looking at you, Nokia).

> *'Brands are a by-product of mass advertising, and mass advertising is dying, therefore brands must be dying too'.*

Even if we posited that advertising really is dying, the syllogism clearly has its limits. It first assumes that brands cannot find other ways to market themselves, while we know branding has been doing well since the dawn of civilisation (cults excelled at branding long before Coca-Cola refreshed our spirits). But more importantly, it correlates the explosion of brands with the growth of advertising as if there was a causality between the two. The only thing this argument captures is the fact that both existed at a time that saw the growth of consumerism. It doesn't demonstrate that brands are a result of advertising. The fact that many people calling the death of brands then sell services to grow them without the use of advertising hints at the reality that brands would, most likely, outlive advertising's passing.

> *'Artificial Intelligence is going to change the way we discover brands'.*

This is so far the best argument I've heard that could indeed change the way we discover products, championed by NYU Stern Professor Scott Galloway, and showing how ordering batteries via Alexa is more likely to lead you to Amazon's 'Basics' range than Duracell's. We know that consumers tend to shop the category more than the brand, and it's therefore possible that product discovery will be delegated to someone, or in this case, something else. But it implies that, first, we will want to delegate that choice, when in fact consumers might actually enjoy the act of discovery more than we think (the thing we call 'shopping'), and secondly, that consumers would still be OK not getting the specific brand they tend to prefer when they do have a preference. Obviously, not every category would be equal to these effects, which is why highly commoditised segments such as batteries (to Scott's example) would become less brand sensitive. But is that really something new?

Now, some of you might think that only the mass brands are threatened. To which I'd respond with a simple observation: have you looked at the most trusted companies in the last few years? Does it not strike you how many of these are mass brands? Seeing no future for mass brands ignores the arithmetic of what makes them mass brands in the first place: it's not because people love them beyond reason, but simply because a lot of people use them. The mistake is to think that certain brands' demise is a result of the weakness of brands, when in fact it's usually a simple illustration of normal market dynamics related to the category: higher maturity and higher involvement categories will show larger repertoires and greater fragmentation. But buyer distribution dictates that there will always be a majority of light buyers, ie people who don't care enough about the brand and/or category to propel mass brands to the top.

The bottom line is, brands are not a result of brainwashing or spamming, they're simply an essential part of our cognitive processes. Predicting the death of brands fails to understand their Darwinian nature: they do not exist because they were imposed unto us, they exist because of us.

References

http://minimaxir.com/2016/01/movie-revenue-ratings/

http://www.bierergroup.com/are-you-blinded-by-the-heavy-buyer-or-are-you-seeing-the-light

https://www.youtube.com/watch?v=3MOwRTTq1bY

3

WHAT AILS MARKETING? MORTIFICATION, TACTIFICATION, COMMUNIFICATION AND DIGITISATION

Written by **Mark Ritson**

With the spirit of current marketing best conceptualised as weary excitement, this chapter questions whether we are really making any progress at all. It highlights four dangerous trends that have had a detrimental impact on the quality and impact of marketing in the early 21st century. The conclusion is that, although much of marketing is indeed 'lost', there is significant personal and fiscal redemption to be found in applying an approach that can be best described as 'old school'.

In some ways it's very hard to pinpoint the current mood of the marketing discipline. On the one hand, the business of marketing products has never been more fluid or exciting. The last decade has seen more change, in a tactical sense at least, than the three that preceded it – and that makes for excitement. On the other hand, marketing has never been so conflicted and tribal than it is right now. The discipline has become a series of warlord states, each vying with each other to gain the upper hand from neighbouring rivals. Each convinced that they, and only they, truly understand marketing.

Most marketers are more focused on the cool new stuff than the concerning lack of clarity or discipline in our field. When you visit the next marketing conference, it's almost certain that you will encounter packed sessions on blockchain, augmented reality and crypto-currencies, plus whatever new toys have been invented between now and the next conference. Marketers have always been the 'magpie discipline': we steal the good stuff from other approaches and bring them into marketing as our own. But with so much stuff around these days, it's perhaps not surprising that marketing has become filled to the brim with nonsense.

And while this distracting ephemera continues to occupy and obfuscate the marketing masses, we are shifting further away from the great tenets of marketing that have served the discipline so well for so long. At this point there is a significant chance that you have arched an eyebrow and are reaching for the next chapter. Hold on! This is not a plea to ignore the new and favour the old; rather it is a plea to beware throwing the strategic principles of marketing out with the new tactical bathwater.

Let me explain with four themes that I think best capture the current marketing malaise.

1. Mortification

The only way to kidnap a century-old discipline and replace its long-thought-through principles is to declare the past dead and the future different. A new wave of wildly ignorant marketers, proud of their lack of marketing training, have appeared, and are intent on reshaping marketing to their own myopic ends. For the past decade, ill-informed, untrained marketing gurus have been declaring various concepts they do not fully understand to be dead. How better to pave the way for bitcoin and AI and the plethora of other jingly stuff that they want to focus on?

The examples are legion: Jason John telling everyone that will listen in *Ad Age* that in 'today's digital world, the sales funnel is dead'; David Baldwin making an equally ludicrous argument to explain 'Why David Ogilvy must die'; research firm Forrester concluding that 'the end of advertising as we know it' was around the corner, while many experts have been regularly predicting the end of television for most of the decade. As 'Ad Contrarian' Bob Hoffman drolly observed recently: 'TV to die again, soon'. Meanwhile, Scott Galloway tells us that Amazon has 'effectively conspired with voice and technology and half a billion consumers to kill brands'. Even I have had my moments, once getting on a stage to explain why the word 'digital' would surely die soon.

It wasn't always like this. If you pick up a copy of *Marketing Week* or *Ad Age* from the 1980s, you won't see a single theoretical funeral. The magazines were busy covering the industry, the main issues and the lessons for marketers. Nothing is dying, just evolving. Of course, picking up 30-year-old copies of marketing magazines is not something any of today's marketers would ever do. The very suggestion would have them scoffing into their lattes. That's a shame. Because the gift of marketing history is two-fold: first, it shows us that not as much has changed as we might imagine; secondly, it demonstrates that, while our tactical mix is always changing, the overall business of marketing evolves at a much slower speed than most of today's trigger-happy predictions might lead you to believe. In many cases the big debates of the 1980s remain the big debates of today.

2. Tacticification

I made up this word, so my apologies for its clumsiness, but it's the only way to capture the current obsession with the tactical elements of marketing at the expense of the other, deeper, more important parts of the marketing process that precede and predicate them.

It may be (and excuse the lesson if you have a training in marketing, but given you are a marketer there is a very strong probability you do not) time for a summary of that marketing process before proceeding any further. There are three phases to all marketing work. First, we diagnose the situation of the brand via consumer research and understand just what is going on. Secondly, we use that diagnosis to build a clear and simple marketing strategy. Finally, with that strategy in place, we select the appropriate tactics to deliver the strategy and win the day.

Strategy is a very complicated thing to work out, but should be a very simple thing to eventually explain. In our world of marketing it comes down to being able to answer three basic questions, and answering them long before we have started spending money on VR headsets and the latest Facebook ads. Who am I targeting? What is my position to that target? What are my strategic objectives for that target market? My current estimate is that around 20% of brands could adequately or semi-adequately pass this test, and the rest have not the faintest clue how to even approach these questions.

There is no polite way to say this, but most big brands are being run without any proper marketing strategy at all. Those in charge delight in the latest gimmicks and tactics, yet remain unable to articulate their target segments beyond the inane and entirely ridiculous concept of 'Millennials'. Positioning is little more than a random strapline or two. Ask for objectives and a dribble of purpose statements and brand love stands in for proper measurable goals. The focus on digital and the latest hot technology has resulted in all too many companies putting the tactical cart in front of the strategic horse.

Talk to agencies about the quality of the briefs they currently receive from clients and you will get the kind of hard stare usually reserved for the most outrageous agency gossip. Time after time, advertising agencies are being instructed on what tactical dimensions a big brand wants to include, but are given little if any strategic input on what those brands are trying to achieve.

3. Communification

This is another clumsy word I made up. It is meant to describe the fact that not only are marketers adept at just tactics (at the expense of diagnosis and strategy), they actually only focus on one small, relatively unimportant subset of marketing tactics – communications – for all their efforts.

I won't get into the eternal debate about how many 'Ps' you should divide your tactics into. Suffice to say, most modern marketers are convinced that the four or seven or 10 Ps are dead. I still like my big four of Product, Price, Promotion and Place. However you slice your tactical pie, there is no doubt that most marketers of the last decade are inherently obsessed with the promotional P, and have virtually nothing to say about pricing or distribution. This is insane, because although it is unfair to play favourites, if you really had to kill one of your four tactical puppies, the promotional one is clearly the least essential in the mix for most brands. Give me a great product, sold through omnichannel in the right way at the optimum price, and it's going to be OK. Sure, a great integrated communications plan will make things sell faster and further, but if you want to choose the one tactic to live without, it would be the one most marketers spend all of their time obsessing over.

At that next marketing conference take a long hard look at the agenda. Now count the sessions focusing on some form of marketing communications versus the sessions on all the other topics. See what I mean? I see marketing as three equal challenges of diagnosis, strategy and tactics. I see communications as one quarter of the tactical challenge. That means it should be about 8% of the stuff we talk about in marketing. Why is it over 80%?

4. Digitisation

Of course, when I say communications I do not mean all communications. The modern marketer has created an entirely stupid dichotomy between 'digital communications' and 'traditional communications'. This is, quite possibly, the most popular and yet ridiculous concept in the history of marketing. With TV advertising almost exclusively digitally delivered, most cities now enjoying far more than 50% of their outdoor advertising via digital screens not paper, British radio now being delivered more via digital channels than traditional broadcast, and most profitable newspapers now making more money from digital subscriptions than print, I continue to wonder exactly what a digital marketer actually does. Everything?

We are deluged with charts that show us the 'digital native who lives in the online world' without any reference to much of the media that these people consume because they are deemed 'traditional'. The ridiculous concept of a 'digital first' marketing plan espouses relegating target consumers, strategy and integration to an afterthought in order to prioritise a meaningless term in an incorrect manner. Recently, Belkin CMO Kieran Hannon was asked by *Inc.*

magazine whether marketers had 'reached a point yet where advertisers and marketers think digital first and traditional platforms second? If not, why not?' Drawing on a proper marketing training and years of experience, Hannon's answer was both exasperated and exemplary at the same time: 'My New Year's resolution for 2016 is to ban the notion of "digital" and "traditional" being separate elements. They're not; it's all marketing.'

It's marketers like Hannon and L'Oréal CMO Stéphane Bérubé that offer some faint hope that all is not lost. 'Marketing needs to move from having digital priorities', Bérubé told *Marketing Week* in 2017. 'We need to stop talking about what is the digital strategy. I am making a big point of this in the culture at L'Oréal.' Bérubé's philosophy also extends beyond his own company to the agencies that L'Oréal, one of the world's biggest advertisers, works with. 'I always smile when agencies claim they are doing digital. Honestly, maybe that was good in 2010, but in 2017 they should claim they just do marketing. We need to stop talking about digital — it's all part of marketing.'

His comments will come as something of a shock to the army of marketers who prefix their title or activities with the word 'digital'. They have spent the last 10 years proclaiming the death of everything from newspapers to television to radio advertising. Now, it's their own sub-profession that has been identified for extinction. Before those from more traditional backgrounds start savouring a move away from digital and back to more 'legacy' approaches, it should be apparent that Bérubé is no more a supporter of the old-school approach to marketing than he is of its newer, digital alternative.

Digital marketing is not going to die, but it is going to be absorbed into the general tactical mix as marketing moves on. The concept, so missed by digital marketers, is not that digital is bad and traditional is good, but that the whole bifurcation was ridiculous in the first place. There are just tactical tools, and they can only be valued and selected once a target and a position and a strategy are in place. What's more, it's clear that most successful campaigns combine multiple channels for optimum success. Most studies suggest that the more channels a campaign includes, the better the ultimate ROI. It was never a question of digital versus traditional. It was always the answer 'yes' and 'yes'. To believe in a 'digital first' approach to marketing is the nadir of this particular period in marketing's history. Too many of my critics point to this argument and claim I am 'anti-digital' and 'pro-traditional'. I reject both labels, and the simplistic inaccurate dichotomy they have created. They are all just tools. I use and reject them with the casual insouciance of someone who looks at strategy first and then makes choices.

Out of the rabbit hole

So, is there hope for marketing going forward? We seem ever more obsessed with tactics, communications and digital toys, and increasingly ignorant of the origins and founding principles of marketing. Again, it is worth noting that, while it may be a wearisome time to work in marketing, it is also the most electric period in our history. That feeling of weary excitement is, I feel, the dominant emotional theme of the current age of marketing. But is it going to change?

Personally, I feel marketing is for the most part lost. A lack of formal education in the subject, an ignorance of the marketing thinkers of the last century, and a rush to adopt the latest tactical candy will surely continue. Marketing effectiveness is on the steady decline no matter what the overly enthusiastic conference circuit might try to tell you.

But we are not curing cancer here. Marketing is a commercial, competitive pursuit, and I continue to make a splendid salary working for large companies that have recognised much of what I describe above, and who have opted to do things in a more strategic, and crucially, more profitable way. The more we forget the successful principles of marketing, the more a small select group of companies and consultants can prosper by remembering them and applying them. Isn't that the ultimate point?

That's the closest I can find to a happy ending. It may not cheer you up. But it's certainly working for me.

References

Dolan, RJ. 'Note on marketing strategy'. Harvard Business School Background Note 598–061, October 1997

Doyle, P. *Marketing Management and Strategy: A reader* (4th edition). Prentice Hall, 1998

Henneberg, S, and O'Shaughnessy, NJ. 'Theory and concept development in political marketing'. *Journal of Political Marketing*, 6 (2-3), 2007

Hoffman, R. *BadMen: How advertising went from a minor annoyance to a major menace.* Type A Group, 2017

http://adage.com/article/digitalnext/today-s-digital-world-sales-funnel-dead/303301/

https://www.businessinsider.com.au/cord-cutters-and-the-death-of-tv-2013-11

https://www.businessinsider.com.au/scott-galloway-amazon-could-eliminate-existence-of-brands-voice-technology-2017-4

https://www.forrester.com/report/The+End+Of+Advertising+As+We+Know+It/-/E-RES137501

https://www.inc.com/jonathan-lacoste/why-the-cmo-of-belkin-banned-the-separation-of-digital-amp-traditional-marketing.html

https://www.marketingweek.com/2015/08/05/mark-ritson-the-death-of-digital-is-upon-us/

https://www.marketingweek.com/2017/11/13/loreal-new-cmo-brands-shouldnt-digital-strategy/

http://www.thedrum.com/opinion/2018/01/22/why-david-ogilvy-must-die

Lafley, AG, and Martin, R. *Playing to Win: How strategy really works.* Harvard Business Review Press, 2013

Yudelson, J. 'Adapting McCarthy's Four P's for the twenty-first century'. *Journal of Marketing Education*, 21(1), 1999

4

SHORT-TERMISM IS KILLING EFFECTIVENESS

Written by **Peter Field**

Marketing effectiveness is facing a pernicious and widely unrecognised threat, this chapter asserts. Focusing on driving short-term sales for brands conflicts with long-term growth, because it leads us to the opposite kinds of strategies and media choices than those that best drive long-term success. The dramatic growth of short-termism in recent years is already playing out in declining effectiveness and weaker brands.

In 2016, for my sins, I travelled to Cannes to present an update of an earlier report exploring the link between creativity and effectiveness. As before, the report was based on analysis of the UK's IPA and *Gunn Report* databases, fused.

The IPA Databank consists of the confidential data submitted alongside entries to the biennial IPA Effectiveness Awards competition, going back over 30 years. The data captured includes a comprehensive range of campaign inputs (such as strategy, media choices and brand circumstances) and campaign outcomes (such as business effectiveness measures, efficiency, ROI and brand measures). The IPA data is less comprehensive when it comes to creative award wins, so that is where *The Gunn Report* data comes in.

The Gunn Report data records the creative award wins of any campaign at the top 46 creative shows worldwide: it is the most objective measure available of the level of creativity achieved. The analysis, in essence, examines how inputs affect outcomes, and allows us to compare the effectiveness of creatively awarded campaigns with that of non-awarded ones.

Although the case studies are all of successful campaigns, and therefore in that sense are a biased sample, they do include a wide range of levels of effectiveness. And most campaigns fail on some metrics. So, it is not unreasonable to extrapolate the findings to the 'real world' of campaigns not entered into an effectiveness awards competition.

There is 20 years of creativity data, so we can look at trends in creative effectiveness as well as the overall pattern. It is in the trends that the worrying findings emerge.

The earlier 2011 *Gunn Report* had come to the very positive conclusion that 'creatively awarded campaigns are becoming more effective', and that 'creatively awarded campaigns were 12 times as efficient as non-awarded'. The intervening five years had been tumultuous in marketing – a deep and lingering recession had modified the mood of marketing, and the evolving media landscape had altered the practices of marketing. In some very important ways, these impacts had been very destructive of effectiveness in general, not just to creative effectiveness. But nowhere was the impact more harmful than on the contribution of creativity to effectiveness: the updated report revealed that, for the first time in the 20-year run of data, creatively awarded campaigns had started to lose their effectiveness advantage. They were still considerably more effective than non-awarded campaigns, but a destructive downward trend had developed. So, the new 2016 report carried the altogether less positive title of 'Selling creativity short'.

'Why should we mourn the demise of creativity?' some will be asking. Who needs creativity when we have social media and 'Big Data'? The simple answer is that nothing else that we can do as marketers even comes close to the impact of creativity on effectiveness. We can play all the clever digital games we like with targeting and retargeting and they will not boost our long-term return on investment by a factor of 12. If we are smart enough to follow Byron Sharp and his research at the Ehrenberg-Bass Institute, we will know that tight, last-minute targeting reduces long-term effectiveness. Creativity builds fame for our brands: it gets them talked about and shared. Consumers are drawn to such brands, and over time, creative brands develop a disproportionately strong position in their minds. If we invest sufficient media money behind great creativity so that its reach is wide, and in media such as TV that have the proven power to spark those conversations, then fame effects can be truly transformational. The much celebrated UK John Lewis campaign is a tour de force of commercial exploitation of creativity. Who would have thought 10 years ago that a *department store* would become a global role model for successful marketing communications?

So, what is now going wrong with this amazing growth machine? In a word, most of the deterioration can be put down to *short-termism*. If we measure success over the short term, we come to completely opposite conclusions about what drives success than if we measure success over the long term. The chart (taken from Les Binet and Peter Field's 2013 book *The Long and the Short of It*) demonstrates how brand-building advertising and sales-activation advertising operate over different timescales, and why timescales of evaluation can lead us to different conclusions.

Short-termists reach for the low-hanging fruit in the market: they reduce their investment in brand building because it takes time to deliver growth, and

Brand-building and sales-activation advertising over time

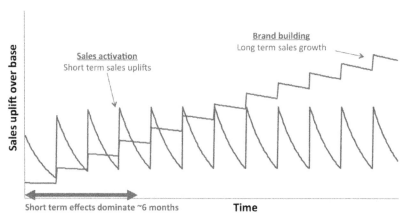

Source: Binet & Field, 2013

they switch ever more expenditure to sales activation and digital sales tools such as search, which can deliver short-term results, but do little for long-term growth. Worse still, they turn away from creativity when they discover it doesn't bring the short-term growth they seek because it takes *time* to work its magic on the brand. At its worse, they end up with a barrage of 'timely and relevant offers' delivered through retargeted online advertising (assuming it isn't blocked by consumers). As you can see, there is no long-term growth, merely a series of spikes. Sales never get easier to achieve, and it can undermine the esteem and appeal of brands. It is a bottomless pit – a bidding war for the last-minute pre-purchase attention of a limited number of prospects.

Brand building is different. It means creating mental structures (associations, memories, beliefs etc) that will predispose potential customers to choose one brand over another. This is a long-term job involving conditioning consumers through repeated exposure, so it takes time; talking to people long before they come to buy. It requires broad reach media, because the aim is to prime everyone in the market, regardless of whether or not they are shopping right now. And because most of the audience are not in the market at the time they are exposed, it cannot assume close attention. So, it relies heavily on emotional priming, since that cuts through regardless of whether people are interested in the product, and it helps create long-term memory structures. But it is vital if we want to make next year's sales easier to achieve than this year's, and so drive long-term growth.

Driven by a relentless diet of short-term digital metrics and a general management culture which fails to appreciate the dangers of short-term digital activation, short-termism is now growing on an industrial scale. Once, only around 8% of IPA campaigns were 'short term', now it is around a third, and growing. Short-term campaigns are defined as campaigns that ran and were evaluated over periods of less than six months. This is not an arbitrary period: analysis reported in *The Long and the Short of It* demonstrated how brand building takes over as the primary driver of growth from sales activation after six months. This places everything up to and including quarterly reporting firmly in the short-term camp. Data-driven real-time marketing is *totally* part of this short-term world: around 20% of IPA case studies now use it. It is perhaps the most dangerous development in marketing of recent times.

A new genre of disposable creativity is arising with the largely futile objective of achieving lasting success overnight. Like fireworks, these campaigns make a lot of noise and light, but are gone before lasting impressions are created. And the legacy of this orgy of short-sightedness is not only the halving of the typical efficiency of creatively awarded campaigns, but also the sacrifice of most of the effectiveness gains achieved since the turn of the millennium amongst campaigns in general. How can we be sure that short-termism is to blame? Because the dwindling class of long-term adequately funded creative campaigns remains as astonishingly effective as ever. The continuing John Lewis campaign success is fantastic evidence of that.

Let's hope that 2018 and beyond sees the birth of a counter-trend towards long-term metrics, and the use of the media and strategies that can deliver long-term success. Otherwise it won't only be creativity that we will be mourning the loss of.

References

Binet, L, and Field, P. *The Long and the Short of It: Balancing short and long-term marketing strategies.* IPA, 2013

5

THE SIGNALLING OF TIME HORIZONS – OR HOW TO PROVE YOU ARE NOT A CROOK

Written by **Rory Sutherland**

How do you show you care about your customer, over the long term? This chapter investigates.

What do the following things have in common?

1. The fact that large, normally carnivorous fish desist from eating 'cleaner' fish, such as wrasse.
2. Those posh rope-handled carrier bags you get when you spend an appreciable amount of money on women's clothes or cosmetics.
3. The free extra scoop of fries they give you at Five Guys.
4. Spending a fortune on a wedding.
5. A hotel waiving your modest minibar charges.
6. The marble and oak lavishly used in 19th century bank branches.
7. That fancy training course your company sent you on in Kitzbühel.
8. A lavish advertising campaign.
9. A restaurant giving its patrons a free glass of limoncello after their meal.
10. Investing in a brand.

Looked at from the standpoint of simple, short-term economic rationality, none of these behaviours makes complete sense. A bank could conduct its business perfectly well from a portakabin. Those rope-handled bags are expensive, but aren't even waterproof. Limoncello costs money, and a lot of people don't like it. Was the training course really worth £5k? These things only make sense if we assume that some signalling is going on.

All of them, I would contend, may signal a variety of things. But they all are examples of a behaviour which is costly in the near term, and which will pay off (if at all) only in the longer term. They are thus, if nothing else, reliable signals that the person, animal or business engaging in that behaviour is acting on the basis of *long-term self-interest* rather than short-term expediency.

This distinction matters. A lot.

Unlike short-term expediency, *long-term* self-interest, as my friend the evolutionary biologist Robert Trivers has shown, often leads to behaviours that are indistinguishable from mutually beneficial cooperation. The reason the large fish does not eat its cleaner fish is not because of altruism, but because *over the long-term* 'the cleaner fish is more valuable to it alive than dead'.

The cleaner fish could cheat by ignoring ectoparasites and eating tasty bits of the host fish's gills instead, but its long-term future is rosier if the big fish becomes a repeat customer. (And they do. Fish, it seems, exhibit surprising brand loyalty towards individual cleaner fish.)

What keeps the relationship honest, trusting and mutually beneficial is nothing other than the prospect of repetition.

In game theory, this prospect of repetition is known variously as 'continuation probability' or 'ω'. Robert Axelrod has poetically referred to it as 'the shadow of the future'. It is agreed by both game theorists and evolutionary biologists that the prospects for cooperation are far greater when there is a high expectation of repetition than in single shot games. Clay Shirky has even described social capital as 'the shadow of the future at a societal scale'. Yet businesses barely consider this at all (in fact procurement, by setting shorter and shorter contract periods, may be unwittingly working to reduce cooperation).

Yet there are, when you think about it, two different approaches to business. There is the 'tourist restaurant' approach, where you try to make as much money from people on their single visit. And then there is the 'local pub' approach, where you may make less money from people on each visit, but you profit more over time by encouraging people to come back. The second type of business is much more likely to generate trust and yield positive sum outcomes than the first.

How might people distinguish the second type of business from the first? Well, the scoop of extra fries you get at Five Guys is one such gesture: an immediate expense with a deferred pay off. It is a reliable signifier that you are investing in a repeat relationship, not milking a single transaction. Likewise, when your company pays your salary this month, it says you are worth that money for now; when it sends you to Kitzbühel, it signals that it is committed to you for a few years at least.

If fish (and even some symbiotic plants) have evolved to spot this distinction, it seems perfectly plausible that humans instinctively can do the same, and instinctively prefer to do business with brands with longer time horizons.

This theory, if true, would also explain some counterintuitive findings in customer behaviour. It has long baffled people why, if a customer has a problem and a brand resolves it in a satisfactory manner, the customer becomes a more loyal customer than if the fault had not occurred in the first place. Odd, until you realise that solving a problem for a customer at your own expense is a good way of signalling your commitment to a future relationship.

The theory of 'continuation probability' would also predict that when a business focuses more narrowly on short-term profit maximisation, it will appear less and less trustworthy to its customers. I suspect that, to anyone who has been awake for the last 30 years, this possibility seems all too plausible.

References

Axelrod, R. *The Evolution of Cooperation.* Basic Books, 1984

Shirky. C. *Here Comes Everybody.* Penguin, 2008

Trivers. R. 'The evolution of reciprocal altruism'. *The Quarterly Review of Biology*, 46(1), 1971

6

FIGHTING NONSENSE WITH NONSENSE

Written by **Ryan Wallman**

Language is meant to elucidate, but all too often it obfuscates, descending into marketing-speak, or plain bullshit. This chapter considers some common offenders, and offers some advice on how to fight nonsense with nonsense.

I think I speak for many people in our industry when I say that it sometimes feels as if we're losing the war of words. And by extension, the war of ideas.

The enemy in our midst is what might be called 'marketing-speak'. Or utter bullshit, to use my preferred term for it.

And the worrying part is that it's not going anywhere. If anything, it's becoming ever more pervasive. Just take a look at any marketing publication.

For many people, the response to all this is 'So what?'

'Ryan,' they probably think to themselves after my fifth unhinged rant of the day, 'give it a rest, will you? Does it really matter if people want to sound like pseudo-intellectual drones?'

Fair enough. But you and I know that marketing jargon is not (just) a silly source of amusement: it corrupts communication and inhibits clear thinking. You need only read a big company's website or a CMO's quote to appreciate the obfuscatory nature of this kind of language.

And this gets to the nub of the problem for you and me: if nonsensical language reflects nonsensical thinking, it's no wonder that marketers are generally held in low regard.

Frankly, marketers often make themselves sound silly. And while that might sometimes put them beyond satire, what follows is a selection of satirical (if not downright facetious) comments on the marketing industry.

First, here's my attempt to decode some of the more common terminology used in modern marketing.

The term	What it means
Customer-centric marketing	Marketing
Omnichannel brand amplification	Advertising
Disruptive	Slightly different
Innovative	Not innovative
Key demographic	A group of customers chosen on a completely arbitrary basis (note: always Millennials)
Influencer	A 14-year-old who makes YouTube videos
Upstream Influencer	The 16-year-old sibling of a 14-year-old who makes YouTube videos
Pre-contemplative prospect	Someone who couldn't give a f**k about your brand

Some marketing terminology, however, is so heinous that it deserves a more rigorous going over.

The first of these is the phrase 'customer journey'. Sure, it may have started out as a worthwhile concept, but suffice to say it has since been hijacked, beaten and left for dead on the side of the customer road.

Travel advice for your customer journey

1. In times past, being a customer was a simple affair. You saw something, and you bought it; or perhaps you thought about buying something for a while, then bought it. Those days are over. Now you're embarking on a 'journey', and you'll need all your stamina to survive it.

2. Before you leave, ensure that your buyer persona is registered with the relevant authorities. If you attempt to go on a customer journey without a recognised buyer persona, you'll confuse the hell out of any modern marketing executive.

3. Plan your itinerary carefully. As with other kinds of journeys, it can be all too easy to end up somewhere you never intended to be (online click-throughs, for example), or to wander around endlessly and still not find what you're looking for (any IKEA visit).

4. Make sure you pack some sturdy shoes, because the grounds for customer journeys can be flimsy to say the least.

5. It's a good idea to learn a few words of the native lingo. A simple, 'Hello, my name is Savvy Millennial' will endear you to the local marketers.

6. Stay safe. Notorious roaming gangs such as 'Adtech' and 'Remarketing' prey on unwary travellers. Do *not* interact with them under any circumstances.

7. Always carry protection. Despite what marketers will tell you about loyalty, customer journeys are often promiscuous occasions.

8. Remember that customer journeys tend to follow rivers of marketing bullshit, which are rife with faecally transmitted diseases. Marketers are immune to these, and even seem to revel in them, but customers are highly susceptible to their effects. If you develop verbal diarrhoea characterised by terms such as 'touchpoints' and 'seamless experiences', seek medical attention immediately.

So, customer journeys are on the nose. But the mother of all marketing bullshit – the one that makes the rest seem noble and sensible by comparison – is surely the term 'Millennials'. Marketers love Millennials even more than they love customer journeys. And they presume to know plenty about them, too.

10 things that marketers have taught us about Millennials

1. Millennials like stuff.
2. Millennials don't like other stuff.
3. Conveniently, all Millennials like exactly the same stuff.
4. Millennials are completely different from every other generation, in that they were born at a different time. That much we can agree on.
5. We can't actually agree on when Millennials were born.
6. Millennials will not persist with anything that doesn't keep them interested. When writing *for* Millennials, you must be unceasingly entertaining.
7. When writing *about* Millennials, you must be unceasingly boring.
8. Millennials will immediately detect if you're being condescending, the clever little scamps.
9. You do not simply ask Millennials what they think, you 'tap into their mindset'.
10. Millennials don't like Apple. They don't like broccoli either, but that's kids for you.

But just to be clear, here is my definitive guide to what makes Millennials different from other generations.

Generation	Born	Other shared characteristics
Millennials	1980–95	None
Generation X	1965–79	None
Baby Boomers	1946–64	None

And if there's one thing I'm sure we can all agree on, it's that there is a worrying dearth of impressive-sounding acronyms in marketing. So, this is my attempt to add to the acronym arsenal (otherwise known as the 'arsenym').

CJO – Chief Jargon Officer

The person who takes company-wide responsibility for the optimal implementation of linguistic overcomplexificationism. Core competency is cross-sectoral alignment of value-adding communicative impenetrables.

BDB – Big Data Baffler

Someone who attempts to baffle you with 'Big Data' (not *actual* Big Data – just the term 'Big Data'). Most BDBs have never studied statistics of any kind, and therefore think that a p-value refers to the monetary cost of relieving oneself in a European public convenience.

ROG – Return On Gobbledygook

A financial measure particularly favoured by CJOs and BDBs. Calculated by dividing net profit by the frequency of use of certain words in marketing communications (for example, 'leverage', 'value-adding', 'innovation'). The ROG acronym is best reserved for those who fully understand its role in leveraging value-adding innovation.

DTL – Down The Line

A contingency strategy activated in the event of a failed marketing campaign. As in, 'Our ATL and BTL activities didn't work. We need to blame this on someone DTL'.

B2S – Business To Self

A type of marketing communication in which a business appears to be talking primarily to itself. Characterised by phrases such as 'We believe ...'; 'That's why we ...'; 'Our philosophy here at ...'; and anything referring to the 'core' or 'heart' of the company. B2S is sometimes abbreviated to just BS.

CTI – Call To Inaction

An element of marketing communication that specifically and emphatically discourages a desired behaviour. Common examples include QR codes, invitations to 'find out more about John's story online', and the phrase 'join the conversation'.

NFI – Newly Fabricated Institute

An attempt to confer gravitas on what would otherwise be an obvious rehash of a marketing concept that's been around for decades. NFI is a phenomenon peculiar to modern marketers.

RTC – Ridiculous Title Creator

One of the most important people in a marketing agency. The RTC is responsible for transforming traditional job titles like 'designer' (BORING!) into cutting-edge handles such as 'pixel ninja'.

N2V – Noun To Verb

The practice of 'transitioning' a noun to a verb, on the basis that it implies more dynamism. While not confined to any one industry, it has been embraced by marketers, who are especially partial to impacting, ideating and gamifying.

As you can see, there's always room for new nonsense in our industry. And the best place to keep up with it all it is at a conference. Like this one.

'The Emperor's New Clothes' conference 2018

Marketing by the cynical, for the gullible

Time	Topic
7.30–8.30	ENERGY SUPPLEMENTATION EXPERIENCE (FORMERLY 'BREAKFAST')
8.30–9.30	Making the simple complex: how to baffle people for profit
9.30–10.30	Emojism: storytelling in the age of illiteracy
10.30–11.30	Completely deluded: taking virtual reality to its logical conclusion
11.30–1.00	SHAMELESS SELF-PROMOTIONAL OPPORTUNITY (LUNCH PROVIDED)
1.00–2.00	Beyond brand love: how do you get customers to actually have sex with your product?

2.00–3.00	Advertising is dead: why hypercontextual data-driven programmatic gamification is the future
3.00–4.00	Rectal insertables: the next generation of wearable technology
4.00–5.00	Buzzword innovation: what's next in the bollocksphere?

But finally, for anyone still struggling with the concepts of modern marketing, here is my foolproof guide.

A 10-point guide to modern marketing

1. Do not under any circumstances try to sell anything to people. Selling is a relic of the 20th century, like humility or non-online porn.
2. You must not 'interrupt' people with your marketing. People must grant you permission before you are allowed to not sell something to them.
3. Whatever it is that you create, make sure it is shareable. The best way to do this is to present it in bite-sized pieces. Like a fun-size Mars bar. Except they're not shareable, come to think of it. Er, forget that analogy.
4. The ultimate aim of being shared is to go viral. Exposing yourself to as many people as possible is the goal. So, in summary: selling = evil; shameless global exhibitionism = good.
5. No matter what you communicate about your business, you must make sure that it adds value. A good way to add value is to write blog posts about how important it is to add value.
6. Modern marketing is all about engagement. You can 'build' engagement or 'grow' engagement, but the best way to achieve an embiggening of engagement is to 'drive' it.
7. Make sure that your marketing efforts are in alignment. With what, you ask? With everything: your culture, your values, your vision and your mission. If you don't have any of these, just steal them from another company; they're the same for every business.
8. Don't get caught up 'doing' things. Instead, you should plan things, or even better, strategise things. Only low-paid chumps do things.

9. An excellent way to avoid doing things is to automate them. Need to measure something? Automate it. Customer service? Automate that too. And if you need some writing done, there are thousands of monkeys on thousands of keyboards out there. Hire one. Hell, hire them all – they work for nothing.

10. Whatever business you're in, you must be innovative. The only thing you can't be innovative about is using another word for 'innovative', because it is mandatory. Say you're innovative. Then say you're innovative again. Innovative.

7

POST-TRUTH TELLY

Written by **Tess Alps**

TV is dead: people no longer watch it, and so there's no point advertising on it. That is the mantra of post-truth telly. But if that is the post-truth, what is the truth? This chapter explores.

Surely there can be no sentient being left unaware that the *Oxford English Dictionary's* 'Word of the Year' for 2016 was 'post-truth'.

It's a fascinating and nuanced word. 'Post-truth' is not just a fancy way to say a lie, a mistake or an untruth. It suggests that the truth is available (a known even), and has maybe been considered, but found wanting. The truth simply doesn't deliver the emotional hit to persuade anyone to let go of their personal prejudices.

The definition in the *Oxford English Dictionary* is instructive:

> *Post-Truth: relating to or denoting circumstances in which objective facts are less influential in shaping public opinion than appeals to emotion and personal belief.*

We in marketing shouldn't be at all surprised that emotion beats facts hands down. Haven't Les Binet and Peter Field done their exhaustive work on the IPA Databank proving precisely that? Marketing campaigns which favour emotional over rational messaging have been shown to deliver more (and larger) business effects, ie greater sales, market share and profit growth.

When 'post-truth' started to appear widely through 2016, particularly in connection with Brexit and the presidential campaign of Donald Trump, it made me realise that marketing and media have been existing in a post-truth world for at least a decade. How many times have we been told that all the rules of marketing have changed, that personalised messages would be more effective than generic ones, that building loyalty was more important than penetration, or that consumers wanted to have a 'conversation' with brands? I've yet to see any evidence to support any of those assertions. Amongst these many 'alternative facts', one of the most prevalent was that the internet would kill TV.

In 2006, I chose to leave PHD to set up Thinkbox; I was frustrated at the ease with which 'alternative facts' about TV consumption and advertising effectiveness had taken root in the British marketing community. When we started, the 'TV is dead' mantra had taken root, and Thinkbox set about trying to pull up the pernicious weed. It should have been tackled much earlier of course, but I think the changes that TV was experiencing in the first five years of this century confused many practitioners, including many broadcasters themselves.

The BBC, ITV and Channel 4 were experiencing significant declines in viewing. This was generally attributed to the growing use of the internet, and this angle was adopted with relish by journalists, fed with mischievous stories from the tech companies, who seemed to have decided that it was not enough for them to grow – TV must die. And so the narrative developed intertwining the growth of the internet with the decline of TV, despite hard evidence to the contrary. So deep-rooted had this belief become that all our attempts to assert the facts about TV were often greeted with accusations that we were lying and trying to deny the existence of the internet.

What was really causing the British public service channels to lose viewing was the growth of multi-channel broadcasters, via satellite or cable, and chief amongst these was Sky. The great irony through the first decade of the century was that, at the same time people were hearing (and believing) that TV was dying, standard TV viewing as measured by BARB (ie live, in-home, plus seven-day playback and on-demand) had never been higher, peaking in 2010 at over four hours a day at the height of the recession.

Chart 1: Standard* TV viewing since 2000, BBC and commercial

Standard* TV viewing remains strong

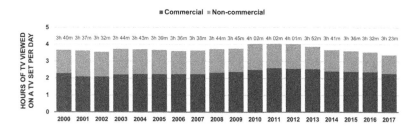

Source: BARB, 2000-2017, individuals. TV set viewing within 7 days of broadcast.

thinkbox

The reputation of TV advertising was, if anything, in an even worse place than that of TV viewing in 2006. The advent of TV recorders (DTRs/PVRs) such as Sky+ was heralded as the TV ad killer. Why would anyone sit through a TV ad ever again? And even if some TV ads were seen, the quality wasn't like it had been in 19blah blah (choose your own 'golden age'), according to people in the industry.

In fact, the viewing of TV ads – at normal speed (BARB doesn't report fast-forwarded ads, and they are therefore free) – grew consistently through the first decade of the century. The numbers of 'impressions' had never been higher within standard TV, as previously defined, in part because the growth of multi-channel TV was taking viewing from the ad-free BBC. But also because live TV was (and remains to this day) the dominant way to watch for the vast majority of people. In 2017, 86% of standard TV was viewed live, even though 60.4% of homes had a TV recorder.

Chart 2: TV ads seen at normal speed 2000–17 within standard* TV

We watched 42% more standard* TV ads in 2017 than in 2000

Individual impacts in billions

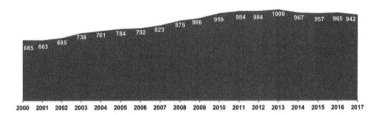

Source: BARB, 2000 - 2017 Base: 30" reweighted impacts. An impact = one person viewing one TV ad in its entirety. Impacts only count when viewed at normal speed

thinkbox

Since the peaks for standard TV viewing and TV advertising (in 2010 and 2013 respectively) occurred, technology has delivered many changes to the way viewers can access TV, with more on the horizon. First of all came catch-up TV services via websites, watched on PCs and laptops, then mobile apps for tablets and smartphones, and more recently, catch-up has come directly to the TV set via set-top boxes. But on-demand TV is now about more than catching up with recently broadcast programmes: broadcasters are clearing rights and starting to make their archives available – the 'box-set' category has arrived. In some instances, they are also making whole series available before they are broadcast, to meet the desire to binge.

All of the above depend on various internet technologies, some of which are very apparent to the user, for instance when a browser is used, but in other instances the internet has become seamlessly integrated into TV technology.

From its earliest days, Thinkbox has resolutely maintained that the internet is not a threat to TV. For a start, it is quite wrong to see the internet as a rival medium. It is a transforming technology that has made banking, shopping and calling your Mum easier. Now it is helping people watch more TV in new ways, at new times. It would be naïve not to recognise that some internet-only media are competitors to TV for advertising money, though even here they work most positively when used in conjunction with TV advertising: TV + search, TV + email.

In addition to broadcasters' new services, the last decade has seen the growth of OTT (Over The Top) subscription video services, such as Netflix and Amazon Prime. These services have largely replaced DVD rental stores; they offer output from Hollywood studios and archive series from broadcasters around the world in addition to some of their own excellent original productions.

All of the above developments are wonderful for viewers – a veritable golden age for TV as widely cited – but something of a nightmare for BARB who is valiantly trying to measure all these new forms of TV to the same high standards as standard TV.

It should be no surprise, given the effort and investments broadcasters have made to encourage people to watch TV differently, that standard TV viewing has seen declines since 2010, albeit ones that show standard TV viewing in 2016 was as high as in 2002. But, in a post-truth world, this trend is gold dust to TV's enemies, who can point to the limited BARB data to peddle their myth that TV is dying. This is too often believed without any further analysis, even by advertisers and agencies who one would hope would be most sceptical and demanding of deeper scrutiny.

BARB's 'Project Dovetail' has started filling some of these measurement gaps, and will continue to work towards total TV measurement of the highest quality, with impeccable transparency, impartiality and integrity. Until that time arrives, Thinkbox has, for the last few years, compiled a fuller overview of the total video world, using a collection of industry recognised sources from UKOM/ComScore and IPA TouchPoints to Ofcom and broadcasters' own stream data.

It's interesting to see how the total video landscape is growing alongside a stable picture for TV. This is not a zero-sum game.

When Thinkbox does succeed in convincing marketers that TV viewing is very resilient, the next 'post-truth' usually thrown back at us is that the numbers are all old people, and that 'Millennials' never watch TV. It's undeniable that young people watch less TV – always have, always will; less video overall, and more of it will be SVOD and YouTube. But the latest numbers are in, and

Chart 3: Total video viewing

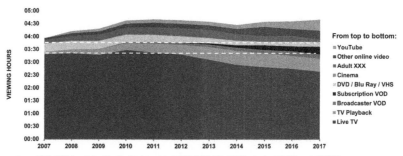

Source: 2017, BARB / comScore / Broadcaster stream data / OFCOM Digital Day / IPA Touchpoints 2016 / Rentrak / OFCOM Communications report / Statista / IPSOS / Thinkbox estimates

it seems young people are just not getting the message: they keep watching TV – it made up a sizeable portion of their total video time in 2017.

Time spent with different media is interesting, but a very poor way to determine where to spend your advertising money. That flawed approach

Chart 4: Total video, all individuals and 16–34s

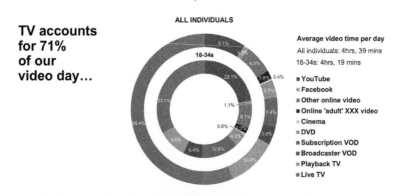

Source: 2017, BARB / comScore / Broadcaster stream data / OFCOM Digital Day / IPA Touchpoints 2017 / Rentrak

has been championed by influential analyst Mary Meeker and her disciple Sir Martin Sorrell; it has led to the overinvestment in all forms of 'digital' advertising. It's not surprising that Ebiquity reports online display ads deliver the worst ROI when you look at how little online video advertising is actually available to soak up all that ad money. And TV advertising continues to defy those 'alternative facts' by accounting for 94% of the video advertising that is actually viewed (91% for young people).

Chart 5: Total video advertising, all individuals and 16–34s

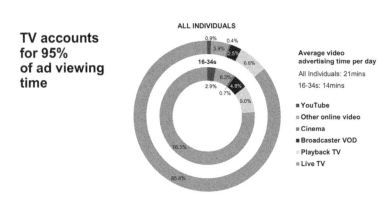

Source: 2017, BARB / comScore / Broadcaster stream data / OFCOM Digital Day / IPA Touchpoints 2017 / Rentrak

thinkbox

I hope that all the data above allows you unbiased and thoughtful marketing people to see that, although TV is changing, it is certainly not dying. And yet, the myths persist.

When we try to understand how and why 'post-truth telly' persists, despite the best efforts of Thinkbox (and many, many others) to put the simple truths in front of the world, we find the following three key factors. We would contend that these three factors can be found in most post-truth situations, from Brexit to Trump.

1. Ignorance

When the world is changing fast, it is understandable that people can't always keep up. And in many cases, there is a genuine information vacuum, as I have described with BARB's measurement of new forms of TV viewing and advertising. When trustworthy information is in short supply, people would rather fill it with any information, however partial or untrustworthy the source.

There is also a strong inclination to 'confirmation bias' here: we more readily believe those sources that agree with our existing opinions. And what we already believe is influenced by our own experience.

Good marketers should be aware of the confirmation bias phenomenon, yet repeatedly we hear very senior people saying, 'I can't believe that impartial research you're showing me because I do X/my children do Y'.

Every couple of years, Thinkbox commissions Ipsos to undertake a piece of research to bring this tendency to life. It's called 'Ad Nation'. It asks the general public to estimate their own behaviour across a range of media channels. Then it asks people who work in advertising (Ad people) to estimate their own behaviour in those same channels, but also asks them to estimate the

Chart 6: Subscription VOD

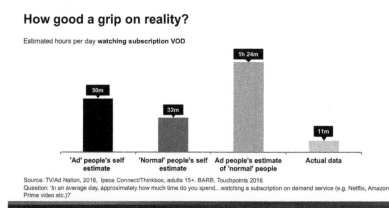

How good a grip on reality?

Estimated hours per day **watching subscription VOD**

Source: TV/Ad Nation, 2016, Ipsos Connect/Thinkbox, adults 15+. BARB, Touchpoints 2016
Question: 'In an average day, approximately how much time do you spend…watching a subscription on demand service (e.g. Netflix, Amazon Prime video etc.)?'

thinkbox

behaviour of the general public. The results are in equal part hilarious and depressing. In 2016, Ad people estimated that the public conducted 24% of their TV viewing on devices other than a TV set, but they believed that it was much higher (at 37%) for 'normal people'. The 'normal people' estimated their own TV viewing via non-set devices at a more modest 16%. But the real figure is 2%. Here are another couple of examples from the 2016 study.

Chart 7: Multi-screening

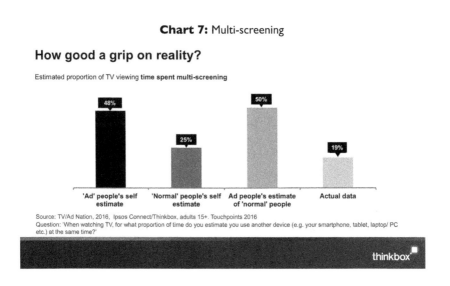

How good a grip on reality?

Estimated proportion of TV viewing **time spent multi-screening**

48% 25% 50% 19%

'Ad' people's self estimate   'Normal' people's self estimate   Ad people's estimate of 'normal' people   Actual data

Source: TV/Ad Nation, 2016, Ipsos Connect/Thinkbox, adults 15+. Touchpoints 2016
Question: 'When watching TV, for what proportion of time do you estimate you use another device (e.g. your smartphone, tablet, laptop/ PC etc.) at the same time?'

thinkbox

There are a number of well-documented psychological explanations as to the reasons why people overestimate these behaviours, but it is extremely dismaying to see advertising professionals so far off the mark, and to have a worse grip on reality than ordinary people. One factor is that advertising and marketing people *are* very different from the average consumer in their media habits. The following is just one example.

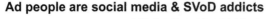

Chart 8: Social media addicts

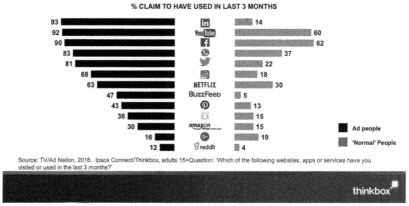

Ad people are social media & SVoD addicts

% CLAIM TO HAVE USED IN LAST 3 MONTHS

Source: TV/Ad Nation, 2016, Ipsos Connect/Thinkbox, adults 15+Question: 'Which of the following websites, apps or services have you visited or used in the last 3 months?'

thinkbox

All we can do is repeatedly tell people in our industry that they are most certainly *not* normal, and hope they don't let that compound their ignorance.

2. Vested interests

We all have vested interests. Some are very easy to spot. Thinkbox's axe gleams away for all to see, for example. The companies licking their lips at the thought of gobbling up TV ad revenue are also easy to identify, and they are often the ones peddling the naughtiest post-truth stories.

TV advertising is worth a lot of money. It's about 40% of the advertising cake globally, though in the UK and other territories with ad-free public service broadcasters such as the BBC it represents a much smaller slice. TV advertising, including broadcaster VOD and sponsorship, takes only about 25% of total UK ad revenue (43.1% of display), but that share has held steady while search and other forms of online advertising have rocketed, mainly at the expense of newspapers and magazines.

But despite their rapid growth and sky-high profit margins, the online tech companies want yet more. They want more ad revenue for its own sake, but they also want it as demonstration of their dynamic growth, which boosts their share price and their investor story. Online advertising has become a 'get rich quick and get out' market, and has led to the unsatisfactory situation we now see. Excessive and creepy advertising has provoked the consumers' response of ad blocking, and there are additional woes for advertisers in the form of walled garden measurement, viewability doubts, fraud and dodgy content.

A big ingredient in the investor stories from tech companies has been the rubbishing of TV. If they can undermine financial markets' confidence in TV, it will divert investment to them and concurrently reduce the share price of TV companies. My personal suspicion is that, as online companies try to develop more video advertising opportunities (and dip their toes into the acquisition of professional film and TV content that would enable that advertising), it is very likely that they will try to acquire TV companies, whether broadcasters or producers. In this scenario, the lower the TV company's share price, the better for them.

As I said, some vested interests are easy to spot, and hopefully that protects marketers from any post-truth propaganda coming out of them. We want people to be as deeply sceptical about anything the tech giants say as they are about what Thinkbox says – including this paper.

However, there are other vested interests that are less easy to spot. We have sometimes been disappointed at how reticent media agencies are when malpractice is uncovered within online advertising, or how reluctant some are to correct 'alternative facts' about TV. We now understand a great deal more about how media agencies make their own money, sometimes pressurised by client contracts that make it hard to make a profit in a legitimate way. 'Post-truth' telly has provided an alibi for them to overinvest in media where they can make more income for themselves at the expense of their clients' marketing effectiveness.

And within marketing departments, where you would expect only proven effectiveness to rule, the creation and self-preservation of 'digital' specialists and silos has enabled 'post-truth' telly to survive to the detriment of the brand's own fortunes.

3. Journalism

Journalists have a tough life. Their lives have changed immeasurably: declining print circulations and ad revenue have led to fewer staff, 24-hour reporting, acres more space to fill, and the hideous culture of click-counting, which makes it all too plain how well-read (or not) their articles are, and hence their individual ad revenue generation. What a stressful existence. They really don't need me to stick the boot in as well.

It's instructive to see how the demands on today's journalists encourage a variety of 'post-truth' behaviours. Given how stretched they are, it is practically impossible for a journalist to check the veracity of every press release they receive. And their need to fill space makes it less likely that they will turn away any possible news story, even if they might have slight doubts about it.

When it comes to our own world of marketing and advertising, the hyping of internet media is evident from the sheer numbers of stories on every aspect of online – be it social, programmatic, personalisation, video, data or content. And this isn't going to stop any time soon.

When I asked the editor of the largest marketing and media website in Australia, Mumbrella, why they publish so many stories about internet marketing (including ones where there was barely a story in it), she was honest enough to admit that they just publish what gets clicked on. For as long as we all keep clicking on those articles, journalists are going to keep writing them. We also, apparently, will always click on something with a 'the death of' in the headline, or anything with a punch-up in it. Can't beat a bit of drama.

As an organisation trying to counterbalance the 'post-truth telly' syndrome, this is a massive challenge. We have a responsibility to help journalists, making facts easy to get hold of, finding as much new news about TV as possible, and responding rapidly whenever we see any 'alternative facts' appearing. If journalists choose to position our corrections as a fight, it's a small price to pay.

In an ideal world, we wouldn't want the defence of TV to turn into an attack on any other online medium. There are a couple of excellent and very high profile columnists who recognise the phenomenon of post-truth telly, and are vigorous defenders of the effectiveness of TV advertising. They are invaluable to us. But their support for TV is often accompanied by a ruthless evisceration of, say, social media marketing or online video. In the real world, advertisers are going to use all the tools at their disposal, and the best thing we can do is help them with integration. It doesn't help 'post-truth telly' to resort to post-truth anything else.

Welcome to our world. Thinkbox has been living with 'alternative facts' and 'post-truth' for its entire existence, and it tests our skill as communicators every single day. So, going back to that *Oxford English Dictionary's* definition of 'post-truth', we recognise that we need to frame our messages in an emotional way, not just a factual, information-rich, rational way. For every marketer who might be persuaded by a paper such as this, or our huge bank of charts, there is another who is more influenced by seeing film from our ethnographic studies: real people captured watching TV at home or on the move, responding to TV ads by laughing, singing, and yes, even buying.

And luckily, we have access to that most potent weapon of persuasion: the TV ad. Our TV campaigns over the last 10 years (latterly starring wonder-dog Harvey) have arguably been extremely inefficient, but by some margin they are the most effective form of marketing we undertake. And not a fact to be seen.

References

Ebiquity. 'Re-evaluating media: what the evidence reveals about the true worth of media for brand advertisers'. 2018

8

IT'S BEYOND TIME TO RETHINK SOCIAL MEDIA MARKETING

Written by **Jerry Daykin**

There are many popularly held misconceptions about social media, which serious marketers need to reassess. While these platforms present substantial opportunities to reach consumers, build brands and drive sales, achieving these goals generally requires applying a much more traditional approach than some gurus would have you believe. In this chapter, we unpack some of those myths, the theory and evidence which challenges them, and how marketers ultimately can maximise their use.

Social media has become a powerful weapon in the modern marketer's arsenal, offering rich opportunities to communicate with millions of people to sell products and grow brands. There is, however, a major divide between the proven approach to these platforms that large companies have privately evolved and the public representation that social media often gets at marketing events or within the industry press. I am a marketer who over the past decade has helped shape the social media activity of some of the world's largest brands, and I wanted to capture here some of what I have learnt along the way.

Social media platforms work far more like traditional media channels than we seem willing to admit as an industry. Yes, they allow for interaction, and have far more information about their viewers, but ultimately, they are valuable to marketers because they attract large audiences which we can reach highly efficiently with paid media promotion. Through surveys, sales tracking, econometric modelling and other research methods, I have regularly seen it proven that social media advertising can influence the opinions and actions of hundreds of millions of people.

The vast majority of those people, however, will never like, comment, share or actively engage with the brand in question at all. In fact, the extent to which social media has introduced a new era of conversational, opt-in marketing – where viral content trumps traditional media spends – is greatly exaggerated. The senior strategic conversations and evidence-based decisions taking place in major brands have long since recognised this, and changed accordingly.

These brands don't chase (or sometimes even bother to measure) engagement; they guarantee scale and impact through their media plans, and they measure success through actual business results, just like their other marketing channels. It's a sharp contrast to the commentary I still see widely shared in the industry where tips are exchanged on how to tweak content to get slightly higher engagement, and 'beat' the nefarious newsfeed algorithms sent to challenge us.

More often than not, these aren't just harmless distractions; they are falsehoods which can completely misdirect marketing efforts and waste sizable budgets. Given that the evidence for what does and doesn't work in social media has been in the public domain for over five years, it's getting to the point of being almost fraudulent that some agencies chose to ignore it, and marketers need to start challenging those who repeat these misrepresentations.

The main players have created much of these challenges themselves, heavily pushing agendas of engagement, conversation, real-time virality and more, before far more quietly backing away from these territories when the weight of their own evidence proved them wrong. Though you may not have realised it, you would have to go back well over five years to hear a Facebook executive or sales person talking up any benefits of fans, conversations or engagement on their platform. Back in 2011, I worked with them on a project to remove all measures of engagement and fans from internal reports at one of their largest global brand advertisers, because they were an unhelpful distraction.

Facebook IQ, a resource designed to help marketers on the platform, has a wide range of articles explaining how important paid reach is on the platform. In contrast, searches for engagement and fans bring up stories about wedding proposals and sports tournaments as their top answers. Of course, I acknowledge that you can easily argue the platforms themselves are conveniently biased in this way as they only make money from advertisers paying to reach more people.

Marketers with a range of other priorities struggle to keep up with regular platform changes, and instead are heavily influenced by often misleading headlines they see in the industry press. The good news is that you can understand effective social media strategy without ever having to worry about the nuances of every single product and ad format. Social media marketing isn't free, most of your consumers don't want daily conversations with you, and you don't have to think about something funny to say about every major event. And that's OK.

Engagement

Social media channels are, by definition, interactive, and the opportunity to move beyond traditional broadcast advertising to something truly interactive and collaborative is hugely appealing. The need to measure, chase and ultimately do everything you can to better this 'engagement' is, however, at the heart of the social media misconception.

A traditional marketing term once used to measure something quantifiable and impactful about a consumer's concept of your brand, engagement has been reduced to a meaningless summation of the number of different clicks your content can attract. As the most real-time measure of success, it is ruthlessly tracked on dashboards and reports around the world. This pursuit of higher engagement rates has encouraged many a brand to post open questions, interaction-forcing 'games', incentivised competitions and a range of content which, outside of this particular lens, unfortunately does little to build brand perceptions or sell products.

Just because you can measure and observe something does not necessarily make it useful. Certainly, there is nothing bad about consumers wanting to interact with (and respond to) your brand; if nothing else, it shows you that they've noticed it in the first place. Unfortunately, at a macro scale, there seems to be an unwillingness to consider whether higher engagement rates actually result in better business results. Of course, it feels perfectly reasonable that they would, and that where more consumers are showing their interest in the content it has a more powerful effect, but the reality is far from this. A 'spot the difference' game posted to Facebook might attract more comments than other posts, but that doesn't necessarily mean it's communicating anything useful about your brand, or that the people interacting with it are even your potential customers. Video remains a powerful communication tool on social media, but tends to attract lower levels of traditional engagement because people are busy actually watching it.

Luckily, the evidence for this goes beyond mere thought experiments. Nielsen carried out a meta-analysis of more than 450 campaigns for which they had detailed ROI and business results. Their analysis showed no correlation between the engagement/click-through rate for campaigns and the ROI they were able to drive. Across the key metrics of ad recall, brand awareness and purchase intent, there was a less than 1% correlation with how often people were choosing to click and engage with the content.

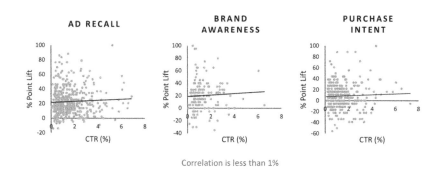

Correlation is less than 1%

Source: Nielsen Brand Effect meta-analysis of 478 online global Facebook campaigns that ran October 2014–April 2015

Big brand social media campaigns are seen by tens of millions of people, but only thousands will ever actively engage with them. It turns out that, just like TV or print adverts, social media can influence decision making without you needing to click and actively engage with it. A 2012 Datalogix study (which used loyalty card data to track sales impact through to offline purchases) I once worked on found that 90% of sales impact came from people who didn't actively interact with the content during the campaign. If only the people who interacted with a campaign were influenced by it, the vast majority of social media advertising would be a waste, but luckily that's not the case.

Unfortunately, however, it is still commonplace for marketers to focus on improving their engagement as a key performance indicator of their social campaigns. Not only is this something of a wild goose chase, it's also potentially actually quite a bad idea: you're likely to create content which gets a reaction rather than effectively communicates; you'll find yourself competing for the most expensive audiences on platforms; and ultimately, marketing science suggests you'll be trying to please the wrong audience altogether.

On social platforms there are some users who are more inclined to click on content and engage with it, and some who are not. With advertisers competing to get in front of the most engaged audiences, the auction price to do so is naturally forced up, effectively putting a price premium on these users. There is, however, nothing to say that the users who click more will be more valuable customers, so chasing them is something of an arbitrary strategy, and paying extra to do so seems a little pointless. Beyond this, the people most likely to respond to your brand are those who already appreciate and buy it, and optimising for their interests may mean you struggle to appeal to the valuable long tail of light buyers you need to attract to grow. There may be insights you can learn from comments and engagement, but don't blindly chase it, or assume it is even representative.

Fans

If that core audience sounds familiar, it's probably because they're the ones we typically call 'fans'. Again, as marketers, we are passionate about our brands, and it's nice to believe there's an audience out there of people as equally obsessive as we are. The reality, of course, is that people live very busy lives, and have very little interest in most of the brands they use every day. Certainly, in smaller businesses, growing a fan base often remains one of the key objectives of social media activity, with the intention that this directly leads to shifts in perception and an increase in purchases. There's certainly a nugget of truth here, but it's distorted to justify a range of falsehoods about what your social media strategy should therefore be.

It is possible to run research which shows that on an individual level your fans and engagers probably do purchase more than other consumers, but such research needs to be treated very carefully. To begin with, there's a high reverse causality at play, with your existing biggest customers far more likely to want to be a fan and engage with you in some way in the first place. Even accounting for this (which is possible with longitudinal research), the evidence suggests that the impact of becoming a fan is short lived, and in fact not dissimilar to the impact of simply having seen a piece of content at that point. Unfortunately, it tends to cost more resources to gain a fan than it does simply to get content in front of someone, and if the benefits are not notably greater, then I would question the intention.

The work of Byron Sharp and the Ehrenberg-Bass Institute to establish greater understanding of marketing science has highlighted the need to reach light consumers to grow your brand (see chapter 1). These consumers likely have limited interest in your brand, or even your whole category, and are going to be the hardest to persuade to actively subscribe to your channel. While fan interactions may be valuable on a micro scale, when you factor in the cost per engagement, it is hard to expand to meaningful scale.

Perhaps the biggest reason that being a fan or follower doesn't have a major impact is that you're still relatively unlikely to see anything that the brand in question posts. Becoming a fan is triggered by some sort of direct encounter with the brand (an ad, a shared post or even a real-world experience) which places them front of mind and explains the positive impact, but the value trails off quickly if you don't hear from them again. Having more people choose to follow (and engage) with your brand is certainly not a bad thing, and can speak to the fact that you are producing interesting and attention-grabbing content, but it shouldn't be an end in itself.

Organic reach

One of the great promises of social media marketing is that it is free. Anyone can set up a Twitter profile or YouTube channel, and post content to it, and before you know it, millions of people will see it. For marketers wary of vast traditional media budgets, that is a hugely appealing prospect, but the reality of course is quite different. Billions of people have set up their own social accounts and post content of their own; somewhat unsurprisingly, it's easy to get lost in that crowd.

It's almost universally believed that Facebook reduced the 'organic reach' of brand pages to force them to pay to reach an audience, but I'd argue this truism is in fact false. With connections to hundreds of friends, celebrities and brands, the sheer weight of content in your newsfeed makes it impossible for you to see it all – in fact, the average user has over 10,000 possible news stories they could be shown at login but will look at just a few dozen of them. As people's networks have grown and more publishers have pushed out content, the share of voice has inevitably been challenged. Facebook's newsfeed engineers are actually on record pointing out that their newsfeed algorithm gives pages more, not less, exposure than a completely unfiltered timeline would provide. If you want to blame anyone for your decreased reach, blame Apple for making it so easy to post holiday snaps from our phones.

Whatever the factors affecting it, many a strategy or tip sets out to game these algorithms in some way to earn a few extra percentage points of reach, and every expert has a new theory when a platform announces changes to how its feed works. Driving more organic reach almost certainly involves finding ways of driving more engagement, which as previously covered is not the best objective for marketers to chase. Such tactics are made almost entirely redundant by the transformative effect that even a small amount of paid media can have on your reach; it's not free, but then neither are the resources you are putting into running your channels. To put that into context, a Coca-Cola executive (Wes Finley) publicly shared that even $500 of media investment can get them in front of more people than an organic post to their tens of millions of fans.

To make matters worse, your fans are almost certainly not the consumers you most need to reach, and you almost certainly don't have enough of them to begin with. A shift from reaching 5% to 10% of your fans may be great on paper, but it's pretty irrelevant if you actually need to reach 100,000% as many people. For this point, I'd again refer to the work of Byron Sharp and his research, that reach and penetration are ultimately what marketers need to aim for, not concepts of loyalty and frequency.

Certainly, you can earn additional reach on top of your paid media approach, and this is definitely a bonus, but we shouldn't overestimate its scale or allow ourselves to believe that in most cases we can earn that media without first investing. In TV, we label the audience we reach outside of our specific target as 'wastage', whereas in reality these are valuable additional eyeballs, and in fact probably a greater 'earned' media boost than social channels provide.

The list goes on

Too much discussion in social media marketing seems to focus on how you drive these above principles, and not enough focus is given to understanding what drives meaningful business results.

I see a lot of discussion about how much content you need to push out, usually built up on concepts around what the consumer 'expects' or what a platform 'demands'. The truth is, consumers expect absolutely nothing from your brand, and wouldn't notice at all if you disappeared for a day, a week or a month. Similarly, most attempts to push out really regular content are based on a desire to game organic reach, the futility of which we've already touched upon. Social media is most effective when simply done on your own terms: when you have something worthwhile/meaningful to say, or more crucially, when you have budget to support that and amplify beyond your limited organic reach. It's more important to put your effort into creating high quality content that works within the limitations of the medium (most notably, often very short impacts with the sound off) than it is to try and churn out regular updates.

Serious Facebook advertisers are planning media to reach large percentages of their audience once or twice a week every week of the year, but even they don't need as much content as you think. Most social posts don't get time to 'wear in' let alone 'wear out', and repeating content (especially high quality video) is much more acceptable than you might think (in fact, in internal research I have worked on, driving frequency of the same pieces of content with media is an effective way of ensuring they actually have impact). With cut-downs, cinemagraphs and later repeats, a brand ends up needing a great piece of content just once every couple of months, certainly not every day.

There may be some opportunities to jump on the latest trend or moment, but in reality most brands disappear without a trace when they try, and the impact of such activities are vastly exaggerated within the marketing bubble. I worked at Mondelez at the time of the infamous 'dunk in the dark' Super Bowl tweet which was credited with inspiring much of the real-time marketing we see today; the biggest internal learning, however, was how much more successful it could have been if paid media had been quickly applied. At the time, Oreo was consistently reaching as many people through a typical week's paid advertising on Facebook as that much talked about tweet delivered.

Perhaps the worst myth of all is that it's hard to measure the success and impact of your social media, and thus none of the above can truly be evaluated. Certainly, some of the world's biggest firms don't continue to invest hundreds of millions of dollars without being able to understand the effects. Unfortunately, most of the real-time metrics you have at hand don't help, but more often than not the best way to measure social success is exactly the same methodology you apply to any other traditional channels. Understand how many people you have Reached, look for ways of measuring how your content has Resonated and what opinions you have changed, and ultimately measure sales alongside to try and identify the business Reaction. Unfortunately, much of the research that major firms carry out to prove effectiveness is never published publicly, but the platform holders do all publish case studies with example data on them.

Making social media marketing work

Through my work I have consistently seen evidence that social media channels can be powerful tools in the marketing repertoire, whether that be Cadbury's Creme Egg persuading millions of consumers to pick one up in a corner shop, or Johnnie Walker selling a high end premium gift. Success usually means cutting through the noise and approaching them similarly to traditional media channels:

- Don't get too caught up in what tactics currently work in social channels, because chances are the latest trend is less important than you think. Brief social media marketing the same way you would traditional approaches: with clear insights, business objectives and a solid view of what your brand stands for.
- Pick your channels based on how you want to position your brand and where your consumers are, focusing on fewer, bigger options to maximise your impact from limited resources. Like other media channels, smaller social networks tend to share their audiences with larger ones, and you're likely to duplicate your reach by going after too many small networks.
- Great social marketing isn't about deep interactive experiences that few people ever get to see, it's about rich, personally relevant storytelling content which gets right in front of them. Being worthy of attention is more important than being worthy of a click.
- Use insights to shape the kind of content you are creating, and then in turn target your media to the people most likely to find it relevant. With paid media promotion you can tailor creative executions to subsets of your audience to deliver true personalisation at scale.
- Scale is a limiting factor to digital marketing success, and the biggest reason it often doesn't have a meaningful impact on business results –

stop creating any content you can't afford to promote, it's a waste of time and effort. Betting for the content to be shared disproportionately ('virally') just because other brands have been able to is akin to betting it all at the casino because someone won the jackpot last month.

■ Think about how digital media channels can improve the effectiveness of traditional ones, extend the reach of them, drive continuity between campaigns or drive scale where you don't have the budgets for TV.

■ Ignore the temptations of real-time engagement data and focus on what really matters: metrics which actually relate to those business measures you set. I suggest using a Reach (how many of the right people did we reach?), Resonance (did it make them think the right things?) and Reaction (did they ultimately take action and buy from us?) approach.

Digital marketing as a whole is facing serious challenges, with questions being asked around viewability, ad fraud, transparency, brand safety and more. While tough, growing pains for advertisers and publishers pave the way for a more measured and sophisticated approach to digital marketing. The same questions are being asked of social channels, and in doing so marketers are unconsciously acknowledging that they do indeed play by many of the same rules. If you put your efforts into making meaningful content, and promoting it to a broad audience, you should be able to drive success you can measure.

References

https://www.facebook.com/iq/articles/reach-matters-driving-business-results-at-scale

https://www.linkedin.com/pulse/paid-social-worth-investment-wes-finley

https://www.linkedin.com/today/post/article/20140605212615-7775134-facebook-s-algorithm-is-actually-driving-more-reach-for-your-page

CHAPTER

TO TARGET OR NOT TO TARGET, THAT IS NOT THE QUESTION

Written by **Shann Biglione**

One of the big contributions of marketing science has been the validation of strategies aiming to reach wider audiences. Meanwhile, modern marketing is offering unprecedented tools to segment and target precise audiences, which often triggers a debate pitting precision versus broad reach. This chapter explores why the two are, in fact, compatible, and provides advice on how to build a strategy that acknowledges the need to build maximum reach while giving a role to precision tools.

Targeting the right people is one of the most established strategic steps in marketing, and often the strategic starting point for media planners. With the advent of data-driven, precision-targeting solutions, we're seeing a fierce debate between the proponents of segmentation and targeting, and those in favour of more mass, large-scale approaches. But the commotion is caused by two forces of advertising that shouldn't be dichotomously pitted against the other: the objective to maximise reach versus targeting the right audience. Backed by the evidence put forward by the Ehrenberg-Bass Institute and the IPA, a lot of marketers have woken up to the importance of 'mass marketing' to build brands, at a time when data marketing has opened up an unprecedented chance to target consumers with an insane level of granularity.

To some, the argument is summarised as buying media with the widest net reach, period. And to be fair, Byron Sharp himself, in his crusade against the old ways of segmentation, has sent signals that could be misinterpreted as an all-out refusal to consider targeting solutions. But I believe it is an unfair and counterproductive representation of the point he makes.

The point is not that brands should target everyone, but rather should aim to target everyone in their category. The category can be huge (say, soap) or small (2,000 USD cashmere sweaters). The way we have interpreted it is that you should favour media strategies that help you maximise the reach of all category buyers, whether heavy or light, young or old, male or female. Sometimes it means 300 million people, sometimes 2,000. People who don't like the sound of mass marketing will usually take the former as the example to scare you off (Look! He wants you to go after *everyone*!), but this is an important and operationally challenging nuance.

Don't get me wrong, in the Ehrenberg-Bass approach there absolutely is an imperative to avoid focusing on very specific segments *only*. But that statement in itself doesn't mean your marketing should never use segmentation and targeting techniques, it merely invites you to think hard about who your target is. As outlined in his book *How Brands Grow*, Sharp's main motivation to reframe mass marketing as the way to go is three common mistakes made by some promoters of the STP (Segmentation, Targeting and Positioning) model.

1. Going for the easy sale

For accountability reasons, marketers are often tempted to only target consumers with the highest conversion value. This is the by-product of a pure ROI approach whereby you must generate maximum efficiencies between a marketing activity and the sales it generates. And it can be a real problem because ROI efficiencies naturally lead you to focus on buyers with a high likelihood to convert. Tim Ambler from the London Business School aptly notes that 'ROI tends to encourage campaigns that target existing and heavier customers. These show higher ROI largely because many of the sales aren't really extra sales but sales that would have happened anyway, or sales that might have merely been brought forward in time'. The problem is that today's targeting tools precisely allow marketers to act on this, and many brands fall for that trap. It looks good for a few months, but usually within a couple of years they wake up with a massive hangover, looking at the inevitable erosion of their baseline. It negates advertising's greatest strength: reaching those who don't care much about you.

2. Going for the one and only

Ehrenberg's research has long attacked the strongly held belief that competing brands have very different buyers. The evidence they put forward shows that the differences within a category are at best minor, or simply correlate with obvious dimensions (you're more likely to have a higher income if you buy a Mercedes S-class than a Skoda, and a higher income correlates with a wide range of other attributes). Marketers often struggle with the idea, but this is mostly a result of their personal or professional involvement in these categories, making it harder for them to see that the minute category nuances they see are not shared by the common consumer.

3. Confusing creative target with media targets

A corollary of the above point, a big portion of brand planning literature tries to establish differentiation through its target audience. Entire workshops can be spent understanding 'who we're for'. While I give very little credit to this approach as a way to truly define who will be buying the brand, it can be a positive catalyst to building more distinctive communications. When a brand wants to project a certain image, it might be worthwhile to use certain segments in the creative material. But it's disheartening to see how many brands confuse this creative segment with their media target. You might want to use young and trendy people in your advertising, but the likelihood is that a lot of your buyers will be older. Use extreme sports in your advertising if you will, but don't forget your buyer might be a dentist with kids whose only favourite sports is football.

And so, the number one issue with segmentation and targeting is not that they aren't relevant methods, but that they're attached to outdated concepts, and are therefore often badly used. They too often rely on attitudes of psychographic profiles which have little strategic meaning for your brand. We should as an industry dramatically scale back their importance, but this doesn't mean they aren't of any use. My response is that there are segments that are meaningful to a business, but less as a way to define the actual target audience your brand will be defined by than to operationally structure your reach. In the long run, as your brand grows your target audience will be the market, ie the category buyers.

But all this doesn't mean focused targeting isn't a viable option, as it remains one of the most common questions asked to media specialists. So, when do I think targeting is a good option? Here are four common examples I have seen.

1. To manage budget limitations

Technically, this is less a targeting option than the 'how much reach can we afford?' question, but it is the most commonly associated with targeting choices. Smaller brands have budgetary constraints, and won't always be able to go after as wide a market as the Unilever's of this world. In this case, maybe you can't afford to reach 100% of the market. But here's how the story should go: this year, you might only be able to afford 20% of the market. So, target 20%. But next year, when you are able to afford 30%, don't limit yourself to 20% reach. Go for the 30%. It might sound like a counter point to mass marketing, but it is in fact a mass market approach *within your means*. Why would you limit your reach if you can afford not to? In the long run, always remember your target is the market, because consumers are not yours, and someone who buys a pair of Nike might one day buy a pair of Reebok, and vice versa.

2. To address temporary gaps in your buyer distribution

Unless you're creating another segment altogether, in most cases your buyer distribution should look fairly similar to that of the category. If your brand's buyers are a lot older than the category norm, for example, you're probably missing out on the chance to sell to younger people. So here, you're absolutely entitled to ensure your marketing does a good job with those younger audiences, and devise activities that go after them. But don't make it a mission to stop reaching the other groups either.

3. To tailor the message

Today's media environment and technology is allowing us to find out more about who we're speaking to, and thus make sure the message is more aligned with their needs. I'm not just talking about context-sensitive or demographic profiles, but about specific behaviours associated with an interest in your category, or even with different levels of category involvements. For example, auto brands can more precisely show you models relevant to your stage in life, while infant milk formula can fully tailor its content to a consumer's concerns. I know a lot of the adtech behind it is raising eyebrows at the moment (sometimes for very good reasons), but this doesn't take away the opportunity from marketers, and is arguably the main reason why the mass market mega-brands are keen on setting up data platforms for one-to-one marketing. And as media has historically been presented as 'the right message, at the right time, to the right audience', it will be very difficult to divert marketer's attention from this potential. There is of course fierce debate whether breaking down campaigns into infinite sub segments is a 'can' or a 'should' for most brands. Having one big idea that resonates with many people will certainly remain a landmark of impactful campaigns. But again, there need not be dichotomy here. We are more and more capable of creating multiple pieces of content, and it is possible for them to sit under a big idea umbrella. What this will likely require is brands to shift from the campaign big idea to the brand big idea. As we know, consistency is key for branding, and the exercise will be to define ideas that have the power to sustain multiple iterations across campaigns (akin to McCann's 'long idea'), while campaigns can be managed not on a calendar basis, but an audience segments basis. The jury is still out on whether this is truly the future of marketing, but it is impossible to not see the attraction these approaches hold in an addressable media world.

4. To identify possible low-hanging fruits

This is probably one of the trickiest tasks, as it can easily backfire into a thinly veiled segmentation of a single audience; but as your brand attacks a market, the reality is that not all buyers will be likely to be interested in your product in the same way. The rule is that these examples are usually related to category behaviours, not attitudes or psychographic profiles of brands. Is your new product more likely to attract light or heavily involved category consumers? Are there buyers of certain products that can more easily consider you? Are there distribution footprints that make it easier to go after certain geographies? Are there decision-makers that influence large volumes? The trick here will be to find ways of tailoring some of your activities towards some of these segments without hurting too much your ability to reach as many category buyers as possible.

You'll notice that all four of these examples are compatible with a mass market approach. As a matter of fact, in my experience they work a lot better with a mass market approach in mind. But the bottom line is simple: whatever you do, please try not to reach below your means.

The reality is that targeting the market is a simple statement, but often a difficult endeavour. It asks your media teams to correlate media choices with behaviours associated with consumption of categories (data that is still difficult to get for many categories) and/or requires brands to use insights and behavioural data to ensure your targeting is going for the right segments. If programmatic data based on behaviour has taught me anything, it's that most marketers have a very approximate, if not totally wrong, definition of who their target audience really is. As a matter of fact, it is often useful to start programmatic campaigns with very little targeting in mind and optimise as we begin defining segments. We're often surprised to realise how some dimensions we hadn't thought of are salient, while others we planned for are mute. It might surprise you, but Tesla buyers are not particularly into saving the environment.

So, if after reading *How Brands Grow* you are either left with the impression that the recommendation is to throw targeting out of the window, or that all this data pointing to mass marketing is only relevant to mass brands, I suggest you read again. Targeting enough of the right people is too important a business to be left to trivial generalisations.

References

Ambler, T, and Riley, D. 'Marketing metrics: a review of performance measures in use in the UK and Spain'. Marketing Science Institute, 2000

Binet, L, and Field, P. *The Long and the Short of It: Balancing short and long-term marketing strategies*. IPA, 2013

http://www.businessinsider.com/tesla-owners-dont-care-about-environment-2013-8

Sharp, B. *How Brands Grow: What marketers don't know*. OUP, 2010

10

PERFORMING SCIENCE ON YOURSELF

Written by **Julian Cole**

Is there a better way to plan planning in an agency? This chapter investigates.

For years there had been commonly held belief in the medical community that stomach ulcers were brought on by stress, spicy foods and too much acid. However, in Perth, Australia in 1984 Dr Barry Marshall had a hunch that stomach ulcers were actually caused by a specific bacteria. He needed to test the hypothesis on humans, but unfortunately he could not find any patients to test it on.

So, he turned to the one person he could ethically test it on: himself. He drank some broth of bacteria and gave himself stomach ulcers, then tested his theory that antibiotics could solve this bacterial infection. He shocked the medical community and proved them wrong, winning a Nobel prize in medicine in the process.

In creative agencies we often turn to our clients to test out theories, asking them for data on their businesses to help them test and make better decisions. However, there is so much data closer to home; and there is a lot we can do by looking at our own agencies and working out how we can improve the process closer to home.

The following are three Barry Marshall-type self-imposed planning tests that I created to see if I could prove a better model for working in the agency.

Experiment 1 – 'Golden window of ideas'

One of the first areas of data that I started to look at in the agency was the date when the client actually signed off on work that would go into production. This involved me trawling through old emails looking for sign-off dates, harassing account directors for sign-off contracts, and quizzing the brains of creative directors about that great meeting they had.

After I was able to compile this list, I found an interesting pattern: 80% of the work got sold 90–120 days out from the go-live date. This data became even more interesting when I looked at when we got briefed on the work – this date changed a lot; we got briefed anywhere between 600 to 120 days out from live dates.

It didn't matter when we got briefed, the date the work sold would always stay relatively the same. In the mind of the client, knowing that there is more time on the clock for ideas means it is hard for them to be certain they have seen the best ideas yet. So, we end up initiating as many rounds of reviews that we can fit into that window.

With this knowledge you can potentially change the way that the agency works with their clients to save the mental burnout for the agency. You could ask the client to brief you later in the process; you could hold the brief in planning for longer to make sure you have the best brief; you could get a junior creative team to help come up with the first couple of rounds of creative to hone in on what the client wants. All these can have a dramatic effect on how profitably you can run an account.

Experiment 2 – 'Show me the money'

For the first 18 months I worked in New York I didn't make one piece of creative that the world saw. I worked as a digital strategy director at a creative agency. Round after round of integrated ideas were killed. Clients would ask for integrated campaigns, and then only buy TV.

Eighteen months gives you a lot of time to do some soul searching on why this might be the case. My hypothesis was that there was no impetus for clients to buy integrated work. With TV, clients inherently understood the pressure to fill a media space, along with an accurate estimate of production. Apart from banner ads and social posts (which other agencies at the time created), there was no media booked for digital ideas. The client was asking us to come up with ideas with no media attached and no production budget in sight. This was all speculative work.

We needed a document that would address this problem at the start of the process, and start a conversation about budget before the creative briefing. We created what we call a blueprint: a document which helps show the client the shape of the campaign in terms of the produced assets along with an estimated cost of each production asset. A blueprint helps break down the production budget amongst the assets we need to create.

This document brought three information sources together in one document: communication tasks, media realities (what has been bought) and production budget. We then look to get sign-off on this document with all key parties (creative director, business lead and client) before they fall in love with any execution.

This has helped to transform the creative process within the agency; it has meant that we are no longer making speculative work, and it is forcing a harder conversation about money earlier, which has reduced the rounds of creative reviews.

Experiment 3 – 'Putting on the client's glasses'

Although we now had timings and the amount of money we needed in place, we realised we had a new problem: speaking the same language as our clients around ideas.

There is a great story about blind men touching an elephant. The men all go up to the elephant and start describing the different parts. A blind man goes up to the trunk and explains that it is like a big tree trunk; someone else goes up to the tail and describes it as a little hair snake; then another blind man describes it as a leather material. They are all correct. This confuses the blind men – how can they all be correct? With a topic it is easy to describe so many different parts of it, and the same can be said about innovative work.

A lot of clients will ask for innovative work – but the topic is so broad, it is kind of like the elephant. People can be speaking about the same piece of work and yet be talking about completely different parts of it, even arguing over the same piece of work. It is important to try and understand where each person is coming from.

One of the exercises that we have started doing is actually trying to get people to explain their perspective, or lens on the work. We show the client a selection of the most awarded innovative work from the year before, and then actually get them to talk about what they like and dislike about the work.

We are using the meeting to listen to the client and how they describe work, rather than the agency bringing them examples which they think are good and explaining why they are good.

This is helping to align our perspective with the client's. This can then help inform briefs that we are given, as we can get closer to the type of language the client is looking for.

Conclusion

Evidenced-based marketing has done a lot to help change our clients' businesses; however, if you take a moment to look at your own business and apply the same mindset to looking at how you can increase efficiency within your own process, there is much that can be done. Within a service-based industry you are always at the mercy of what a client wants to do; it is up to them whether they take your advice. The great thing about applying this evidence mindset to your own work is that you are the master of that domain; you can apply your theories without anyone telling you otherwise.

SOMETHING IS NOT ADDING UP IN ADLAND

Written by **Becky McOwen-Banks**

The percentage of women in creative departments remains woefully small. Yet female spending power and share of voice is ever-growing. The world of advertising is no longer representing the world it purports to reflect – and business should be worried. This chapter takes a closer look at why the numbers on gender diversity continue to not add up, and at how small changes can make a big difference.

I am one of few.

Not creative directors – there are literally hundreds and thousands of those all around the world. I'm talking about female creative directors.

Women make up just 14% of creative directors in London, and the stats for New York are even worse, at 11%. According to 2015 IPA research, the stats for girls within creative departments are also shocking, at just 26% – just a quarter of the whole department.

And all this in an industry that purports to be a mirror on society; the very industry that reflects our world.

Creative directors are the governors of ideas. We create, curate, sow the seed and nurture along the way. We create those moments of cultural change – those moments we all remember: Diet Coke man, Levi's, Paralympics, Meerkats (yeah, sorry about that). Women are making up just 14% of this world.

In the world advertising purports to reflect, women account for **85%** of all spending – across auto, electrical, tech, DIY… you name it, it's women in control of the wallet; yet, **70%** of women say they are alienated by advertising, and a huge **91%** saying advertising doesn't understand them, doesn't reflect them.

Well, no surprise that's **70%** who are asking 'Where?' 'Where are the brands that understand and talk to me?' 'Where are all the ads that recognise me?' 'Where are the ads that show insight into my life?'

Seventy percent say advertising doesn't understand them, doesn't reflect them – and worse than that, think it actively repels them. What a massively missed opportunity. Something is not adding up in Adland.

Why does this matter?

With everything that's going on in the world – Brexit, refugees, Trump, Syria, Trump – why does any of this matter?

Well, advertising should help shape our world: it shares big ideas and informs us about life-changing technologies and how they impact on our lives. It steers and directs our understanding of the world, and to truly resonate, it needs to reflect the make-up of that world. Women should be forging the way at this leading edge.

It really started to matter to me when I rose to a certain level in my organisation, when I started asking 'Where?' 'Where did everyone go?' 'Where have all the senior female creatives gone?' 'Where have all the brilliant brains I studied with, and graduated with, gone along the way?' 'Where has all that important insight disappeared to? All that understanding, all those ideas. And with 70% of women saying advertising doesn't reflect them, what is the cost of this disappearance?'

It also matters because it has been proved again and again that greater diversity means greater creativity, which (especially for our industry, but for any) is better for business.

We're all familiar with the many *Forbes* reports on the subject, the many experiments and business-led examples that have appeared over recent years.

Way back in 2015, Lord Davies said, 'Britain is beginning to see the full extent of female talent unleashed', which, he claimed, was 'good for business and good for the economy'. And at organisational level, in a growing body of evidence from 2016, McKinsey linked greater gender balance in leadership to better organisational performance and corporate governance.

It makes sense, doesn't it... the more diverse brains, coming from all of those differing accumulated experiences, together come up with better results – better results creatively, for team structures and ultimately for the bottom line. And yet, these missing senior creative women are a voice that isn't being heard. The collective voice for that 70% who say advertising doesn't understand them.

But I'm not here to tell some terrible story of personal woe, simply to work out the *why*. Why the numbers fail to add up.

Stacking up the story around the stats

I love Adland; it's an amazing, brilliant career – no day is the same. You find out all sorts of crazy facts, meet dazzling, brilliant people, and get to create amazing things that all start as just a black and white scribble that comes from your head. But though my journey has been good, that's not to say it's right for all – there may be a few clues along the way as to where we are losing this important set of brains.

The frequent-enough-to-make-a-difference-2am pitch nights haven't been too much of an issue for me, as I've chosen not to have children. The predominantly male environment with the dull sporting bants and joshing come as second nature to me, where others might feel excluded – I am super-close to my older brother so am hardwired to joke; I even played rugby for my university.

The norm culture for Adland is overwhelmingly a male norm. Girls are the minority; I see them skulking off as the sport chat begins, or heading home before the heavy drinking kicks in. The occasional loudest-volume-wins meeting style can be hard to adapt to.

Let's be clear here – there is no mal-intent, it's just how it is, how it has been. The status quo continues because good people are unaware how to do better

– or indeed, that there's anything wrong. We need to dig deeper, to discover why these brilliant female brains are deserting the industry in such numbers.

Coming out of university the numbers look peachy, with girls graduating from creative arts and design at 61% ('The gender gap at universities'), and frequently outstripping the chaps on results. And yet just 14% are at creative director and leadership level.

Something's not adding up in Adland.

Imagine a creative graduate with a book full of creative ideas comes to town to ply her wares and secure an opportunity at an ad agency. The first thing she will encounter is people who are not like her. We've heard the numbers. If girls make up just 26% of creative departments, then it only follows that the faces they meet at interview will more than likely be male. It's not out of mal-intent – it's just the way things are right now.

It may start our young women thinking 'Where?' 'Where are all the female creatives?' 'Where are the faces I can emulate? Those minds that understand my positioning, my experiences, my perspective. Should I even join if I can't see someone like me succeeding?' After all, as they say, we can't be what we can't see.

And the first face you see does make a difference. One global CCO of a large ad agency put her female junior creative team in charge of first-stage recruiting and immediately saw a more diverse set of faces coming through the door: different ethnicities, different religions, different in every way from 'standard issue' white male. One simple change, but a massive difference.

Women are the minority in the creative workplace, that means we are more used to seeing and welcoming voices and faces that don't look as our own, more used to hearing stories that differ from ours – as such we engage and see the potential in a wider circle.

Sadly, as has been discussed time and time again, boys are frequently employed on potential and girls on proof, when unconscious bias comes into play. When male creative directors see male junior teams, they may see people who remind them of themselves in their early career, and how they have progressed: 'They remind me of me when I was that age'. This leads them to take a leap of faith and make an offer based on the potential the boys offer.

When girls, on the other hand, sit in front of male senior creatives, they do not look or sound similar. No fuzzy feelings or memories are triggered, so unconscious bias does not kick in. So, the seniors ask for proof, look deeper at women's portfolios and ideas, and scrutinise their qualifications.

And so it continues.

Happily settled in an agency and working hard on every brief that comes along, our creative is enjoying the agency vibe and agency life. Briefs are coming across her desk, which she is dedicating herself to with aplomb.

But what can tend to happen in agencies is that brands become allocated to specific teams. We see it time and time again in freelance call-outs: 'Looking for female creative to work on beauty brand'. 'Need female creative director for fashion perfume launch'. 'Need brave creative rock star to be right-hand man to creative director'. Telling, isn't it?

While I am veering here towards anecdotal evidence gathered over many years, it is sadly true that girls are more likely to be given the warmer, fluffier brands (because all women are warm and fluffy, right?). She may finally get the chance to do that face cream or tampon ad she's always dreamt about (finally a chance to break out those roller skates.) Or charity ads – because women care, don't we?

Meanwhile, one of the chaps at the agency who started at the same time has also been plugging away on his briefs – but here we'll see a different mix: say booze, or cars, or banks, or a sports brand. Now the difference here is that beauty or charity brands usually don't want to rock the boat. They don't usually want to make a big splash. Budgets may be smaller, ambitions lower. Agency ambitions lower. This sets boys on the road to becoming that brave creative 'rock star' we heard of earlier.

Exiting college with the same projects, the same briefs – boys and girls, no difference – just exciting fresh ideas. But now, only a few months later, we'll see a difference, and one that will really make a difference should a fabulous opportunity arise.

Now we see that the mix of briefs has had an impact. One book is filled with softer, potentially sassier (but ultimately 'fluffier') brand work – while one may have more edgy, brave, energetic brands. Both books have hugely successful campaigns, but which do you think will be selected for a once-in-a-lifetime opportunity?

So, even if they make it through the door, girls are having their creative potential limited – unknowingly – through the briefs they are being asked to do.

Again, no one meant to do this. There has been no mal-intent. Another small, unconscious bias – big difference. And the cumulative result means girls have more typecast briefs creating typecast books – and as such, less creative opportunity. So, it's not just 'Where are the creative girls?' but 'Where are the opportunities to develop them?'

We can start to see how the numbers story erodes... from 61%... to 26%... down to just 14%.

From where to here

The question of 'Where are the women?' isn't just about advertising – it's every business, every industry. The paucity of female politicians has been highlighted, and the way in which they are reported compared to male politicians (Theresa May's wardrobe anyone?). Speaking of reporting, how about the inane questions asked only of women on the red carpet... to the lack of women in the C-suite, to too few female board members on the FTSE listings. Or on conference panels, awards and judging panels; even how women's achievements were reported in the press at the Olympics.

The lack of women at the top (and the effect it has) is widely reported, and not easily solved. Our industry in particular has hangovers from the boys' club that are beginning to lift, but need applied action to adequately address. Awareness is not enough.

I have to say that, for me, there was no epiphany. No key moment of awakening. No shaking of fists. No 'Enough already!' Just a growing realisation that things needed to change.

The realisation that my awesome creative partner had cut her days down so she could look after the kids, when her equally creative husband continued five days a week.

The realisation that when I was speaking, people took my words as a voice of my gender, rather than the opinion of a single creative.

The realisation that I was bored of being proud to be stamping out the use of the 'c' word in agency spaces – and even more bored of having to explain why I objected to it.

A growing realisation that things needed to change to balance the numbers in creative departments – and if they were to change, then it would take me. As one of the few senior female creatives, I needed to do something. I couldn't invent lots of senior women to fill the gaps and even the balance at the top level. I needed to create change for those following.

It was this realisation that led me to join forces with another female creative director and partner the launch of Creative Equals. Creative Equals is a not-for-profit providing a practical set of tools, and most importantly, a standard for agencies – to help them attract, attain and retain women at every step of the career ladder.

It was this realisation that led me to champion a pilot project of 'The Girlhood' within my agency to find new pathways for girls to enter the industry from non-traditional backgrounds.

It was this realisation that meant I put myself forward to lead the amazing 'Girl Effect' in Rwanda – changing the course of girls' lives; to allow their value and abilities to be seen as more than childbearing and homemaking, for their talents and skills to be acknowledged and nurtured, for them to shine and even possibly get careers.

It's no longer about moaning about the lack of women at the top. Let's create change. Let's start to open pathways to even the balance, round the sums, add more female voices to Adland. Let's enable the move from 'Where are creative women in advertising?' to 'Here are the creative women!'

Here is a statement of visibility.

Here is a statement of belonging.

Here is a beacon to others following in the path.

To women and girls: Be here – be visible. Have faces, have voices, speak up, opt in to meetings, lead presentations, write editorial pieces, write blogs and comments; take the opportunities you deserve.

To men: Be here – be present. Be aware of your decisions and possible biases. Lead with openness and share a path of potential.

This isn't about people being bad. It is about balancing those numbers that really matter. It's about finding small ways that will enable a big change. Being aware of the first face you meet new teams with. Being open to stories and ideas that differ from your own. Being aware of the type of brief stereotyping that can occur. Checking your default choices for your own bias, so we can spot potential in all people, not just a chosen few – and enabling that to grow.

Let's hold Adland to account, address the imbalance and begin to appeal to the 70% of spending power that is currently not being understood.

Let's make the numbers work for better creative and a better business.

References

Business professors Cristian Deszö of the University of Maryland and David Ross of Columbia University studied the effect of gender diversity on the top firms in Standard & Poor's Composite 1500 list – a group designed to reflect the overall US equity market. First, they examined the size and gender composition of firms' top management teams from 1992 through 2006. Then they looked at the financial performance of the firms. In their words, they found that, on average, 'female representation in top management leads to an increase of $42 million in firm value'. They also measured the firms' 'innovation intensity' through the ratio of research and development expenses to assets. They found that companies that prioritised innovation saw greater financial gains when women were part of the top leadership ranks. https://www.scientificamerican.com/article/how-diversity-makes-us-smarter/#

Creative Equals research 2016, http://www.creativeequals.org (down to 12% in 2017 https://www.campaignlive.co.uk/article/creativitys-female-future/1428824)

https://www.cranfield.ac.uk/press/news-2016/women-on-boards-ftse-100-company-has-full-gender-balance-for-first-time

Greenfield Online for Arnold's Women's Insight Team – According to Greenfield, women's accounting for 85% of consumer purchasing includes 91% of new homes; 66% PCs; 92% holidays; 80% healthcare; 65% new cars; 89% bank accounts; 93% food; 93% OTC pharmaceuticals; 58% of total online spending.

According to 2010 Women.drivers.com research (via M2W.biz), women buy more than half of the new cars in the US and influence up to 80% of all car purchases. Women also request 65% of the service work done at dealerships and spend over $200 billion on new cars and mechanical servicing of vehicles each year; 45% of all light trucks and SUVs are purchased by women.

Evidence for the benefits of diversity can be found well beyond the United States ('How diversity makes us smarter', Katherine Phillips, *Scientific American,* 2014). In August 2012 a team of researchers at the Credit Suisse Research Institute issued a report in which they examined 2,360 companies globally from 2005 to 2011, looking for a relationship between gender diversity on corporate management boards and financial performance. Sure enough, the researchers found that companies with one or more women on the board delivered higher average returns on equity, lower gearing (that is, net debt to equity) and better average growth.

12

MAKING AND MEASURING WHAT MATTERS

Written by **Anjali Ramachandran**

The advertising industry is obsessed with numbers, but the incessant pursuit of clicks and views has come at a cost. Even as advertising technology continues to impede upon the reading experience online, people are taking matters into their own hands by using ad-blocking technologies. There is a better way, asserts this chapter… If brands shift their focus to measuring their real impact in the world in an iterative way, as many grant-making organisations and media organisations do, it might work better for everyone.

In the 16th century, the nobility could commission artists to create works of art, theatre or music – a refined form of recreation, which was available for those who could afford it. For the lower classes, on the other hand, entertainment came in the form of executions, amongst other things. Public beheadings and torture were open to the public, and the galleries were usually packed. The resulting blood and gore were not too far from the decrepitude of their own lives – this was the time of the bubonic plague – but perhaps the poor thrilled in the fact that, however bad their lives were, it wasn't as bad as the people whose lives they were witnessing being extinguished.

There are echoes (if distant!) of this imbalance in modern media: those who can pay get access to content without the constant interruption of ads, and they don't need to put up with trackers sneakily deployed on the pages they visit – or at least, not to the extent that they otherwise would be. Those who don't (or can't) pay get the sudden loud videos, the pop-ups, the trackers. Online security can't be guaranteed for this group, and web pages can take their time to load, given the number of scripts they need to parse. Steven Englehardt and Arvind Narayanan from Princeton University talk about their latest research on web privacy in their 2016 paper 'Online tracking: a 1-million-site measurement and analysis'. They created the largest dataset on web tracking to their knowledge: a census of over 1 million websites. In the process, they found an overwhelming number of third parties present on at least two first parties, where 'a third party is defined as typically hidden trackers such as ad networks embedded on most web pages' and 'a first party' is the site the users visit directly. These third parties can obtain users' browsing histories through a combination of cookies and other tracking technologies that allow them to uniquely identify users. The scary part? In their words, 'How many third parties are there? In short, a lot: the total number of third parties present on at least two first parties is over 81,000.'

In 1994, the first banner ads (created by HotWired, which we now know as Wired.com) hit the web. They were treated as a novelty for a while – simple banner ads for the most part – till advertising technology started trying to outdo itself. Formats became more and more interruptive.

The ambitiously named Coalition for Better Ads, formed in 2016, is a consortium that includes brands like Unilever and Procter & Gamble, publishers such as those of *The Washington Post*, and internet giants like Facebook and Google. It surveyed over 25,000 consumers in North America and Europe in 2017 about some of the most interruptive formats. The results were unsurprising: they included 'pop-up ads', 'prestitial ads', 'poststitial ads' that require a countdown to dismiss, 'flashing animations' and auto-playing videos with sound – when you think about it, all terms that normal people probably don't even understand, beyond the fact that the interventions themselves are annoying.

Today, a growing number of people are taking things into their own hands and using the weapons they have easy access to, to wit, ad blockers. The usage of ad blockers grew 30% in 2016, and now covers 11% of the global internet population, according to PageFair's *2017 Adblock Report*. Some 615 million mobile devices use them, and the average ad blocker is more likely to have a bachelor's degree – in other words, is a valuable customer.

The issue of tracking has huge implications for data and privacy, as Facebook have discovered to their detriment following the Cambridge Analytica scandal in 2018. Facebook stock dropped 19%, with $120 billion wiped off its value, as growth slowed, and users left the platform – of which 3 million are said to have left after the scandal broke.

Tracking users is also not limited to just websites. In 2017, a strong backlash caused Uber to retract its policy of tracking users even *after* their journeys ended within the app, which they claimed was done with users' physical safety in mind. Uber admittedly has many more problems than this, but the fact that they deployed the philosophy of tracking people with such impunity was one of the straws that contributed to breaking the proverbial camel's back. It's probably no coincidence that a company with such low moral standards had $10 billion knocked off its value in 2017, according to a report by industry news publisher *The Information*.

So, we've established that apart from it being morally questionable, there is a financial effect on the bottom line of companies which decide that they're comfortable holding customers' attention and data to ransom. But this is the thing: there are better ways for a business to make an impact on its audience.

Let's focus on social impact first, which is becoming the goal of more companies today, as documented by Suntae Kim from Boston College and Todd Schifeling from the University of Michigan in their 2016 paper 'Varied incumbent behaviors and mobilization for new organizational forms: the rise of triple-bottom line business amid both corporate social responsibility and irresponsibility'. In the paper, they discuss two main reasons companies are looking to get certified as 'doing good' for the larger community through membership of movements like Benefit Corporations or B-Corps: 1) to establish that their intentions are genuine; and 2), as an admission of their new belief in the importance of creating a new, fairer economy. B-Corps, as of 2016, number over 2,000 and, include not only much loved eco-conscious companies like American outdoor clothing company Patagonia, but new additions like French multinational food corporation Danone.

Measuring the impact of companies that have a social objective is hard, beyond the feelgood walls of CSR. Yet measurement is important, because without a real sense of impact, it isn't easy for audiences to believe in a company's products and actions. It might be useful to take a leaf from organisations involved in activities where it actually is hard to make a correlation between action and impact, such as grant-making foundations like the Gates or Rockefeller Foundations, or even publishers who work on important journalism projects. When a project you are funding has the potential to change people's lives, or a story you break can alter the course of someone's life, the communication of that impact is in many ways as important as the impact itself. It is the reason for sustained funding of a project, or in the case of brands, the reason they retain old audiences and attract new ones.

Independent news publication *ProPublica's Annual Reports* do a great job of documenting their impact. One of 24 impact stories in their 2016 report included their story on Facebook's role in perpetuating bias:

> *When ProPublica reported that Facebook allowed advertisers to buy credit, housing and employment ads that exclude anyone with an affinity for African-American, Asian-American and Hispanic people from seeing them, it sparked a wave of criticism aimed at the social network. Four members of Congress wrote to Facebook demanding that the company stop letting advertisers exclude viewers of housing ads by race. The federal agency that enforces the nation's fair housing laws began talks with Facebook to address what experts said was a clear violation of federal anti-discrimination laws. Two weeks after our story ran, Facebook announced that it would bar advertisers from excluding users by race in ads that involved housing, credit and employment. The company said it would build an automated system to spot ads that discriminate illegally.*

Tracking and reporting impact is important to maintain brand image, and actually to be seen to be making a difference. But for brands that have never really done this before, or even those that have (but would like to apply a more rigorous process in their reporting), where do they start? In the 2013 report 'Deepening engagement for lasting impact: a framework for measuring media performance and results' produced for the Gates and Knight Foundations, media measurement is discussed in terms of being a live, working process instead of a record of hard numbers that are less relatable, and easier to manipulate, for example by bots. The report says: 'For ultimate success, evaluating media must be approached as a discipline that is built over time and integrated within a program's core.'

This is an important point. Most measurement in media happens at a moment in time, or is considered within a defined period, such as quarterly or annual cycles. That in turn lends itself to quantitative metrics, like clicks and views, as opposed to the more emotional real-world impact, such as being instrumental in changing a policy, as in the ProPublica example above.

Thinking of media impact as a working process can also give brands a sense of where new business prospects may lie, which is the other important impact-related factor to discuss: commercial benefit.

Increasingly, brands can't have commercial impact if they don't wield some amount of control over the environments they choose to be in. But they don't have that control. Over time, depending on platforms like Facebook for reach has ceased to be a trustworthy business model. Given the general upward trend in digital advertising revenue, and the growth of younger, digitally native audiences, companies need to contend with the fact that audiences they don't own are not theirs to reach. This is clear from Facebook's latest about-turn regarding the way it deploys its algorithms: as of January 2018, they are no longer supporting brand pages, instead upweighting news from friends and family in the newsfeed. This strategy makes sense for them: Facebook have realised, with the expanding tentacles of fake news taking hold over media, that they are best staying out of being a publisher. It also reinforces what Englehardt and Narayanan say in the privacy paper discussed earlier in this chapter: 'Larger entities may be easier to regulate by public-relations pressure and the possibility of legal or enforcement actions, an outcome we have seen in past studies.'

So, what business models should brands be thinking about? One of the most straightforward routes to profit, in publishing at least, is the subscription model. This makes commercial impact easier to measure, but also allows a crucial relationship with customers. John Ridding, CEO of The Financial Times, said in an interview with *Fast Company* in 2018 that the *FT* was ridiculed for charging for subscriptions when they started doing it in 2002, but it didn't matter because 'the primary responsibility for any publication is to its readers and not its advertisers'.

This is true of all businesses (a business only exists if it wants to sell a product or service): the primary responsibility is to its consumers, because doing right by them will do right by shareholders. That ain't rocket science, but it's too often forgotten in this age of constant interruption. And constantly measuring how successfully you discharge that responsibility through an iterative process rather than a static set of numbers is the best way to keep track of your goals.

Measuring impact will then no longer be a matter of trying to game the system with technology, as we discussed at the beginning of this chapter.

If you want impact, you will do what matters.

13

THE SILENT AD THAT SPOKE VOLUMES

Written by **Ryan Wallman**

Do you have to make a lot of noise to get noticed in Adland, and beyond? This chapter investigates.

Many years ago – too many for my liking – there was a TV commercial for a brand of garden sprinkler.

No, wait. It gets better, I promise.

This ad was remarkable. It wasn't famous, mind you. You won't have read about it in advertising textbooks, and I doubt that it would have won any awards. In fact, it was for a fairly obscure Australian brand that you've probably never heard of, unless you lived in Perth in the 1980s (if so, my condolences).

Anyway, the remarkable thing about this ad was that nothing really happened. And it was silent. The ad was little more than a black screen overlaid by a super that read (something to the effect of): 'This is the sound of one of our sprinklers'. It ended with a shot of a lush lawn.

Aside from the fact that it neatly demonstrated a benefit of the product, the really striking aspect of this ad was that it stood in stark contrast to everything around it. All of the other ads at that time, and indeed most of the TV programmes, were loud and tacky. It was the 1980s, after all. In that context, this unassuming little ad was almost impossible to ignore.

And it made a huge impression on me at the time. Funnily enough, I can still remember thinking 'I would like to go into advertising so that I can make an ad like that', which is saying a lot, because gardening products interest me about as much as white papers on programmatic marketing.

So, would that ad work today; in this era when all available space must be filled?

I think it would. Given the bluster and blather of advertising in the 21st century, such a simple idea would probably be more effective than ever. Because for all the 'noise' that characterises modern marketing – the convoluted strategies, data dashboards, media plans, contextualised targeting, concept testing, and what have you – the single most important rule of advertising is that it must be noticed. This rule does not change with the times. It will always be true that if an ad doesn't get noticed, it is pointless. Totally, utterly pointless.

Consider the last ad that you put out there. And be honest with yourself. If you saw that ad, would it stop you in your tracks? If your answer is something like 'Probably not, but the message is on-brand and the images are correctly placed in accordance with our style guidelines', you've got a problem.

Nobody looking at your ad has your brief on hand. Nobody is checking it off against your strategy, or wondering about your message hierarchy, or measuring the height of your logo. Indeed, the difference between how you see your ad and how your audience sees it might be summarised thus:

What people in advertising think when they see an ad

Hmm, I'm not sure about that headline-image combination. Might be too obvious. And the headline gets lost. It needs to be about 4 point-sizes bigger. I wouldn't have used Calibri, personally. And that kerning needs work. Could do with a touch more white space. Surely the supporting copy is redundant? I don't think the use of borrowed interest really works. And that logo isn't anchored properly. Mind you, the payoff line isn't bad. Reminds me a bit of that campaign from last year. I wonder who did it. I think Tom's agency does their stuff, come to think of it...

What everyone else thinks when they see an ad

Isn't the TV guide supposed to be here?

So, the first question to ask about any advertising is, 'Will it be noticed?'

Then, sure, ask the other important questions. Is this the right message? Is the ad believable? Does it demonstrate the benefits? Is there a strong incentive? And so on. But if the answer to that first question is 'no', all of those other questions are irrelevant. If the answer is 'yes', on the other hand, then your message might get through. It might be remembered. It might be written about some 30 years later. Hell, it might even inspire a career.

14

WAGING WAR ON RADICAL INCREMENTALISM

Written by **Rich Siegel**

What ever happened to swinging for the fences, to making ads with a difference? Is it going to be more bore? This chapter considers.

We visited some friends recently who had just finished painting their living room. Naturally, as guests (and being of excessive politeness), we said it looked beautiful. Unable to let a sleeping dog lie, however, I made further enquiry.

'What colour was it before?'

'It was Snowbound White 7004.'

'And now?'

'We went with Toque White 7003.'

'Lovely. Just lovely.'

And that, in a nutshell, is where we are at in advertising in 2018: trying to move an apathetic, largely uninterested audience with fragmented media and a monumentally bland message that is barely two angstrom units to the right or left of the same incomprehensible strategy used by the nearest competitor.

Witness the Lexus commercials that look like Acura commercials, Coke spots that could easily be mistaken for Pepsi spots, and Windows ads that bear an uncanny resemblance to those from Apple (though to be fair, that seems to be Microsoft's entire modus operandi).

I'm happy to take money from clients and marketers who think terms such as 'Motivated Achievers', 'Ambitious Challengers' or 'Extroverted Innovators' are useful demographic delineators. Or agencies who believe their insightful one-of-a-kind briefs are different from another agency's identical, insightful one-of-a-kind briefs. Or anyone who thinks they can build a successful brand with tweets, Insties and Snapfaps.

The truth is, they're all playing in the same sandbox. And at some point, the turd left by the cat has to be removed.

It's all such small ball.

And maybe when you're dealing with parity products and parity services it's impossible to raise the flag of true differentiation. But hell, what happened to swinging for the fences? To saying something nobody else was saying? And doing it in a way no one else was doing?

The other truth is, if you're not doing something radically different, you're doing everything radically wrong.

But I don't expect anything to change.

And until then, I'll just keep creating social media scavenger hunts that will never get produced, conjuring up brand activation stunts that will never get activated, and writing meaningless, micro-targeted TV spots aimed at 'Perseverant Non-Traditional Influencers'. Whatever the fuck that means.

15

DEATH OF A SALESWOMAN

Written by **Rich Siegel**

We're talking advertising, not curing cancer here. So, don't get gruelling, advises this chapter.

Turns out a woman in Japan, working for Dentsu, a giant advertising company, committed suicide when she could no longer keep up with the gruelling workload.

First off, we're talking about advertising here. Nothing should be gruelling about advertising. Let's not forget our products are frivolous TV commercials, meaningless interweb scavenger hunts, and the occasional print and outdoor board – shiny print pieces meant to bait witless consumers into a frenzy of mindless consumerism.

We're not curing cancer. In many cases, we're pimping it – with brown fizzy sugar water, hormone-injected meat tubes and carbon-burning 400-horsepower crossover vehicles.

It's just huckstering. And it doesn't merit gruelling anything.

It was reported that the young woman put in 105 hours of overtime in one month. That's roughly 25 hours a week. Meaning she put in about 65 hours a week, for four weeks straight.

Sadly, this is not unheard of. Years ago, while working on a pitch, I maintained that pace for about nine weeks.

The whole team did. And it was brutal. And nerves were frayed. To the point where one creative director, unhappy with the specifics of one highly forgettable storyboard, literally turned to the art director, and in full tantrum mode blasted... *'Frame #5 is all wrong. It's supposed to be a male dog. Where is the dick on the dog? Have this redrawn and put a damn dick on the dog.'*

Oh yeah, that happened. If I'm lying, I'm dying.

Of course, I'm not dying. And don't plan to off myself in the pursuit of writing the great American 15-second BOGOF spot, or the world's greatest 'call to action'.

Because, after all these years in this business, I now have something that unfortunately the overworked Dentsu employee did not: perspective.

16

BEST PRACTICE – IS IT REALLY?

Written by **Mark Earls**

While marketers and advertising professionals are beginning to embrace the idea that consumers (aka 'people out there') use copying and 'social learning' to shape their choices, we are by and large resistant to seeing ourselves using the same mechanics to solve problems. Except, that is, in copying 'best practice': this seems altogether a different, more respectable kind of copying. This chapter argues that while copying is the smart thing for marketers to do in the face of strategy challenges, big and small, we need to take care around 'best practice'. All too often 'best practice' really isn't 'best' – and copying it can disappoint.

Copying success

There was a time when IBM really was 'Big Blue' – when its sales people all dressed in the same blue suits, crisp white shirts and plain black ties; when they all wore the neat short hair and respectable black wingtip shoes of the born-again evangelist. When I first encountered the corporation, early on in my career, some of the dress code had been relaxed (but not much), but the way they pitched and presented was strangely out of time: very stiff and old fashioned. It was (I was told) still the same as it always had been. It was 'the IBM way'.

An old hand once explained the origins of the IBM pitch. One day, the founder, Thomas Watson Senior, bemused by the repeated outstanding sales performance of his number one salesman, called the star employee into his office to explain his method and approach. 'Is this how you always pitch?' I can imagine the old man asking. So taken was the old man with what he saw that he ordered it to be written down and circulated to all sales staff: *this is the IBM way of doing things.* Just like the suits and the haircuts. And the no drinking rule (exception was later made for that when the EMEA HQ moved to Paris).

Now, whether or not this story is true (I have never been able to confirm it in the many management histories of IBM), doesn't really matter. It represents a phenomenon that most of us have seen in other contexts, in other organisations and other situations: *when in doubt, copy success.*

It's hard to argue with copying success. Behavioural scientists happily point out the long history of copying as a decision-making strategy; its abiding utility and ease of use – if you want to know how to hunt, copy the hunter with the best hauls; if you want to know how to cook, copy the best cook selecting their ingredients and watch them as they work around the fire; if you want to know how to fight, you know who to copy. If you want to be cool... go copy the cool kids.

As a strategy, copying success is credible, easy to understand and easy to implement; don't bother thinking about the complications, just copy the winners. No wonder the bestselling business book is Stephen Covey's blockbusting *The 7 Habits of Highly Effective People.* But when you look more closely at 'best practice' – what it is, who decides what it is, and how we might tell what it is – it's far from clear that it's the thing to do.

Out there (but not in here)

Over the last decade, the empirical cognitive and behavioural sciences have given us unprecedented insights into the consumer behaviour we seek to change, and helped us rethink how our tools, like advertising, work. What we've learned about the role of emotions in decision making has, for example, helped us revolutionise the way we think about, and measure, advertising's effectiveness. That said, the importance of social influence and learning – copying by any other name – has taken rather more time to work its way through into what we do every day. In the individualist culture through which we and consumers swim, it is easier to accept a different account of behaviour (which stresses the primacy of what goes on between our ears) than to really engage with the possibility that the action is to be found beyond our individual crania, in the space between individuals.

Our reluctance to accept something doesn't mean that it isn't true. Copying is central to how many consumer decisions are made, as I described in a 2011 *Admap* article and book I co-authored with Professor Alex Bentley, *I'll Have What She's Having*. From the music we listen to and the gadgets we buy to the names we give our children or the way we lay out food on a plate (and even what counts as food), we all copy.

Figure 1: Map of choice styles adapted from *I'll Have What She's Having*. The eastern side of the map denotes copying-shaped choices; the western side, independent choices

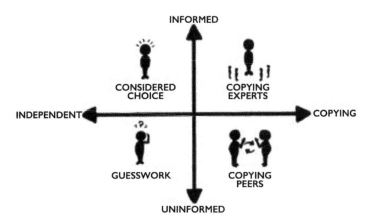

Great work by a number of hands – including the UK government's erstwhile Behavioural Insights Team (the so-called 'Nudge Unit') – has demonstrated the importance of copying-based strategies to changing consumer behaviour. It is now much more widely accepted that consumer behaviour is shaped a lot of the time by 'social proof' and norms, and that these are very good levers for behaviour change.

However, even if we accept the importance of copying 'out there', we still baulk at using the power of copying in the creation of strategy – copying other people's strategies. Outside it's OK that consumers copy, but in here, we'd never do such a thing. (Except, of course, that we do.)

In my book *Copy Copy Copy*, I make the case for copying as the number one hack for strategists: if you want to know how to solve a problem, then why try to do it all on your own? Why not find what other people have done with similar kinds of challenges, and use that as the start point for your strategic thinking? Why not use the experience of others – their success in solving similar kinds of challenges – to template your own? I describe that, if you do this well, a number of possible strategies (not just one) emerge, which reflect what we all know in our hearts. Despite our love of the singularity, of narrowing down our thinking to one solution, we know that there is always more than one answer to any given problem.

The best way or the highway

You could see the practice of best practice as a subset of this. However, it is different in an important respect: it assumes that at any time (and in any context) there is a single 'best way', a demonstrably superior practice to follow.

Part of this is an inheritance from the early 20th century 'Scientific Management' movement of Frederick Taylor and his collaborators. They all believed that through observation, careful measurement and experiment the 'best way' of doing something could be established. This could then be taught to companies, teams and employees, thus raising both the quality and efficiency of the workplace, and its output.

But working out the very best practices in many fields is not so easy – even Taylor's close collaborators, Frank and Lilian Gilbreth, were concerned with the subjective nature of his approach to measurement of 'best'. They recognised that, in the absence of doing these hard yards, he was leaving the door open to subjectivity.

Very often when we say best practice we take a much looser approach than was intended by these pioneers: we mean good things to do, or rather, 'things that appear to be good'. 'Social media monitoring best practice' in this sense becomes more like 'how experts in the field generally agree you should be doing it' (see, for example, the excellent IPASocialWorks guides to Evaluation, Insight and Personalisation, available from the IPA). Of course, the next question to answer is who those experts or authorities are, and how they make their recommendations – are they empirically based or are they merely anecdotal (remember the plural of anecdote is not data)?

Success and 'best'

Often, rather than bother with the detail of 'best', we use success as an indicator of 'best' – as the IBM sales pitch illustrates. Surely, if something is successful, it has to be the best? Well, maybe.

For example, success may only be 'accidental' (as sociologist Duncan Watts observed in his trenchant criticism of the science behind Malcolm Gladwell's 2000 book *The Tipping Point*): if a thing is successful it may be because it has spread from person to person (like music and many drinks brands), not because it is better in any way. Try this thought experiment: if you were to 'rewind the tape' of history, fast-forward it and rewind it a few times, do the same things come out on top every time? Evolutionary biologist Stephen Jay Gould coined this analogy to describe the actually very unlikely evolutionary success of homo sapiens. The implication being that if you follow 'accidentally' successful practice, you may just be copying what a lucky person or company did/does. Without the key component in their success – *luck*. Assuming success is a sign of better or best now has its own name in cognitive science: 'survivorship bias'.

Another way in which success misleads is if the practice we admire is only partially responsible for the success we're seeking to replicate. So for example, while we marketers love to explain Lego's renaissance over the last decade in terms of its brand and incredible consumer focus (letting the adult Lego fans and their obsessions in), the truth is that without a fundamental reworking of their supply chain the business would almost certainly have had to be sold (and nothing like Mindstorms or short *Star Wars* YouTube animations would be around to distract us and/or our kids).

Or, we might find out that what looked like success is anything but – it's just that the data we use to evaluate success isn't able to show this, or the timeframe is too short to make that judgement. Many great authorities, whose ideas are otherwise very sound, have fallen foul of this trap. Michael Porter was famously criticised for using examples of successful companies that subsequently failed. Clay Christensen, the creator of 'disruption', was more recently criticised for choosing arbitrary time periods for comparisons that make his point better than a longer term comparison might make. This is something to bear in mind when you hear someone proclaim that they have identified the best practice from successful companies.

The thing about case studies

Case studies make great reading. The best illustrate (in compelling style) points, ideas and practices to be admired; they bring alive what might otherwise be dry and impenetrable. However, they are poor ways to establish what's what – what's best and what's not.

Case studies are written (by necessity) after the fact. And as with all history, they are written by the victors. As with all stories told by human beings, they are subject to the risks of self-aggrandisement biases – just as each of us has a tendency to be over-optimistic about the future, and the likely impact of our own choices, so the stories we tell about business and its performance tend to overstate the importance of our/its actions and decisions on positive outcomes, and downplay the positive impact of other factors like competitors, the environment etc.

From over there to over here

The practice of best practice raises many problems around the notion of 'best': what it is; how do you or anyone else tell what 'best looks like etc?

However, perhaps the most important watch-outs are to be found in 'how' you copy.

First, when you port a set of practices or protocols from one context to another, this transposition is unlikely to be neat, mechanical and surgical. The practices that work particularly well in one context don't necessarily work at all well in another. In some ways, the efficacy of the practices in the first context is dependent on the context for success; for example, the 1990s fad for US firms adopting Japanese factory processes struggled because those practices depend on a shared national culture that the exemplary Japanese firms enjoyed. One of Scientific Management's biggest fans was Lenin – the Soviet Union's centralised approach to economic planning is straight out of Detroit. But the replication of one set of practices in another context may not deliver what the transplanter is seeking. Of course, sometimes it does, as Professor Martin Elliott and the Great Ormond Street paediatric heart surgery team demonstrated, in *adapting* protocols from one context (in their case, Formula 1 racing) to their medical practice to reduce human error count in operating theatres by 42%.

In *Copy Copy Copy*, I highlight the difference between 'replication' (a machine word) and 'copying' (the human word): one seeks precision and accuracy and the other allows for (or indeed embraces) error and variation. One is singular and the other multi-headed. I suspect that behind the practice of best practice is the assumption that replication is both required and possible. And that there is a singular answer to the challenges we face.

Conclusion

Copying – outsourcing the cognitive load – is one of our greatest gifts as a species; marketers and their agencies have perhaps been rather too embarrassed about their use of copying as a means to solve strategic problems and to create new solutions. We should use it more than we have done, as a central part of our problem-solving and creative arsenal. And feel OK about doing so.

However, it does matter who, what and how we copy. Sam Bowles, the evolutionary economist, identifies these as the central questions on which to focus, as individuals, as organisations, societies and as a species. Copying best practice has problems in all these areas. Especially in defining 'best' and ignoring the context of what is copied, and the context it is copied into.

Maybe we ought to be a little more humble, and re-label 'best' practice 'good' practice? *Good practice* in advertising effectiveness measurement. *Good practice* in multi-channel real-time content development. *Good practice* in brand building? It doesn't sound nearly as scientific or grown-up. But that's probably a good thing. Probably.

References

Covey. S. *The 7 Habits of Highly Effective People: Powerful lessons in personal change.* Simon & Schuster, 1989

Earls, M. *Copy, Copy, Copy: How to do smarter marketing by using other people's ideas.* Wiley, 2015

Earls, M, Bentley, A, and O'Brien, M. *I'll Have What She's Having: Mapping social behavior.* Wiley, 2011

Gladwell, M. *The Tipping Point: How little things can make a big difference.* Little, Brown, 2000

17

WHERE DID IT ALL GO WRONG?

Written by **Eaon Pritchard**

'A bag of money never scored a goal.'

Never attribute to malice that which is adequately explained by stupidity. Or as Goethe noted in *The Sorrows of Young Werther* in 1774, 'misunderstandings and neglect create more confusion in this world than trickery and malice. At any rate, the last two are certainly much less frequent'. Of course, you should never rule out malice completely. Either way, this chapter asserts, somewhere advertising took its eye off the ball, forgot what it really does and how it works, and allowed both stupidity and malice to take control of the game.

According to legend, one night in late 1974 ex-Manchester United soccer superstar star and Belfast's most famous sporting export, George Best, had just spent a very successful evening in the casino accompanied by the reigning Miss World.

They had just won a silly amount of money – around £15,000 (that's over a hundred grand in today's money) – brought it back to their hotel room and ordered up a magnum of the hotel's best champagne, which was shortly delivered by an Irish room service waiter.

The waiter looked at George, looked at Miss World, the piles of cash surrounding the pair all over the bed. The champagne was popped, and before leaving the waiter famously asked…

'So, tell me now, George... where did it all go wrong?'

Our waiter's typically dark Belfast humour aside, on the surface George certainly didn't look like he had too many problems, but something, somewhere, had fundamentally gone wrong for world soccer's first superstar.

Whether this particular casino story is exactly true or not is not important. What *is* true is that even as early as 1971, George's hectic off-field celebrity lifestyle was widely believed to be reducing his effectiveness on the pitch.

That was the popular view, but perhaps also true was that the slow, steady decline of Manchester United's status and fortunes since the departure from the dressing room of legendary coach Matt Busby was taking its toll on George's enthusiasm for the game.

In just a couple of years, following the spectacular European Cup win of 1968, the ageing United had effectively become a one-man show: George was carrying the whole team.

That alternative explanation is worth its inclusion. This is a book that is principally about advertising, after all. And if there's one thing that has remained constant over time, it is our ability to consistently get cause and effect the wrong way around.

Either way, while arguably the most talented footballer of his generation (or just about any other subsequent age), the wayward Best was now rapidly developing a reputation for general unreliability, and regularly going AWOL rather than participating in training sessions. And he was now even missing matches.

This erratic behaviour coincided with Best's developing problems with alcoholism, and he eventually parted company with his beloved United (and football) during the 1973/74 season, at the end of which the once mighty Manchester giants were relegated to the second tier of the English Football League.

George was only 27 when he quit – an age when most players are usually regarded as being at or near their peak – and without the distraction of football, George was now free to pursue his other principal interests: the aforementioned drinking, gambling and company of glamorous women.

The notion of a self-fulfilling prophecy is often overused and overstated. Ideas that become a reality simply because an individual believes them do not usually turn out, and despite the claims of the self-help book industry (and as Sean Bean would concur), you do not just simply think yourself rich.

But there is something to be said for how expectations may come to pass when many people hold the same beliefs. George's boozy exploits, alongside the 'wasted genius that threw it all away' narrative, were never far from the tabloid headlines. So, believe it we did.

If we follow the money, then the advertising business would appear to be in rude health.

Global ad spending is said to be growing faster than at any time in the digital era. The most recent eMarketer Worldwide Adspend Forecast estimates that total spending will reach around $725 billion by 2020. That's growth of between 5% to 9% year on year, with digital and mobile spend contributing to about 36% of that at present, growing to nearly half by 2020. Big bucks.

And the glamour?

For George Best, the constant company of a sequence of Miss World winners ticked that box, while the Rosé-fuelled, celebrity-splattered and yacht-propelled Cannes Festival is our thing.

These extravagant festivals are not going away any time soon; however, many influential agency types are starting to question the value they create.

For some, *Cannes has become a parody.* Tom Goodwin calls it a 'self-serving fetishisation of the newly possible and the highly improbable'. Yet Cannes is also predictable and formulaic, awash with novelty technology for its own sake, and about as far from the everyday concerns of the average shopper as it is possible to be.

It's hard not to agree with that point of view – at least in part – when observing some of the winning entries from 2017. Much of the silliness seemed to abound in the 'Innovation' category, of course.

Awarding a Gold Lion for a *Grand Theft Auto V* mod seems like a bit of a stretch, while the Innovation Grand Prix was awarded to a smelting project for recycling handguns.

What these activities have to do with brand communications is anyone's guess, but they are symptomatic of the real and bigger problems for this industry that are only now starting to unravel.

There's money all over the bed, but pull back the covers, and there's a horse's head.

We'll never know for sure, but when the horse's head was attached to its body, the whole horse almost certainly hated advertising.

These days, everybody seems to hate it.

It's not just those cheeky 'authenticity-seeking purpose-driven Millennials' that claim to hate advertising. Even 'old' people (that's over 45 in ad-speak, by the way) will say they hate it, while the advertising and marketing trade press definitely hate it.

And lastly, most of the people who work in advertising and media agencies seem to hate their jobs – and hate the idea that they are selling brands, products and services rather than the more noble aim of solving society's problems: 'Our best trained, best educated, best equipped, best prepared troops refuse to fight. As a matter of fact, it's safe to say that they would rather… switch, than fight!'

With apologies to Chuck D and Thomas N Todd, maybe it's more charitable to say that we've now 'successfully' produced a generation of advertising professionals who have never even known what advertising is for, and how it works.

And who's going to teach them? Well, the rest of us appear to have forgotten entirely.

Being even more cynical, we could say we've turned a business that used to value ideas and creativity into 'a pig's breakfast of insufferable bullshit, dreadful jargon, stupid gimmicks and amateur bumblers producing horrific crap', to use a classic Hoffman-ism.

Who needs creativity when you can be *'growth-hacking a well-integrated purpose and empowering organisational pivots to navigate today's disrupted environment and engage with digital ecosystems!'* Or something.

Talk of disrupted ecosystems probably goes some way to explaining why the big consulting firms are among the few who seem to be interested in the advertising business. Now we've started to talk a Dunning–Kruger approximation of their language, we are fair game.

Just like George Best's dwindling interest in football, the advertising industry seems to have lost interest in its own game. Or we've forgotten why we're in it.

So, where did it all go wrong?

At the close of the 20th century, a powerful idea caught the imagination of the media industry and then the advertising business.

The emerging digital era was to herald the swift death of mass media and mass communications – blunt instruments like TV and newspapers were about to become the forgotten relics of a latter-day dark age – as the new technologies ushered in the brave new world of one-to-one communications.

It all seemed pretty plausible.

At the time, none of us even questioned the circular logic of Don Peppers and Martha Rogers in their 1993 bestseller *The One To One Future*, as it quickly became the blueprint for the 'new' marketing thinking.

> It is information about individual consumers that will keep a marketer functioning in the 1:1 future. Without individual information, as opposed to market or segment information, 1:1 marketing would not be possible.

This is 1993, remember. It would be another seven or eight years before the term 'marketing automation' was first uttered, but for the CFOs of the world who saw the money spent on advertising as suspicious at best, a total waste of time at worst, this was the kind of accountability and efficiency story they liked to hear. No more wastage.

Somewhere around this time, the seeds were sown that allowed two fundamentally wrong assumptions to become the dominant narratives in advertising and marketing in the digital era.

The first of these is the widespread acceptance and assumption in the industry that 'advertising online' almost exclusively meant 'highly targeted direct response'.

The second is the widespread acceptance and assumption that for 'advertising online' to be effective, it must always employ the tracking and surveillance of consumers.

Doc Searls said it best (in 'Separating advertising's wheat and chaff'): 'Madison Avenue fell asleep, direct response marketing ate its brain, and it woke up as an alien replica of itself.'

When asked, people don't like the idea of being overtly tracked and profiled.

In some quarters (the above-mentioned Doc, in particular), there's close to a moral panic over tracking. I'm not sure I subscribe to that view. We're too far in to go back.

Fundamentally, it's what the internet is *for*: information.

Co-founder of *Wired*, Kevin Kelly, suggests that our central choice now is whether the surveillance economy is going to work one way only, or more of a kind of 'coveillance'.

> ...So that we make tracking and monitoring as symmetrical and transparent as possible. That way the monitoring can be regulated, mistakes appealed and corrected, specific boundaries set and enforced.
>
> A massively surveilled world is not a world I would design (or even desire), but massive surveillance is coming either way because that is the bias of digital technology and we might as well surveil well and civilly.

Who we are being tracked by, and to what end, needs sorting.

I agree with Doc that adtech, in its current guise, is full of fraud and malware, incentivises bullshit content over journalism, and gives fake news a business model.

But apart from that...

Of course, being followed around the web by ads for stuff you have already bought is annoying. This cheap, clumsy targeting has a knock-on effect in that it may even actually harm those brands that are doing the following.

Implicitly, this sends the wrong signal to consumers, especially if an established brand is the signaller.

Signalling theory shows that when we can intuit how much money a company has laid out for an ad campaign, this helps us (unconsciously) make distinctions between brands that have put their money where their mouth is and brands that have not.

Even if (as much of the rhetoric goes) people are demanding and responding to more personalised and relevant 'advertising', why isn't ad-blocking adoption going down?

But from an advertiser's point of view, and aside from any ethical considerations, the single biggest failure of adtech is that advertising online to date has simply not been able to deliver on the brand advertising part of the picture.

The internet's spectacular inability to deliver on brand advertising means it is (today) not really a place to be if you want to build a brand, because we have set up the web to only deliver direct response marketing pretending to be advertising in the form of impressions and clicks and an assortment of vanity metrics (coincidentally, the easiest things to fake).

We've forgotten the basic idea that brand advertising creates demand, and direct response fulfils it. The adtech-ers and our Silicon Valley robot overlords stepped up, wanted the whole game, and we handed it to them on a plate.

The ball has been stolen by the worst kind of *used car salesmen (and their mechanics)*, and the actual drivers have had no input.

So where do we go from here?

Psychologists will tell you that humans are pretty good intuitive biologists. We have innate abilities to be able to identify the kinds of plants that are safe to eat or animals that are likely to be predators or venomous.

We are also pretty good intuitive psychologists. We can identify what others are thinking and feeling, or what kind of mood they are in, with very few cues.

I'd also argue that people are pretty good intuitive media strategists.

We don't know how much a full-page ad in the broadsheet newspaper costs, exactly. But we do know that it was pretty damn expensive. We don't know exactly how much that retargeting banner ad costs, but we know that it's pretty cheap.

Likewise, we can quickly and intuitively detect high or low production values that reflect the level of economic investment in any piece of communications. All these indicators are signals.

The kinds of signals that carry an implicit sense of 'cost' on behalf of the signaller can be trusted, to a degree. Costly signals are reliable. The signaller has put their money where their mouth is.

Researchers Tim Ambler and E Ann Hollier quantified this in their important study 'The waste in advertising is the part that works'.

> *High perceived advertising expense enhances an advertisement's [persuasiveness] significantly, but largely indirectly, by strengthening perceptions of brand quality.*

Quality online publishers, for example, are beginning to come around to the idea that a viable strategy might be to restrict their premium online inventory, creating scarcity, and therefore an opportunity for 'signal' or brand building. (I worked with a premium fashion title a couple of years ago, and this was their exact model. There was no way they were going to sully their web presence with anything other than premium ads and premium-branded content – the same strategy as for the print magazine.)

The way an ad is perceived in any vehicle is influenced by both the editorial content, and by the other ads it shares space with. So, ads in this particular publication were not just sold to anybody who could pay for them. If anything, the ads were as integral to the experience as the editorial. But what about efficiency? Adtech makes everything more efficient, right?

In so-called 'Madmen' days, the media owners took 85% of an advertiser's dollar (Dataworldbase.org), while the agency took the other 15%. The advertiser could then open up the newspaper or switch on the TV or radio and see their ad.

Full transparency? What? This was clearly a broken model!

By way of an amusing aside, I recently had a client who was justifiably alarmed to discover, via a tweet by a vigilant employee, that one of their online ads had appeared on the right-wing news/satire website Breitbart.

The agency was alerted, and the ad was removed, but the incident opened up a can of brand safety worms that we could have all done without at the time.

I never mentioned this to the client, but was tempted to say that their ad was:

1. Seen by an actual human being for long enough that they were able to screengrab the page and post it on Twitter.
2. Regardless of whether we agree or disagree with the political sentiment of Breitbart, it is a legitimate news site, written by real journalists – albeit journalists of questionable viewpoint.

This means that the ad in question was already doing somewhat better than 75% of online display. (The employee herself had been retargeted from somewhere else and followed to Breitbart. Whether she went there deliberately in order to make a point or this was an indicator of her individual political leanings is not known.)

The quote that follows is pulled from Onora O'Neill's 2002 Reith Lectures series 'A question of trust'.

Her comments are as apt today as they were then.

In the fifth of her lectures, 'Licence to deceive', the Cambridge emeritus professor of philosophy was principally referring to the state of journalism, but today, we can apply her insight into what has happened to advertising in general, and to advertising technology in particular.

> Do we really gain from heavy-handed forms of accountability? Do we really benefit from... demands for transparency? I am unconvinced.
>
> I think we may undermine professional performance and standards... by excessive regulation, and that we may condone and even encourage deception in our zeal for transparency.

The final sentence is perhaps the most disturbing.

How can we discern the trustworthy from untrustworthy? O'Neill argues that we should perhaps focus less on grandiose ideals of transparency, and rather more on limiting deception.

O'Neill was some 15 years ahead of my Google/Facebook crunchy-on-the-outside-fluffy-on-the-inside metaphor.

> The new information technologies may be anti-authoritarian, but curiously they are often used in ways that are also anti-democratic. They undermine our capacities to judge others' claims and to place our trust.

We need to make measurement sexy. It's a topic we need to embrace and give a lot more love to, say, the likes of the IAB.

Good luck with that.

Not everything that counts can be counted. And when trust moves out, measurement moves in.

Full transparency and exposure to skulduggery may even backfire, strengthening the norm that unsavoury behaviours are widespread, and therefore those behaviours are (implicitly) permissible. Or that the practice is necessary in order to succeed – a muddling of norms.

We are where we are, and it's going to be a long road back, but the biggest challenge is not that evil criminal masterminds populate agencies – or even some areas of advertising technology – although they do exist. It's more of a cock-up than a conspiracy.

People who fundamentally do not understand what advertising is for, or how it works, are increasingly being handed far too much influence in the industry.

In the words of Hanlon's eponymous razor, 'never attribute to malice that which is adequately explained by stupidity'. But how much can be attributed to stupidity?

The legendary Theodore 'Ted' Sturgeon was (and still is) widely acclaimed as one of the greats in science fiction and horror writing, and would have been no stranger to the odd slash of a razor.

He wrote a number of novels, was an early scriptwriter on the promising TV series *Star Trek* in the 1950s and '60s, and also one of the foremost critics in the sci-fi genre, penning over 400 reviews before his passing in 1985.

After many years of pushing back attacks on the science fiction genre from critics, Sturgeon had a moment of insight. This insight became known as 'Sturgeon's Revelation', later shortened (less dramatically) to 'Sturgeon's *Law*'.

Speaking at the World Science Fiction Convention in Philadelphia in September 1953, Sturgeon responded to 'proper' literary critics who claimed that '90% of science fiction is crap'.

Ted agreed: 90% of science fiction is indeed crap. But, he argued, to say 90% of science fiction is crap is meaningless because science fiction conforms to the same trends of quality as all other art forms.

Sturgeon's Law, therefore, states that 90% of everything – all film, literature, products, culture and advertising – is crap.

Less often reported is Ted's proposed solution to the problem. If we agree that 90% of everything is crap, then what's important is to study, learn from and promote the 10% that isn't crap. (Maybe 90% is generous; it's more likely closer to 99%, but you get the idea.)

In advertising there seems to be a period when any new approach, platform or technology that comes along seems, for a time, to somehow be viewed as exempt from this law. In the beginning, all TV and radio advertising – such was its shiny newness – was likely to be exempt.

Social media marketing, content marketing, QR codes, VR/AR, chatbots, and most recently, programmatic delivery and adtech, have all arrived, been heralded as 'the next big thing', then gradually landed in a ditch of disappointment, or as in the case of adtech in its current guise, murky nefariousness.

But if we had remembered Sturgeon's Law, perhaps we could have been more critical of practices and theories from the outset, and avoided a lot of unpleasantness.

The shortcomings of the majority of adtech have now been fully revealed. (As another aside, it is peculiar that in this age when information is supposed to disseminate at warp speed, mainstream media has only just caught up with what many of us have been discussing for about four or five years.)

Somehow, we have to shift focus and look for the 1%.

Look for the good.

Where is the good practice? If there is none, then how do we create some?

As an industry, we've been duped and cheated, but now we have had our eyes opened.

Will we get fooled again?

Probably, Madison Avenue has often been the road to Abilene.

Anyone who has sat through campaign or brand-tracking presentations by supposedly reputable research companies and thought '...am I the only one in this room who thinks this is bullshit?', please raise your hand now.

I thought so. Just about everyone. But we never raised our hands at the time.

The only way to break out of these cycles is to speak up, ask questions, be sceptical and ask for evidence.

A decent rule of thumb would be to *demand* that the more extraordinary the claim of any technology platform or gizmo, the stronger the evidence must be to support that claim.

This is not a Luddite rant. Far from it.

Programmatic delivery, automation and advertising technology are inevitable.

Very soon all media will be bought and distributed in this way.

Surveillance is also inevitable, but if we can work towards balancing symmetry and transparency, there's much value to be derived from real behavioural data at this scale.

Crappy-ness, however, need not be inevitable.

Not if the programmatic, automation and advertising technology is operated by people who understand how advertising works, what it is for, and why we urgently need to figure out and evaluate existing and emerging technologies on their ability or future potential to actually build brands.

The used car salesmen and engineers have had their turn, and the results were substantially less than optimal.

Factor in blind-sided publishers, winner-takes-all multinationals being allowed to mark their own homework, the deluge of shitty content, open season for fraudsters and criminals, and we've got a big mess to clean up.

At least 90% of the whole internet advertising shooting match was total crap. But It's out in the open, and we have to move on.

And 90% of everything will always be shit, but it's only a relentless, sceptical, demand for quality and creativity that points the way forward.

The impending death of something or other is reported every other week. The death of this, the death of that, the death of the other, and the death of the next thing. The death of advertising in particular.

Mea culpa. About 10 years ago I probably was that douche-bag. I called it my own *Dunning–Kruger peak.*

But if you are lucky, eventually you get over your own bullshit, to a degree. Or at least go into recovery. (I'm taking each day as it comes.)

Perhaps it all went wrong when we forgot the simple fact that the purpose of advertising is to bring brands, products, services and behaviours to the attention of the people so that they might buy them, or buy into them at the next opportunity.

What if the change the industry *really* needs is to refocus itself towards producing the kind of brilliant, insightful, creative advertising that will get noticed and remembered by consumers. We've more ability to screen out crap than ever before, so should the solution be better ways to do advertising, not worse?

If advertising is really dead, can it come back to life?

Back in 1979, the emerging young painter Julian Schnabel presented his two breakthrough solo exhibitions at Mary Boone's gallery in New York. The shows mainly featured his signature neo-expressionist wax paintings and plate paintings.

Amid the popular and influential art world narrative of the time were widely read articles with titles such as 'The end of painting' and 'Last exit: painting' in respected journals such as *Artforum*.

It should be noted that those essays (penned by critics Douglas Crimp and Thomas Lawson, respectively) should be approached with some caution unless readers are particularly fluent in academic postmodernist mumbo jumbo.

The final nail in painting's coffin had barely been hammered into place when at the exact same time other commentators began to herald Schnabel's works as 'the *return* of painting'.

In later years (and looking back), Schnabel somewhat wryly reflected (*Artforum*, 2003):

> *I thought that if painting is dead, then it's a nice time to start painting.*

It strikes me that there is a real, live emerging opportunity for those advertising agencies that actually want to take advantage of the expanded 21st-century media and technology canvas to actually make killer advertising. A crazy idea, but it might just work...

It's worth presenting Schnabel's full remark on the 'return to painting', but mediated through the lens of advertising:

> *I thought that if [advertising] is dead, then it's a nice time to start [doing advertising]. People have been talking about the death of [advertising] for so many years that most of those people are dead now.*

Advertising's many detractors are not dead yet, unfortunately. Even more unfortunately, a great many are the ones who are supposed to be driving the industry forward, but perhaps their time is coming to an end. Here's hoping.

In later years, and reflecting on his career, George Best famously joked, 'I spent most of my money on booze, birds and fast cars. The rest I just squandered.'

George got it: it's the *waste* that is the part that works.

As for us?

We have neglected imagination, creativity, originality and intelligence – all the fundamentals that make our product occasionally great – and instead squandered a lot of advertising money on dubious adtech and poor quality direct response that creates no value for publishers, advertisers or consumers, and is sending the next generation(s) of real creative talent elsewhere, somewhere more *sexy*.

So, tell us George, where did it all go wrong?

It had nothing to do with women and booze, car crashes or court cases.

It was purely football.

The great players I'd been brought up with were replaced with players who should not even have been allowed through the door.

Boom!

References

Ambler. T, and Hollier, EA. 'The waste in advertising is the part that works'. *Journal of Advertising Research*, 44(4), 2005

Crimp, D. 'The end of painting'. *Art World Follies*, 16, 1981

Goethe, J. *The Sorrows of Young Werther*. Penguin Classics, 1989

Kelly, K. 'Why you should embrace surveillance, not fight it'. *Wired*, 2014

Lawson. T. 'Last exit: painting'. *Artforum*, October 1981

Peppers, D, and Rogers, M. *The One to One Future: Building relationships one customer at a time*. Doubleday, 1993

18

APPLE, WALT DISNEY AND HARLEY-DAVIDSON – EXCEPTIONAL BRANDS!

Written by **Robert van Ossenbruggen**

It is tempting to look at successful cases to learn something about how to be successful. But as logical as it might sound, this approach leads to misleading conclusions. People turn out to fool themselves in a broad range of situations, as this chapter reveals.

What do the iconic brands Apple, Walt Disney and Harley-Davidson have in common? An exceptional customer experience? An inspiring purpose? Level 5 Leadership perhaps? And could what they have in common help you build your brand?

It's often the same set of brands that shine in books and blogs. Brands that have been successful for a long time. Or brands that have become successful in a very short period. Or brands that for whatever reason appeal to your imagination. But these exceptional brands have one problem: they are – what's in a name – exceptional.

Exceptions can easily fool you. Imagine the following (hypothetical) situation. The past two years a thousand new dairy products have been launched. A hundred of those sold well, and the rest of them have been taken from the shelves because they didn't. Of those well-sold products, 80% are low fat, low calorie, or some other light version; 20% are of the regular kind.

It is tempting to infer from the above that a light dairy product has a larger chance of success than a regular one. Without the 900 failed products, however, you can't draw any conclusion. The products that have been taken from the shelves might have been light products for 80% as well. That would imply that the attribute 'light' has no effect whatsoever.

This is an example of 'survivorship bias': you only observe things that have survived some process for whatever reason. You simply look at one side of the medal which could lead to misleading conclusions.

Mark Zuckerberg, Oprah Winfrey, Steve Jobs and Bill Gates all dropped out of college. But we don't encourage students to drop out because of these successful examples, do we? Still, we draw this kind of conclusion in similar but less obvious situations.

Take, for example, your loyalty programme, which at first sight might look like an impressive business case. Your customers that participate in the programme buy more, more frequently and stay longer. The programme works! But survivorship bias is at play here too: loyalty programmes attract exceptional customers. Participants enrolled in your programme partly because they were more engaged with your brand in the first place – of course they buy more! You are comparing apples and pears.

Once you recognise it, you will see it in many situations. The 'Ice Bucket Challenge' was a very successful campaign, but exceptional. Many tried to copy the seemingly successful elements to go viral. But many found out too that this award-winning ad did not spit out a set of rules for setting up a successful social media campaign.

Steve Jobs was no doubt a successful entrepreneur, but exceptional. Reading his biography will have inspired a great many minds, but studying Jobs doesn't teach you how to be a successful entrepreneur.

The growth of Google has been quite impressive, but exceptional. Jeff Jarvis's book *What Would Google Do?* is a very interesting read, but it cannot live up to the promise that we can learn from the 'fastest growing company in the history of the world'.

Several popular business books that attempt to reveal the secrets of a successful company make the same methodological mistake: the authors collect successful companies and ask themselves, 'What do they have in common?'

The only commonality you can be sure of is that they are all exceptional.

There are many examples simply because it's so tempting to learn from somebody else's success. Successful individuals, brands or products must be successful for a reason – there must be a common theme, a logical explanation. Yet successes are always a minority, and are partly random flukes.

Trying to learn from successes is risky business at best, and misleading at worst. To reveal the underlying pattern, you need the whole range of observations: successes, failures and all the 'more or less reasonable' cases in between. In research-speak, you need a representative sample.

It is important to recognise survivorship bias, as every day you will stumble upon new ideas about how to grow your brand, how to make customers happier, or how to lift your conversion rates. Often, the 'evidence' consists of several examples that fit the new idea. The many examples that don't fit are conveniently ignored.

Survivorship bias will survive, as the brain is easy to fool. We tend to stop asking questions when something makes sense. That's what makes this cognitive trap so persistent.

Don't get me wrong; I don't mean to encourage you to stop reading about interesting cases – just don't believe you have learnt anything from it. Inspiration and knowledge are two different things.

References

Jarvis, J. *What Would Google Do?* Collins, 2009

19

EVERYBODY LIES – THE IMPORTANCE OF PSYCHOLOGICAL VALIDITY IN CONSUMER INSIGHT

'Everybody lies.'
House M.D.

'You want to know how two chemicals interact, do you ask them? No, they're going to lie through their lying little chemical teeth. Throw them in a beaker and apply heat.'
House M.D.

Written by **Philip Graves**

Over the last 30 years, behavioural psychologists have demonstrated that we routinely don't understand our own decision making. This presents significant challenges to brand owners who want the reassurance of consumers' opinions to validate prospective decisions or recent marketing activity. For many years, the 'clever' question to ask of any market research was, 'How many people were asked?' – a nod to the statistical validity of the responses being referenced. But there is a better question to explore first, this chapter argues: you need to know if the research you're referencing is psychologically valid.

If someone tells us something, we have a complex decision to make about whether or not we believe what we've been told. Does it sound believable? Can it be verified elsewhere? Does it fit with our existing knowledge and beliefs? Do we regard the source as credible? Like most complex human decisions, this evaluation is handled largely by our unconscious mind. It provides us with a feeling about what we've heard, and it is this feeling that determines whether or not the 'information' alters our future behaviour. As with most facets of unconscious processing, they endure because they work well for us most of the time.

Unfortunately, in most organisations, this complex, unconscious evaluation is bypassed when it comes to interrogative market research. Information arrives from a survey or focus group, and is propagated around the organisation as a fact – because it has been said by consumers, we believe it must be true.

This faith, like most faith, is entirely understandable. Faced with uncertainty and complexity, someone somewhere (quite possibly with admirable intentions) manufactures a solution that offers comfort, at a price. Reassurance comes either from one of two places: a knowledge of statistical methods that tells us how mathematically confident we can be in our number given the sample referenced, or from the belief that the conversations that led to the insights were sufficiently deep that they must be well considered, and therefore true.

Regrettably, when it comes to trusting what people say in research, this faith is entirely misplaced, for two reasons:

1. People have no access to the unconscious mental traits that drive most of their decision making. These traits are termed 'unconscious' because they are outside of conscious awareness. We see this whenever an experiment is conducted where a component of the decision-making environment is changed and a change in behaviour occurs. Participants almost never identify accurately how the environmental factor was a part of their decision-making process. Instead, they routinely provide an alternative (and entirely plausible-sounding) version of events that paints them as sensible, rational agents.

2. The process of asking people what they think exerts its own unconscious influences to quite an extraordinary degree. A subject covered at length in my 2010 book *Consumer.ology*.

Of course, typically organisations resort to asking consumers questions when they don't (or can't) know the answer to something from any other source. They may well console themselves with the notion that they can 'triangulate' to a good understanding by combining what they 'learn' from research with other sources of information. Anyone leveraging this argument would do well to reflect that triangulation with an unreliable data point is as likely to send you in the wrong direction as to get you closer to the right one.

How significant can the problem of inadvertent research influence be? When researching *Consumer.ology* I happened across two research studies on the same topic that had been conducted independently by well-known polling organisations (a rare occurrence). Despite high profile polling failures in recent elections, there continues to be a faith in survey results. The research was exploring people's opinions on what should be done with money that was left over in the UK Television Licence fee after the transition to digital television. The money had been taken to ensure that vulnerable customers weren't left without TV access, but with the process successfully completed, the money was surplus to requirements. A political debate arose between the government and the BBC, which led the Department for Culture, Media and Sport and the BBC Trust to commission research to 'find out what people wanted'. Both chose to interview 2,000 people, thereby ensuring that, in statistical terms, they could be confident that their answer represented the nation's view.

The two surveys produced an answer 60 percentage points apart! One found that 66% of respondents supported the idea of using the money to help fund regional news on commercial channels. The other reported that just 6% of people thought that the money should be used in this way. When I analysed the trail of unconscious influence in the two, I reached two conclusions: first, that neither answer was reliable, and secondly, that there was no reliable answer to the question because people didn't have any firm belief on which they were basing their replies. It was this lack of conviction that made people's responses as malleable as they were.

From my work researching how consumers make decisions, and how the market research process influences them, it appears to me that much of what passes for customer insight is an unhelpful distraction to the organisations who commission it.

Without question, the best way to predict consumer behaviour is to conduct live trials and see what people do. Ultimately, you may not know exactly why people acted as they did, but you will know that they did it. In other words, the best option is to observe people's behavioural response to the stimuli provided and deduce what they were thinking. The more you understand *how* people think, the easier this becomes. Why does this help? First, you are starting with a fact (ie people's behavioural response), and secondly, you acknowledge that you are surmising what they're thinking was at the time, which is infinitely better than presuming that you *know* simply because enough people told you when you asked them.

All too often those who commission surveys and focus groups are victims of the psychological need for consistency and confirmation bias: having made a decision to spend tens of thousands of dollars asking consumers questions, there is an inbuilt psychological need to believe the answers that come back. Likewise, they will be quick to forget the times when the research led the organisation astray. When a project is a success, their role and contribution is reinforced. When a project goes awry, they mirror the well-documented response of gamblers, and either forget the resultant losses or dismiss them as minor aberrations in a 'winning' sequence. What's undeniably good for these individuals' psychological health is at odds with what's in the best interests of their commercial organisations (unless their business is selling market research).

While live trials are undoubtedly the gold standard for insight, there are numerous occasions where they simply aren't practical. If an alternative is needed, or being presented as evidence on which to make a decision, how can business managers gauge the value of the consumer insight that they're being encouraged to use when making commercial decisions?

The good news is that they can do considerably better than trotting out the most clichéd question anyone conducting market research will hear: 'How many people did you ask?' While there is a point at which statistical validity matters, it is sufficiently far down the path to be very nearly irrelevant (and I write that as a statistics graduate). There are five questions you should ask about any piece of consumer insight before you place confidence in it: the more times that you can answer 'yes' the more confident you can be that the insights you have are valid.

The 'AFECT' criteria for evaluating the psychological validity of market research

1. Is this an analysis of behaviour?

If you have data that indicates what people currently do, you have something very valuable: a fact. Yes, it's a fact about now and not the future; however, predicting the future is a precarious business, and there's no reason to believe that aggregated consumer opinion is any better a guide into what people will do than reading tea leaves or studying star signs. Understanding what consumers do *now* is crucial if you want to make smart commercial decisions. Sales data and (covert) behavioural observation should always be the start point.

Asking people what they have done can also be useful. If I asked you whether you visited a pharmacy last week, you would probably answer accurately. The data would not be perfect – people forget things; they often remember things as having happened more recently than they did; they may be confused about the definition of a pharmacy etc. However, the use of a question to establish recall of a recent factual event has some merit if it is your only means of identifying what consumers currently do.

2. What frame of mind were respondents in?

Where evidence comes from data that is captured in the real world (without the subject being aware that their actions are being monitored), you have the confidence that the way in which that person's mind was working is realistic.

In contrast, when research data comes from an artificial process (such as asking questions about people's decisions), or from an artificial context (a viewing facility is the worst by some distance), or from an atypical social setting (such as a focus group where a respondent is surrounded by strangers discussing a purchase he makes on his own), there are good reasons to be concerned. In short, the respondent's frame of mind is likely to be very different from the one he'll have in the real world.

3. Were environmental cues present?

The amazing, amusing and intriguing clues to the way in which people make decisions that have emerged from behavioural psychology usually have one thing in common: they are the result of experiments where a contextual variable is changed and a difference in behaviour observed. It is almost always the case that the participants fail to attribute their behaviour to the altered variable; instead they tell themselves and the researchers a version of events that reflects how they perceive themselves. The priming, framing or social proof that have influenced them to act differently are routinely not given credit. So, when it comes to considering the value of any insight, it is vital to consider to what extent the environmental cues were present at the time. If they weren't present, the likelihood is that a very different response will occur when they are.

4. Is the focus of the research covert?

When people are mindful that they are being observed or measured, their behaviour changes. This can occur for several reasons. The most significant is that simply knowing that someone is watching induces a degree of self-consciousness; this introspection changes how people think, and what they do. You only have to watch someone who is nervous about speaking in front of an audience change from a confident, knowledgeable expert into a mumbling, stuttering mess to see how powerful this effect can be.

Making the focus of the research overt, while it feels like a good, open and honest practice, is intrinsically biasing. It leads to priming, sensitisation, mental rehearsal of responses and idealised claims that, in the moment of real-world behaviour, would very often not be present.

5. Was the response timeframe realistic?

In life, time is precious. In many consumer goods purchase scenarios decisions are made swiftly because there are more important or rewarding things to think about. When your insight into a product is the result of lengthy introspection or discussion, but your product is purchased in a few seconds, you should be concerned about how different the thought processes involved are likely to be.

Buying a product is often impulsive or habitual. This in itself is an indication of *how* the mind of the consumer is working at the time (possibly the most useful insight). Before accepting that what consumers have said is true, it's worth considering how well matched the research response and consumer response are in terms of the time allocated. Where they are different you may well be getting the wrong response from the wrong part of someone's mind.

So what?

It makes sense, when taking significant commercial decisions, to weigh up evidence from a wide range of sources; sometimes people in market research refer to this as 'triangulation'. The analogy with this surveying technique is sensible, but it highlights an important consideration: if you have a rogue data point in your calculation, it will pull you away from the right position, not help you find it. Just because consumers have said something in research doesn't mean it is true (even if lots of them have said it). Instead, ask the five AFECT questions and decide whether you should trust the data that you have.

The AFECT criteria underline the benefit of conducting randomised controlled trials. Real-world trials typically meet all the AFECT criteria. You get to find out what consumers do without influencing how they think, without them realising they are being evaluated, in a realistic timeframe. and with all of the environmental context in place when that (real) decision is made.

Experiments (like Implicit Association Testing) and lab experiments can be optimised by considering the AFECT criteria. They will usually be limited in their ability to represent the environment accurately, but their ability to capture a behavioural response covertly make them a useful tool for understanding how consumers think, enabling primes, frames and social proof to be manipulated with different samples so their role and influence in decision making can be explored.

As I alluded to previously, there is essentially no psychological validity to focus groups. They create a cocktail of influence that is a million miles away from most consumer scenarios. There is no harm in using them to brainstorm ideas with consumers, but it is a huge mistake to attach value to a consensus opinion that emerges from them. What a group of people say, when they've been thrown together, asked to think about something at length in an abstract way, and cope with the uncontrolled priming of the facilitator's questions and respondent's answers, is not a good representation of most consumer purchase scenarios.

There is a sweet spot for insight involving consumers that is rarely referenced: the recent past. Here there is an opportunity to identify what people did, and dig into what has driven this behaviour. Understanding this well, in particular *how* consumers are thinking (rather than *what*), provides the optimum foundation for developing whatever creative intervention is being considered. It doesn't guarantee success, but it makes it more likely.

Evaluation of new initiatives requires considerable care. Without randomised controlled trials (and even, sometimes, with them), any consumer insight technique is an attempt at creating a proxy for what will happen in the real world. As such, it's vital to keep in mind what its limitations are, and to validate the technique over time empirically; ie in light of the behavioural response that's seen when the initiative goes live.

As all marketers know, changing behaviour is a challenge. It follows, therefore, that bad market research habits will take time to break. It's clear why surveys and focus groups appeal – part of the allure is in their comparative ease, and they also have the implicit benefit that they defer decisions to the 'voice of the consumer'; add in the human capacity for confirmation bias and you have the perfect cocktail for an erroneous belief. However, those organisations that consider more carefully the psychological validity of the data they reference have the potential to gain a considerable commercial advantage. Without the corrupting aspect of what people *say* they think being a factor in commercial decisions the scope to be creative is infinitely greater, and the opportunity exists to find better proxies to evaluate initiatives and be more successful more of the time.

References

Graves, P. *Consumer.ology: The truth about consumers and the psychology of shopping.* Nicholas Brealey Publishing, 2010

20

FACTS, FRAMES AND FANTASIES

Written by **Robert van Ossenbruggen**

In the world of marketing, 'fact based' is a popular phrase; it suggests we are objective and don't get distracted by sentiment. Unfortunately, facts are never neutral. Our ideas of how the world works shapes our choices in what data we show, how we show it, and how to interpret it. As a result, as this chapter describes, so-called 'facts' can easily turn into fantasies.

If you think your glass is half full, you have a different view of the world than someone who thinks their glass is half empty. Both proverbial glasses contain the same amount of liquid, but the interpretation is the exact opposite. This is framing: information does not get meaning through *what* is being said, but *how*.

You know someone is not a proponent of abortion if the phrase 'killing babies' is being used. Someone who talks about 'tax relief' is more likely to be on the conservative side of the political spectrum. Meat that is '80% lean' is more attractive than meat that contains '20% fat'.

Frames are everywhere, especially when numbers are used. Infamous for number framing is the conservative Fox News: all 'facts' are presented in such a way that it makes Republican policy look smart. Everything that just smells of Democrats gets burnt to the ground. They fool around with graph axes, and the data points that are selected for their charts or tables must fit the predefined narrative.

You will find this kind of deception also in marketing. For example, recently an Australian survey about brands and social media was published. The agency asked, among other questions, about the number of brands respondents followed on social media. They presented the results as Table 1.

Table 1: Number of brands followed on social media (Australia, 2015, Q4)

# brands	Total (%)
1 to 3	46
4 to 6	37
7 to 10	8
10+	9
	100

Table 2: Like Table 1, including 'none'

# brands	Total (%)
None	66
1 to 3	16
4 to 6	13
7 to 10	3
10+	3
	100

From this table it is tempting to conclude that consumers are quite engaged with brands on social media. However, if you take a closer look, you'll notice an important category is missing: there should at least be some people who do not follow any brands on social media. Indeed, if you comb through the piece, you will find most people don't – two-thirds to be more precise. So, the table should have looked like Table 2. This one paints quite a different picture.

Obviously, in this example some essential data is deliberately omitted to make it fit with the pre-selected frame ('social media are important for brands'). Often, framing is much subtler, and not a deliberate choice, as it is a natural result of our set of beliefs of how the world works.

The following example illustrates this. Suppose you compare two customer segments on several attributes, as depicted in Figure 1. The significant differences between the two customer segments are marked. The frame here is, 'these customer types are different'.

But you can display the same numbers as shown in Figure 2. Here the numbers are sorted from high to low and the correlation between the two rows is added. Now, the frame reads 'these customer segments are very similar'. Same data, opposite story.

Figure 1: Customers are different

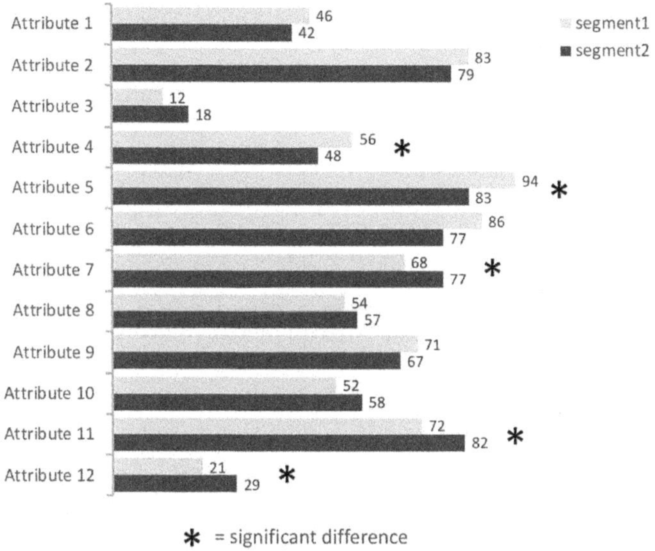

∗ = significant difference

Figure 2: Customers are similar

	Segment1	Segment2
Attribute 5	94	83
Attribute 6	86	77
Attribute 2	83	79
Attribute 11	72	82
Attribute 9	71	67
Attribute 7	68	77
Attribute 4	56	48
Attribute 8	54	57
Attribute 10	52	58
Attribute 1	46	42
Attribute 12	21	29
Attribute 3	12	18

Correlation = 0.96

This is not an arbitrary example. In marketing, we are used to looking at how our brand is *different* from other brands, how certain consumers have *different* perceptions and behaviours than others, and how our product is perceived *differently* from that of the competitor. It's the Kotlerian legacy most marketers have been spoon-fed. As a result, marketers look through differentiation glasses, which makes them blind to similarities. By using the differentiation frame by default, you create a very one-sided view of customers, brands and products.

The above leads to the logical question: which frame is true? The answer is straightforward: the frame that corresponds most with performance should be the dominant one. For the last example, that means that the differentiation frame only works if you can capitalise on the observed differences. Does the extra revenue generated by a differentiated approach exceed the extra cost? In my experience, the answer is 'no' most of the time. The problem is that often this question is not asked in the first place, let alone that it is measured. As the differentiation frame is so self-evident, the similarity frame is not even considered.

Framing is a tricky business, but you can't escape it either. Language is never neutral, nor is data. You can communicate proper facts, but by employing a misleading or one-sided frame you can still communicate a fantasy. Which makes you wonder about the usefulness of the term 'fact-based marketing'…

21

BIG DATA, BIG NOISE

Written by **Robert van Ossenbruggen**

We tend to believe that more data means more value. In some situations this might be true, but in others it is exactly the other way around. The problem is that we don't take the latter situation into account. As a result, we identify things that aren't real, which as this chapter explores, is dangerous.

I think nowadays most marketers would consider themselves 'fact-based' marketers: facts instead of intuition will guide their decision making. But all too often, even though they might be measuring all sorts of stuff, their assumptions of how things work hampers smart decision making. One of those errors that I think is particularly fascinating is the so-called 'randomness fallacy'. Although a very well-documented error, even trained intelligence professionals tend to confuse *noise* (chance, randomness) for *signal* (logic, explanation).

Take for example A/B testing. Two alternative ways of presenting something to a consumer are tested in a real (usually online) environment. The alternative that generates the most clicks, or has the highest conversion rate, wins. Most tools that facilitate A/B testing will flag a winner as soon as the test yields a 'statistically significant' result.

Many winners flagged with his approach, however, will not give you any uplift in clicks or conversion. Simply because most tools have simplified the criteria for a proper test. A proper test would be: 1) setting a minimal effect size in advance; 2) determining a sample size that has the power to 'prove' the minimal effect with a certain probability; and then 3) letting the experiment run until it is finished. For many, this is too much trouble, or worse, they are not aware these are minimum requirements to run a test.

The A/B test example is an illustration of a serious problem in marketing intelligence: often the criteria we use are simplified or flawed. The solution in this case is straightforward: you should set up the experiment as prescribed in any solid textbook about testing and experimenting. Just as importantly, don't let an automated tool make decisions for you, without having a firm understanding of its underlying assumptions and criteria.

Even if you are aware of all the assumptions and criteria, your mind can still play tricks on you. The other day I had a conversation with a skilled and experienced analyst who was comparing the conversion rates of two groups. One group got a specific treatment that should raise conversion, the other one was a control group. The analysis showed no difference between the two.

The analyst's first reaction was a natural one: 'This can't be right… It surely must work… I must have overlooked something…' So, he turned the data upside down and tried to tweak the data, in an attempt to get the expected result. In this case, the data didn't confess, and the analyst felt like he lost the battle.

I have seen many versions of this example. It illustrates another persistent issue: our expectations affect what we see, and how we see it. If the data doesn't live up to our expectations, we usually don't give in very easily, and start tweaking until it restores our view of how we think the world works. It's called 'motivated reasoning'; again, a very thoroughly documented phenomenon that tricks our minds. As a CMO of a Dutch corporate recently acknowledged to me, 'We are a data-driven company, as long as the data confirms what we believe'.

Finally, our assumptions about how the world works can lead us astray. For example, as marketers and analysts are often focused on finding variation in their numbers, they use various tools that do exactly that. Indexing, significance testing, brand mapping and segmentation algorithms (just to name a few) tend to exaggerate the variation that's hidden in the numbers. Hence, it doesn't take much effort to see a bit of signal in a sea of noise.

Take the brand map for example. If a company measures how various brands in the category are perceived, it often looks like a lot is going on. Some numbers are low, others are high (an example is given in Table 1). What is often ignored is that the variation in these numbers is almost always in line with a very predictable pattern. First, bigger brands get higher scores on all attributes, simply because they are used more often, and they are more visible.

Table 1: Raw brand scores (% agree)

Attribute	Brand					
	A	**B**	**C**	**D**	**E**	**F**
Personal	10	13	11	6	17	6
Reliable	12	36	28	8	41	9
Well organised	9	34	26	6	39	8
Specialist	10	16	11	5	17	7
Cheap	3	20	19	3	33	3
Seductive	2	14	10	2	14	2
Easy going	9	18	17	7	23	6
Distinctive	5	12	9	2	13	4
Craftsmanship	12	21	17	7	26	7
Helpful	12	29	23	9	34	8
Clear	8	36	28	7	41	8
Grand	2	32	18	2	35	4
Special	6	13	9	3	12	3
Good quality	13	39	29	8	40	10
Up to date	8	38	27	7	39	8
Fresh	5	25	19	4	25	5
Expert	12	24	19	6	28	8

Secondly, some attributes are more associated with the category than others, and therefore get higher scores. Consumers will probably associate their favourite brand of yoghurt with 'good quality' or 'value for money', but they will be unlikely to think of this product as 'innovative' or 'unique'. When you take these patterns into account (see Table 2), the variation that is left is often not much more than sheer sample noise (Table 3, overleaf).

Table 2: Same as Table 1, now sorted horizontally and vertically from high to low

Brand

Attribute	E	B	C	A	D	F	Average
Good quality	40	39	29	13	10	8	23
Reliable	41	36	28	12	9	8	22
Clear	41	36	28	8	8	7	21
Up to date	39	38	27	8	8	7	21
Well organised	39	34	26	9	8	6	20
Helpful	34	29	23	12	8	9	19
Expert	28	24	19	12	8	6	16
Grand	35	32	18	2	4	2	16
Craftsmanship	26	21	17	12	7	7	15
Fresh	25	25	19	5	5	4	14
Cheap	33	20	19	3	3	3	14
Easy going	23	18	17	9	6	7	13
Specialist	17	16	11	10	7	5	11
Personal	17	13	11	10	6	6	11
Special	12	13	9	6	3	3	8
Distinctive	13	12	9	5	4	2	8
Seductive	14	14	10	2	2	2	7
Average	28	25	19	8	6	5	15

Table 3: Relative brand scores – % deviation given the average brand and attribute scores

Attribute	Brand					
	E	B	C	A	D	F
Good quality	−3	1	0	1	1	0
Reliable	0	0	0	0	0	0
Clear	2	1	2	−3	−1	−1
Up to date	0	4	1	−3	−1	−1
Well organised	2	1	1	−2	0	−1
Helpful	−1	−2	−1	2	0	2
Expert	−2	−2	−1	3	1	0
Grand	6	7	−1	−6	−2	−4
Craftsmanship	−2	−3	−2	4	1	2
Fresh	0	3	2	−2	−1	−1
Cheap	8	−2	2	−4	−3	−2
Easy going	−2	−4	1	2	1	2
Specialist	−3	−2	−3	4	2	1
Personal	−2	−4	−2	4	2	2
Special	−2	1	0	2	0	0
Distinctive	−1	0	0	1	1	−1
Seductive	0	2	1	−2	−1	−1

Brand maps (Figure 1), however, suggest that brands are perceived very differently, simply because the brands are spread throughout the map. Most of us are not aware what's going on under the car bonnet, and thus have no idea that the variation shown in the brand map is totally blown out of proportion. Often, you are trying to make sense of sheer noise.

I have been in several situations in which I addressed the uncomfortable situation of working with (near) random data. Once, someone questioned my analytical skills. Fortunately, a case of random data is always easy to demonstrate. You just generate random data just like the format of the actual

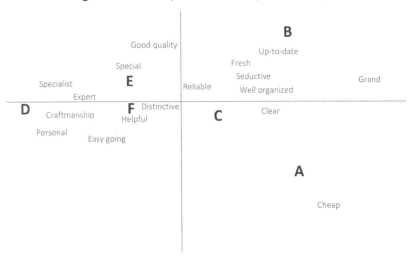

Figure 1: Brand map based on correspondence analysis

data you have. If the results coming from your fake data looks suspiciously like that of your real data, you know for sure you are looking at merely noise. Noise doesn't translate to value, ever.

In the 'Big Data' era, it is tempting to believe that the impact of data-driven decisions will only increase. But as the availability of data grows, so does the level of noise. If we don't get better at separating the wheat from the chaff, the value of the 'new oil' will prove quite disappointing.

22

CAN NEUROMARKETING REALLY HELP BRANDS?

Written by **Brandon Towl**

Part of managing a brand is managing people's perceptions and experiences of that brand. As brain science has grown in leaps and bounds, it was only natural that marketing professionals would try to incorporate its insights into how those brand perceptions and experiences are formed. All too often, bad logic and poor experimental design lead to unsupported conclusions and bad strategies. As this chapter asserts, knowing a little neuroscience can help find the more promising studies, and avoid the misleading claims.

Part of managing a brand is managing people's perceptions and experiences of that brand. The last several decades have brought huge strides in our understanding of how perceptions and emotions come about in our brains. So naturally, marketing professionals have begun trying to incorporate insights from neuroscience to learn how those perceptions and emotions are formed, predict them, and find novel ways to provoke them.

Unfortunately, this new 'neuromarketing' is often done quite poorly. As a case study example of this, we can take a look at one of the flagship books in this area, Martin Lindstrom's *Buy.ology*. My goal is not to discourage people from reading the book, but rather to hold up parts of it as an example of our flawed ways of thinking about the brain, especially when that thinking is done by business people concerned with building a brand.

Once we understand some of these flaws, it will be easier to spot the neuroscience that is done well, and that might have some bearing on marketing. Though such science is much harder to find, it may well inspire new ideas for marketers and brand managers.

Neuromarketing and 'buyology'

One mistaken way in which we think about the brain is that it is divided into parts that are 'for' certain behaviours. Part of the job of neuroscience, so the thinking goes, is to uncover what these various parts are for. If and when it succeeds, it then provides justification for seeing some behaviours as part of our 'human nature' or 'natural endowment'.

It is true that much of neuroscience is concerned with finding which areas of the brain become active during certain tasks. But just because we find our brains are active during certain tasks does not mean that those areas are 'for' that task, or for any other task we have measured before. This is one of the big fallacies behind neuromarketing.

As mentioned above, the flagship book for neuromarketing is *Buy.ology* by Martin Lindstrom. Lindstrom's book garnered a lot of attention, and Lindstrom has gone on to share many of the ideas in that book in other venues, including *Fast Company* and *The New York Times*.

Buy.ology tries to pinpoint factors that make us identify with brands, and ultimately buy them. Lindstrom certainly has a flair for storytelling, which comes out in the engaging way he describes the experiments and draws conclusions from them. But those very conclusions are what is suspect. Let's take a look at a single case as an example.

In chapter 6, Lindstrom describes an experiment involving well-known brands such as Apple, Guinness, Ferrari and Harley-Davidson, as well as Microsoft, BP and others (the former have intense consumer loyalty, the latter do not). Subjects then sat in an fMRI scanner while objects with these various brands were flashed before their eyes, along with various religious images (and, for another experiment, images of famous sports figures).

The results? As reported by Lindstrom:

> *Strong brands brought about greater activity in many areas of the brain involved in memory, emotion, decision-making, and meaning than weaker brands did... [and] that when people viewed images associated with strong brands... their brains registered the exact same patterns of activity as they did when they viewed the religious images.*

So far so good – nothing to argue with, yet. But then Lindstrom goes on to say:

> *Our research showed that the emotions we... experience when we are exposed to iPods, Guinness, and Ferrari sports cars are similar to the emotions generated by religious symbols... Clearly, our emotional engagement with powerful brands (and to a lesser extent sports) shares strong parallels with our feelings about religion.*

Is this conclusion warranted? Do we know that the same emotions are in play? And what exactly are these 'parallels' Lindstrom alludes to?

The logic of this chapter (and indeed a logic that runs through most of the book) goes something like this:

1. Subjects in the current study showed activity (or an increase in activity) in brain area(s) X when the subjects were doing/looking at Y.
2. Subjects in the current study also showed activity in X when they were doing/looking at Z (where Z is some brand or buying impulse).
3. And so, X is doing the exact same thing in Y and in Z.
4. Further, we can infer: doing or seeing Z is a kind of doing or seeing Y.

This is the kind of logic that leads Lindstrom to claim that seeing a strong brand, and feeling brand loyalty, is a kind of religious experience. But that logic is bad, in several ways...

1. You cannot infer that, because **X** showed activity, it is 'for' doing **Y** (or **Z**, for that matter)

This is because brains are just not divided up that way. If they were, there would be way, way too many behaviours to be represented in the brain! Here's an example... Humans can play a number of different sports that require hitting or kicking a ball and timing that activity just right. Imagine how many brain areas there would be if we thought of those activities like this:

▨ Hitting a forehand in racquetball.
▨ Hitting a backhand in racquetball.
▨ Hitting a serve in racquetball.
▨ Hitting a forehand in tennis.
▨ Hitting a backhand in tennis.

...and so on. Repeat for any possible sport you might play, and you'll have a nearly infinite list of activities human beings can engage in. It would be silly to think that there would be some one brain area involved with each.

Instead, the brain has a general motor system attached to a general visual system and bodily kinaesthetic system. Those systems work in tandem, drawing on past experience to fine-tune a whole range of movements. Insofar as there are regions of the brain that 'do' specific tasks, they carry out specific steps in information processing for a wide range of behaviours (Steve Petersen and Julie Fiez, two of the original pioneers of using PET brain imaging to study cognition, write about this well).

Likewise, there are no 'religious feelings' areas of the brain, nor are there 'prayer' areas of the brain, nor indeed any 'recognising religious icons' areas. What we would expect (and indeed what we find) is that any activity increases the use of a wide network of brain areas, and these networks tend to have parts in common. But that tells us precious little.

2. Brain area **X** might not be doing the same things during **Y** and **Z**

People assume that if a brain area is active during two tasks, it must be doing some one thing during those tasks. This isn't always the case. It is quite possible that some brain areas do multiple things, just as some organs, such as the liver, do multiple things.

3. Even if brain area **X** is doing the same thing, that 'thing' might not be obvious from the nature of **Y** and **Z**

For example, it could be the case that the brain areas identified in the studies Lindstrom discusses were actually involved in visualisation generally, or recognition, or even recall of religiously valued objects. It doesn't take a great leap to see why these general areas would be active during a task like prayer. But we need to keep in mind that praying, or having a religious experience, is not the exact same thing as looking at a picture of a cross to begin with.

4. Finding that brain area **X** is active during different tasks does not make **Y** a type of **Z**

Is viewing a strong brand a kind of religious experience? Maybe. But there's an equal amount of evidence that religious experience is an association with a strong brand (just not a *corporate-backed* brand). Or that both religious experience and brand experience are subtypes of a more general kind of activity. Or that both tasks overlap in the neural resources subjects need to complete the tasks, but are themselves quite distinct.

Playing fast and loose with these kinds of correlations happens all the time, unfortunately. (It seems that every election cycle someone trots out some poorly done studies to try to figure out how the other side could *possibly* find their candidate at all appealing. Just watch.) But we can clearly demonstrate the faulty logic used with an example constructed to show just how silly the conclusion really is:

1. Studies show that the brain's amygdala becomes more active when subjects are exposed to fear-inducing stimuli.
2. Male subjects in one study also showed amygdala activity when they looked at pictures of Ferraris (see Sally Satel and Scott Lilienfeld's book *Brainwashed*).
3. And so, for men, looking at pictures of Ferraris is fear inducing.
4. And the hidden implication: Ferraris are threatening.

Hopefully, this example helps expose the failures in the logic. The logic must be faulty, because the results are so ridiculous. *Now imagine if you were in the auto industry and basing your sales strategies and marketing campaigns partly on 3) and 4) above.*

Turns out we are suckers for a good brain story

Why does bad neuroscience – or rather, bad reporting on neuroscience – get around so much? Part of it is confirmation bias: we are more likely to believe evidence that supports previously held positions. And so much reporting on neuroscience merely shoe-horns actual neuroscience into our preconceived ideas and biases.

Another part of it is *authority*. Neuroscience is hard, and the studies are very complex. But these very facts make us lend extra credence to neuroscience studies… even when it is unearned.

For example, in a 2008 study done by Deena Weisberg and colleagues at Yale University, subjects were given explanations of psychological phenomena that were either 'good' or 'bad' as rated by respected experts in the field. Additionally, some of the explanations were accompanied by neuroscientific information *that the experts agreed was irrelevant to the explanations provided*. Subjects were then asked how satisfying those explanations were, among other things.

For the most part, even people without extensive training in psychology and neuroscience could tell a good psychological explanation from a bad one when the explanations were couched completely in psychological terms. The interesting finding was that subjects judged that explanations with logically irrelevant neuroscience information were more satisfying than explanations without. Indeed, simply introducing some neuroscience information, *even though the information was irrelevant*, could make an otherwise bad explanation for a psychological phenomenon seem plausible. The information somehow 'masked' the glaring problems with those explanations.

Other studies are beginning to bear out this phenomenon as well. The moral is clear: *we should be wary of messages that use neuroscience as 'evidence', especially if there is not a good business case or behavioural study given as well.*

Should we roundly reject all neuroscience?

No, of course not. We just have to be careful. Well done neuroscience builds on (and extends) the existing corpus of neuroscientific and psychological knowledge. It also goes well beyond trying to identify areas 'for' certain tasks, and instead tries to find evidence for one hypothesis over another.

Here, then, are a few examples of interesting neuroscience that may well have some bearing on the ways in which companies grow their brands.

1. Music preferences in teens are based more on social pressure

It is clear that people's behaviour might reflect multiple competing preferences. But how does a piece of information affect those preferences? One set of studies found that teenagers' preferences for music follow what they think is popular. No surprise there. But do teenagers' tastes change as they interact and discuss music with friends? Or do they just learn to suppress their own preferences when interacting with others? One series of studies set out to answer these questions. It turns out that teens' tastes in music converge not because the music is 'felt' as more enjoyable, but rather because teens mask their true preferences when presented with social information. This is the kind of thing neuroscience can get traction on, and it's likely to be of real concern to marketers in the music industry.

2. But for luxury brands, perception really does change the experience

On the other hand, some external forces may well change our preferences by changing our experiences. One famous experiment looked at wine consumption and asked why people tended to prefer more expensive brands, all other things being equal. Is this because they are rationalising the high price tag, or do they actual have a better wine experience? Brain-scanning results indicate that the actual taste experience is different with the higher priced wines, even if the wine is physically the same as a cheaper brand.

3. Technology affects interaction

The 'ultimatum' game has been studied extensively. In this 'game', subjects will reject a deal they deem 'unfair' in order to punish another player, even though it would be irrational to do so (because both are then worse off). This effect goes away, however, when the deal is generated by a computer at random. If, however, people are told that the computer is an artificial intelligence, the effect re-emerges. This has all sorts of things to tell us about human–computer interaction and the emotions involved, especially when it comes to digital customer journeys.

Final thoughts

Neuroscience is hard. So is marketing. No doubt finding the intersection, so far as it exists, is extremely difficult as well.

But you can inoculate yourself against misleading claims about how our brain works. A few things to read:

- *Discover* magazine online has a 'Neuroskeptic' column worth checking out. Look for articles with the tag 'bad neuroscience': http://discovermagazine. com/tags?tag=bad+neuroscience.

- Read Joseph Devlin's blog post, 'Five warning signs of neuromarketing snake oil' (Devlin is a neuroscientist at University College London). https://www.ucl.ac.uk/pals/research/experimental-psychology/blog/five-warning-signs-of-neuromarketing-snake-oil/.

- Check out this cool study demonstrating 'neuroenchantment' and our penchant for believing that technology can, somehow, read our minds: https://www.ncbi.nlm.nih.gov/pmc/articles/PMC4034606/.

- Finally, read up on some of Dorothy Bishop's work on 'bad neuroscience', starting with the summary of her work at the blog *Neurobonkers*: http:// neurobonkers.com/2012/08/21/the-science-of-bad-neuroscience/.

As for brands, you don't need validation from neuroscience to understand their emotional appeal. Sometimes the best tool for good brand management is just good brand management.

References

https://fastcompany.com/1814327/we-know-what-you-want-and-when-you-will-buy-it

http://scienceblogs.com/mixingmemory/2006/11/14/computers-are-people-too-and-d/

https://scientificamerican.com/article/in-teen-music-choices-fear-rules/

Petersen, SE, and Fiez, JA. 'The processing of single words studied with positron emission tomography'. *Annual Review of Neuroscience*, 16(1), 1993

Plassmann, H, et al. 'Marketing actions can modulate neural representations of experienced pleasantness'. Proceedings of the National Academy of Sciences of the United States of America, 105(3), 2008

Satel, S, and Lilienfeld, S. *Brainwashed: The seductive appeal of mindless neuroscience*. Basic Books, 2015

Weisberg, DS, et al. 'The seductive allure of neuroscience explanations'. *Journal of Cognitive Neuroscience*, 20(3), 2008

23

THE SCIENCE OF EFFECTIVENESS

Written by **Phil Barden**

Marketing's purpose is behaviour change. We've been pursuing this for decades, yet with, for example, 80 to 90% of new products failing, there is significant room for improvement. How can we make our activities more effective and our budgets work harder? By leveraging what science knows about human behaviour. The vast majority of us didn't get into marketing or advertising for the love of science, but there's more science to what we do than we probably realise. This can give us greater explanatory, and predictive, power than we've ever had, and can be harnessed to greater effect. This chapter explores how science can help.

How many times do we hear the word 'effectiveness' in our everyday work lives? Perhaps an easier question is when *don't* we hear it?! Effectiveness is crucial for marketing, and rightly so, because brands provide the revenue which is the lifeblood of any business. How might we leverage learnings from science to help us be more effective? Science? What's that got to do with marketing I hear you cry. Up until 2008 I'd have agreed with you. Then, as brand VP for T-Mobile in Europe, I experienced what science can bring to the party: a step-change in effectiveness so powerful that it made me change careers. Science was behind T-Mobile's relaunch, which first manifested itself in the UK with the flashmob 'Dance' ad at London's Liverpool Street station. That increased sales by 49%, share by 6%, tripled brand consideration, and to date, has had more than 41 million YouTube views. Science was subsequently applied to other touchpoints, and the UK brand VP was happy to attest to this approach being effective in halving customer churn.

If we use the *Oxford English Dictionary* definition of effectiveness being 'the degree to which something is successful in producing a desired result', then my T-Mobile experience of what science can bring to the party might now sound more interesting. So how should we think of effectiveness? There are two aspects. First, marketplace effectiveness, which means creating some sort of 'value' so that customers are willing to choose your brand rather than another at the same price – it's not simply about selling more, because that could be achieved by cutting price. The second aspect is internal (within the organisation) effectiveness – if you're using the wrong model of how brands work, then you won't be as effective as you could be. Let's look at how science can help with both of these aspects.

Customers don't read our strategy papers, so we have only our marketing activities to trigger the desired impact. It might sound obvious, but if something isn't perceived by our senses, it doesn't enter the brain, and hence has zero chance of being effective. Perception is a key point here; Nobel laureate Professor Daniel Kahneman's real insight wasn't the dual System 1 and System 2 theory (System 1 being fast, automatic and reflexive mental processes and System 2 referring to slow, controlled and reflective processes), but that our perception is bounded by stimuli. This is what is meant when he talks about WYSIATI (What You See Is All There Is), so the first step in mobilising System 1 is that our marketing activities/touchpoints have to be perceived. Taking this in the visual sense, the saying 'out of sight is out of mind' is literally true for the brain. This is acknowledged by our marketing objective to 'cut through' the clutter; we want attention to be paid to our ad among thousands of other messages, or we want our pack to stand out on the shelf. So, if gaining attention and being correctly perceived are key to cutting through, what does science contribute to how this works, and how we can harness the learnings from science to increase our effectiveness?

Science tells us that the vast majority of our 120 degrees of vision is peripheral, and that this is blurred and loses colour saturation; only a tiny fraction of our vision is in focus and in full colour. So, there is a huge difference between a customer walking around a store, surfing online, reading printed matter or passing outdoor advertising, and a marketer or agency executive spending hours focused on a piece of creative. Our System 1 is constantly scanning our environment for threats and rewards, and this will then direct our focused attention, but the majority of perception happens under blurred conditions of vision. So, what are the implications for marketing? How can we increase branded cut-through under less than ideal conditions? A simple (yet powerful) way to check what's perceptible in peripheral vision is to blur images (you can do this in PowerPoint), show them quickly to someone who is not familiar with the image, and ask them what it is. Figure 1 shows an example

Figure 1: The new design is not effectively perceived in peripheral vision

from a Tropicana relaunch where the new design, shown on the right, fails this simple test as it's no longer perceptible as Tropicana.

Another insight from science is that faces are powerful magnets of attention, and people will attend to faces in preference to objects and text. We used this to help British Telecom understand why a direct mailing was not achieving its desired response rate, and how a simple change could significantly increase results.

Figure 2 (below) shows the original (left) and revised (right) versions, together with a visual impact prediction. The attentional 'hot spot' in the original is the face at the bottom of the page. While faces can be used to direct attention, in this case it was a problem as the face was drawing attention away from the call-to-action roundels above it. This created dis-fluency (difficulty to process), because reading from the bottom upwards goes against our natural reading pattern. So, our recommendation for a short-term solution was simply to remove the face. The call-to-action roundels then became the hot spots (because science tells us that contrast is a way to grab attention, and the roundels stand out due to colour and shape). As a result, response rates went up by 31.8%.

Figure 2: The face drew attention away from the call to action. Removing it increased response by 31.8%

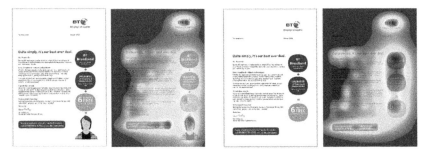

Science knows much more about the principles of attention and perception, and this can really help us not only to achieve cut-through, but also to ensure that attention is paid to key elements of communication. This helps us in the critical first step towards effectiveness — but it doesn't mean that customers will choose our brand. What's perceived now needs to be understood and assigned to the correct brand.

When decoding incoming data, the brain metaphorically asks two questions: what is it, and what does it represent? It answers these questions via System 1, accessing our vast associative network of memory structures, which has formed over many years. Figure 1 is again useful here to show how the new design was ineffective: those packaging 'codes' (the orange and the logo) that had been learned, and which activated the brand, were absent from the new design and, with that, branding disappeared. The new design looked like any other orange juice, and was not decoded as Tropicana.

I was frequently faced with writing a design or communications brief and wondering which codes or assets I should keep and which could be changed or removed. Something we hear often from our clients is 'I don't want to throw the baby out with the bath water, but I don't know which is which!' Fortunately, science can help us to bring more precision to our design and comms briefs by identifying those codes which automatically activate our brand, as well as their implicit meaning. An example can be seen in Figure 3. This shows a result from our 'Iconic Asset Tracker' study in the ice cream category. The brain uses shape, among other things, to decode data. This shape has high branding power for Magnum: it activates the brand automatically, with high uniqueness and certainty. The print ad on the right in Figure 3 is for a Häagen-Dazs product. With an average dwell time of 2.1 seconds on print ads, and with the shape attracting attention due to contrast, this ad has a

Figure 3: The bar shape is an iconic asset for Magnum, not for Häagen-Dazs

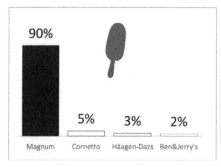

high likelihood of being ineffective for Häagen-Dazs as the product shape will activate Magnum.

Assuming that our activity has been perceived and decoded correctly, that still doesn't mean that people will choose our brand. How can science help us in understanding how the brain makes a purchase decision, and what we can do to ensure that ours is the brand chosen?

A seminal 2007 study by Brian Knutson et al, using brain imaging, showed that pictures of a product or brand increase the activation of the so-called 'reward system', which is known to be triggered when we value something. It's as if the brain says, 'I want this'. This wanting is based upon the value that we expect the product to deliver. In our associative memory, we have experiences with the brand – from using it, processing its advertising or seeing other people using it. Based on this associative learning, we have an expected value delivered by the brand. If this expected value is high, then the reward system shows a high level of activation. If it is low, then the level of activation will also be low. When price was exposed to the respondents in the study, an entirely different area of the brain was activated: the insula. This area is normally activated when we experience pain. Prices imply giving away something we already own and which is of significant value to us: money. This is coded as a painful experience in the brain. The scientists uncovered the underlying (and simple) principle that determines whether a brand or product will be bought or not: if the relation between reward and pain exceeds a certain value, people are willing to purchase this item for this price.

Further studies support this key finding. For example, a 2016 study (Figure 4) showed a high correlation between activity in the reward system and sales: the higher the reward activation, the higher the sales.

A major learning from this study (as well as others) is that reward activation, or 'wanting', significantly outperforms explicit, subjective judgements of 'liking' in terms of predicting sales. The reason for this is that the two are not causally connected in the brain, so it's possible to like something, but not buy it. The implication for marketing is that we can increase effectiveness by focusing on, and measuring, wanting – but how? How can science help us to understand 'wanting' in a way that we can start to apply it to brand building? Wanting is based on the value that we expect the product/brand

Figure 4: Higher reward activation = higher sales
(illustration from Kühn et al, 2016)

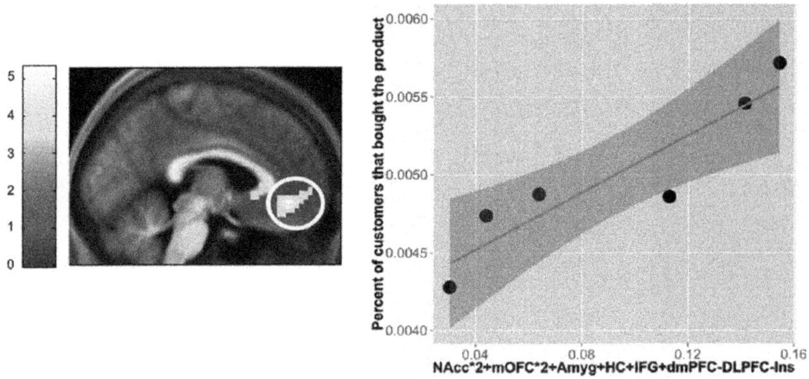

[figure: brain scan image and scatter plot with regression line. Y-axis labeled "Percent of customers that bought the product" ranging from 0.0040 to 0.0060. X-axis labeled "NAcc*2+mOFC*2+Amyg+HC+IFG+dmPFC-DLPFC-Ins" ranging from 0.04 to 0.16]

to deliver. Put differently, this 'value' is the outcome that we desire in a given context. The brain ascribes high value to a brand/product if it's perceived to be an effective means of accomplishing the desired outcome. It's useful to think of outcomes as Job/s To Be Done (JTBD). These jobs can be functional and neuropsychological, and we can describe them in terms of what a customer wants to have, do, be or become.

Let's look at an example in order to bring this to life. Figure 5 shows some product choices.

If we wanted to predict sales of these products, typical research questions such as 'Which do you like best?' or 'How likely is it that you will purchase X, Y or Z next week?' are unhelpful because the answer depends on (and will change with) the context for the decision. Imagine that you are on a diet, for example. Which products would you choose? Or you want to satisfy

Figure 5: Choice is context dependent

your child's hunger while at the same time getting a hug from your kid? But what if you want to satisfy your kid's hunger while at the same time being recognised as a good parent by others? And what about the pain side of the equation? Which would you choose to eat if you were driving? The orange is too effortful, and this equates to pain; therefore, the value of the orange is low.

So, context and the desired outcome change the value of exactly the same product. Putting context and the outcome we desire into the equation is therefore critical, and when we do this, 'wanting', and hence purchase decisions, become very clear.

To recap briefly, value (reward activation) is high if our choice (product/brand) is perceived as an effective means to accomplish the desired outcome (in a given context). Perceived value is high if our products/brands 'fit' to what customers want to do, have, be or become. The fit to a JTBD determines the value and relevance of brands.

We're all familiar with functional JTBD; these are category-specific benefits or goals that people want to achieve. We want to have clean clothes, satisfy our hunger and rely on our broadband, and while delivering against these is fundamental because brands need to be relevant within a category, we often find that brands perform similarly to each other at this level, particularly in mature categories. So, if we want to be truly effective, we need to find other ways to be distinctive. What about the neuropsychological level? Science can help us here too. At this level, goals/JTBD are those representing higher level purpose, universal human needs, personal values, self-identity, emotional and social outcomes that are linked with using the category. To find out which goals drive purchase in a category, how brands match with these to create relevance and distinctiveness, as well as how touchpoints trigger goal associations, we use a model derived from neuropsychology, and test using implicit methods. Figure 6 shows how this deepens our understanding of why the Tropicana redesign failed.

All customers have to work with are the codes we send, and a core benefit of the JTBD approach is that it links directly to codes. Codes are how we signal the match between our product/brand and the JTBD. The design codes trigger very different goals, hence the new design has a poor match with the JTBD of the original. The orange and straw automatically trigger the concepts

Figure 6: Decode's Goal Model shows why the new design was ineffective

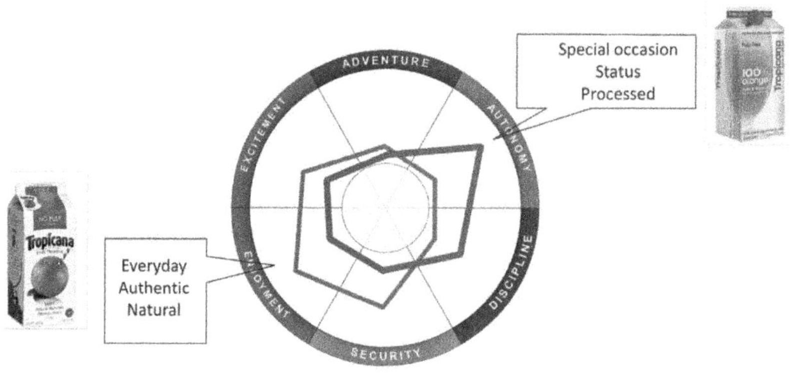

of 'everyday' and 'natural', whereas the fluted wine glass conveys 'special occasion' and 'processed'.

The brief for Tropicana's redesign called for the new pack to be 'more modern', 'fresher' and 'cleaner' than the original. There is no doubt that the new design met these objectives when viewed on a designer's Mac, the brand manager's desk or in a focus group. The point is that those are irrelevant objectives when it comes to what drives purchase. Aside from the perceptual and brand assignment issues cited earlier, the new design simply didn't signal a match to the JTBD. Therefore, its perceived value was low, and the brand lost $27m in sales in six weeks.

The JTBD approach is validated not only in science, but also in market. The successful T-Mobile relaunch cited at the start of this chapter was based on JTBD. More recently, for a global FMCG client, we studied over 60 brands in 20 categories amongst 100,000 customers, and found a correlation of .86 between brand equity (defined as relevance and distinctiveness versus JTBD in a category) and 'willingness to pay' (based on actual market shares). So how should we think differently if we want to use this approach to increase our effectiveness?

First, stable segmentations, for example socio-demographics, are not particularly useful, because humans are very flexible in determining value based on context and the outcome we desire. When these change, so do our behaviours and our decisions (remember the apple, orange and doughnut example), so the same person can inhabit multiple segments.

Secondly, we need to know how to communicate 'value' so that customers can decode the fit with their JTBD (think Tropicana, and see further commentary below).

Thirdly, we need to recognise that many metrics we use, rather than being drivers of purchase, are actually outcomes of goal/JTBD achievement. We may ask about 'brand love', but the causes of this can be very different. We tested four different skincare brands, all of which had similar brand love scores among their users, and found significantly different matches with JTBD. All the users loved their respective brands, but for different reasons. The same holds true for attitudes, trust and satisfaction. As marketers, we need to work with the causes, not the outcomes. Not only is this crucial for effectiveness, but science tells us that JTBD also drives other mental processes such as attention, mental availability and brand recognition.

Science can certainly help us to increase in-market effectiveness. In the short term, we can adopt the principles by which the brain processes information (perception, attention, cognition) to make our activities more effective. Try blurring images of any visual touchpoint – POS, displays or web pages – to check for perception, for example. In the longer term, we can increase our effectiveness by using the same model for how the brain deals with brands (goal/JTBD). Indeed, using the wrong model for how brands 'work' mitigates against effectiveness.

The clear insights from science are that when people buy brands:

- Context matters.
- The JTBD in the (sub-) categories is the consumer reference point.
- A brand intuitively signals high fit to consumers' current JTBD.
- A brand offers superior value when it is the superior means to accomplish the current JTBD.

Marketers, therefore, need to know the JTBD at the category and brand level, as well as the brand codes with the best fit to JTBD at the functional and neuropsychological goal levels.

References

Barden, P. *Decoded: The science behind why we buy.* Wiley, 2013

Kahneman, D. 'Maps of bounded rationality: a perspective on intuitive judgment and choice'. Nobel Prize lecture, 2002

Knutson, B, et al. 'Neural predictors of purchases'. *Neuron*, 53(1), 2007

Kühn, S, Strelow, E, and Gallinat, J. 'Multiple "buy buttons" in the brain: forecasting chocolate sales at point-of-sale based on functional brain activation using fMRI'. *Neuroimage*, 2016

24

PUTTING 'NUDGES' IN PERSPECTIVE

Written by **Byron Sharp** and **Amy Wilson**

This chapter puts behavioural economics and its rise to fame in perspective for marketers. It presents some of the latest evidence, and explains what lessons marketers can learn.

The 'new' guy on the block

Behavioural economics has won the hearts of many professionals, including marketers, environmentalists, doctors and politicians. Behavioural economists claim to have developed groundbreaking consumer insights through the application of psychology to economic decision making.

At its heart, behavioural economics rejects 'homo economicus' (the model of people as rational utility-maximisers with perfect information, zero search costs and unlimited time). This relates to the idea that while we might like to think that we are fully aware and in complete control over our decisions, this is not necessarily true. We are rationally bounded, and factors that influence our decision making (be it consciously or subconsciously) include stress, fatigue, emotions, multi-tasking, time constraints, and more. It is not practical to consciously think about every step and breath that we take, otherwise there would be no time left to do anything else. When we have had a bad day, we reach for a chocolate bar instead of an apple, despite our healthy intentions. We buy products on promotion assuming that they will be good value and because it is easier than comparing all the options. Subconscious (or habitual) behaviours occur without much, if any, conscious awareness. These behaviours tend to satisfy immediate desires (ie save us time/energy, curb our cravings etc), usually regardless of our stated intentions and future goals.

While this all sounds like a step forward, the publicity that behavioural economics has received, along with the Nobel prizes and bestselling books, has been accompanied by a lack of critical examination – at least in the marketing realm. Academics and practitioners have accepted (sometimes outlandish) implications for marketing practice too readily. Some rather bizarre 'supporting evidence' has been waved around. For example, from neuroscience: 'Oh look, this part of the brain lights up when people see a brand they know well and buy – this proves that brand preference is due to brands forging strong subconscious emotional bonds'. This is a gigantic leap of logic! It is worth noting that no serious neuroscientist has made such a claim, nor been willing to support such a claim.

Weird claims are made about brand values being underpinned by manipulated/seduced consumers. Yes, brands are worth a fortune, but that's because they have built a customer base which is likely to buy year after year. Through successful trading and distinctive advertising, brands have built mental and physical availability that is very valuable. This enhances the probability (ie reduces the risk) that many people will buy, and for many years, therefore, profits will continue. Brand value is not acquired because consumers are coerced into irrational loyalty and buying things they do not need. As Philip Kotler pointed out many years ago, consumers are not stupid, nor highly susceptible – their garages are not full of cars they do not drive, pantries are not full of food they do not like, and so on.

We need to be wary of a return of the (discredited) theory of brand image besotted/manipulated consumers. Advertising is a weak force, and equally importantly, most advertising isn't persuasive, nor does it need to be. Advertising can do an amazing job without shifting beliefs and attitudes. For example, the 'mere exposure effect' was first documented in the late

1800s. Studies conducted since the 1960s have documented the power of familiarity. Familiarity is an important and simple notion, and there is little need to complicate it with more theory.

Today there is much interest in subconscious decision making – as there should be, because buying rarely involves a great deal of conscious deliberation. Unfortunately, along with this sensible interest in 'fast buying' and 'low attention', comes a belief in the power of psychological effects. History seems to be repeating itself. Years ago, there was considerable hype around subliminal advertising. Hidden messages in advertising were quickly believed to have a strong influence on buying behaviour. Market researcher James Vicary was infamously most responsible for the rise (and fall) of subliminal advertising: according to his research in 1957, flashing subconscious exposures of 'drink Coca-Cola' and 'eat popcorn' in movies increased their sales by 18% and 58% respectively. However, Vicary's research was a hoax. The joke would (again) be on marketers if we fell for a new version of the subliminal advertising story. Yet the conditions are ripe. Marketers are often frustrated that advertising and media decisions are the only decisions they can control. Therefore, advertising strategies that 'work magic' on consumers are very attractive. Advertisers have shown, many times, a willingness to invest in advertising tactics that lack scientific evidence. Witness the recent rush into 'earned media' and 'viral video'.

The rise of behavioural economics

Behavioural economics stems from years of psychological and economic research, including insights into heuristics and biases, framing, loss aversion and bounded rationality. However, the rapid rise of behavioural economics came in 2008 with Richard Thaler and Cass Sunstein's book *Nudge*. A nudge was defined as 'any aspect of the choice architecture (environment) that can be altered to influence behaviour in a predictable way, without forbidding options or changing economic incentive'. It is important to note (as it is often overlooked) that price changes are not a nudge (ie price promotions, taxes etc).

Nudging became popular, quickly, and 'revolutionised' thinking in many sectors, including financial services, healthcare and policy. Government institutions established teams dedicated to the application of behavioural economics – including the UK's Behavioural Insights Team (aka 'The Nudge Unit'), The Behavioural Economics Team of the Australian Government (BETA) and the White House's Social and Behavioral Sciences Team (SBST).

The evidence

Due to the popularity of nudging and choice architecture interventions, many researchers are actively adding to the evidence base. A series of studies conducted at the Ehrenberg-Bass Institute provide interesting insights into nudging; these studies included a systematic review and two real-world experiments focused on the use of nudges to influence dietary choices, including strategies that relate to marketing activities.

The systematic review revealed that there are many different types of nudges which can be used individually, together, or in combination with other behaviour change approaches. The most common are priming and salience nudges. However, many of the nudges are not particularly novel.

Research on the effectiveness of nudges shows they can work, though overall the evidence for their efficacy is less than compelling. Replication research is the cornerstone of science; it checks on the fragility and generalisability of a finding. Much experimental psychology research produces highly fragile results that often fail to replicate. This doesn't mean the original study was necessarily plagued by error (or fraud), it is impossible to perfectly replicate any experiment (you'll be in a different time and date to start with, different researchers, respondents, and so on), so when an experiment fails to replicate, it suggests the 'finding' is very fragile. Unsurprisingly then, outside the lab, in the real world, these results seldom (if ever) occur, and when they do they are usually far weaker.

In 2012, when interviewed for the world's top-ranked science journal *Nature*, Daniel Kahneman tried to defend the fact that so many psychology results fail to replicate under laboratory conditions: 'The conduct of subtle experiments has much in common with the direction of a theatre performance... trivial details such as the day of the week or the color of a room could affect the results, and these subtleties never make it into methods sections'. But this raises the question of whether there is any difference between a result that is so sensitive and no result at all.

To understand the value of nudging in real-world applications, real-world experiments are crucial. As salience nudges were found to be among the most effective, an experiment was developed to investigate the influence of a salience nudge in the form of a health message (as is often seen on supermarket shelves or product packaging) very close to the point of consumption. A label saying, 'Pick me, I am low calorie' was placed on the skimmed milk in a workplace kitchen for 12 weeks. Initially, consumption increased – but for both skimmed and full-cream milk. This increased consumption faded after two weeks, with a variable influence after that.

Such findings raise questions regarding the consequences of nudging, of which there is little evidence. First is the issue of 'spillover effects', which is when a nudge influences the selection of both the nudged option (ie skimmed milk) and the non-nudged option (ie full-cream milk). Spillover effects have been identified in several nudging interventions. The milk finding is closely related to the potential for compensatory effects, which is when the nudged choice is selected and then offset by a subsequent choice. In health contexts, this is typically a healthier choice being subsequently compensated for with an unhealthy choice, such as 'the salad I had for dinner was healthy, so now I can have the ice cream for dessert!' While compensatory behaviour may be difficult to avoid, interventions should ensure the measurement of more than just the nudged option to determine whether there is any 'backfire'. This could be an easy mistake to make when looking at the sugar-sweetened beverage tax research; for example, are people sacrificing a soft drink for an equally sweet fruit juice? While taxation is not a nudge, the potential spillover effects and backfire of nudges is something for marketers to be wary of.

The second issue relates to the 'life' of a nudge, being the length of time a nudge will influence the targeted behaviour. However, the research in this area is scant. Findings from the milk experiment suggest that the effects of a nudge wear off after a short period of time, especially for behaviours that are frequently made. The life of a nudge is important to know as these insights could determine which decisions and behaviours might benefit most from a nudge, ie frequent versus infrequent behaviours, high versus low involvement decisions, and so on.

There is also an ongoing ethical debate about the transparency of nudging. Some argue that changing the environment to influence behaviour in a particular way, for a specific outcome, is a form of manipulation. Therefore, one proposed solution is to inform people about the nudge. However, this may compromise its efficacy, given that the purpose of a nudge is to have a subtle influence on subconscious decision making. So far, evidence regarding transparency is inconclusive. A randomised controlled trial tested a 'self-nudging' approach, where people that were trying to maintain weight loss were provided with a variety of nudging items to implement into their daily lives (ie a mug with images of healthy breakfast options, a shopping bag with an image of fruit and vegetables, a portion control plate etc). People were informed as to the purpose of the nudges, and were advised that they were free to choose which items to incorporate into their lifestyle. While people reported using a variety of the nudges, they were ineffective for assisting with weight loss maintenance. People used the nudges and liked them; however, there was no difference in weight maintenance between those who did or did not receive the nudging items. It is, then, possible that transparency was the issue because people knew how they worked, which inhibited their ability to subconsciously influence behaviour.

Interestingly, there was an additional finding, a (thin) silver lining, where people who did maintain weight reported using more of the nudging items than those who did not. This suggests that a variety of nudges may improve effectiveness, and be important for extending their life. However, further research is required.

All in all, the literature suggests that nudges have some potential; but there is still a lot to be learned before marketers can implement nudging and be confident of their intended consequences.

The dodgy few

Sadly, another reason to temper enthusiasm for nudges is that the research findings are not always trustworthy. Unfortunately, James Vicary was not an isolated case. Experimental psychologists have also been guilty, and multiple times. One of the worst offenders, Diederik Stapel, has had over 50 articles retracted! While outright fraud is rare, there are less serious (and more subtle ways) of manipulating the truth, and the majority of academic psychologists admit to having used questionable research practices; whether this was because they were tempted, or were simply not diligent, we do not know. Sometimes these questionable practices are identified, and the research has been retracted, for example consumer behaviouralist Brian Wansink, well-known for his research on nudging food choices, has had a number of articles retracted. Consumer psychologist Dirk Smeesters has also had articles retracted from peer reviewed journals. It is quite plausible that there are many more publications circulating where questionable practices have not yet been detected. The preoccupation with laboratory experiments, rather than working with publicly available real-world data, opens up unique opportunities for questionable research practices to remain hidden.

The silver ~~bullet~~ lining

While behavioural economics has received too much hype, too quickly, we don't want to suggest that there haven't been discoveries that are of practical value to marketing.

Yes, consumers use heuristics to make 'good enough' decisions. This has been well documented by researchers for many years. Yet psychologist Gerd Gigerenzer suggests that heuristics do not represent irrationality; rather, they are adaptive cognitive tools that do not follow the formal logic, which have practical outcomes such as better decision making. We use heuristics because they work rather well, not because we have been coerced by clever (evil?) marketers who use sneaky tactics to convince us to do something that we would otherwise not do. For example, the assumption that higher priced items are better quality works pretty well because it is largely true; and larger pack sizes are better value because they generally are. It is through experience with brands and a need for efficient decision making that people rely on heuristics, because they make our lives easier. It is important to understand these heuristics, and to know how marketers can account for them. It is also important to consider how the environment and our natural instincts may alter the heuristics used.

Yes, consumers can be nudged by presenting things in different ways (framing effects), and they may have more affinity for brands that they buy (the 'mere exposure effect'); however, this is not the biggest story in marketing. As marketers, we must remember that advertising is a weak force. People live in a cluttered, chaotic world where advertising and brands fall very far down the priority list (if they are even on the list at all). We screen out advertising by leaving the room, switching stations and walking head down looking at our phones, thereby missing much of the advertising that is attempting to reach us. As marketers, capturing people's attention is the primary challenge. The main focus, then, should be on reminding people your brand exists, and refreshing memory structures that give your brand more of a chance of being chosen in choice situations.

In summary, psychological manipulations, such as framing effects, can create more demand under some conditions, but these conditions aren't well known, and in many cases, the effects will be less than what is advocated. The view that demand for your brand depends on psychological manipulation of consumers is a massive exaggeration, and a distraction for marketers.

So, a word to the wise – do tests to see if specific nudges can do what you hope they will do. Meanwhile, don't lose sight of the main game; if sales are not where you would like them to be, consider that it's probably due to insufficient physical and mental availability.

References

Blumenthal-Barby, JS, and Burroughs, H. 'Seeking better health care outcomes: the ethics of using the "nudge"'. *The American Journal of Bioethics*, 12(2), 2012

Bovens, L. 'The ethics of nudge'. *Preference Change*, Springer, 2009

Bruns, H, et al. 'Can nudges be transparent and yet effective?' WiSo-HH Working Paper Series, Working Paper 33, 2016

Bucher, T, et al. 'Nudging consumers towards healthier choices: a systematic review of positional influences on food choice'. *British Journal of Nutrition*, 2016

d'Adda, G, Capraro, V, and Tavoni, M. 'Push, don't nudge: behavioral spillovers and policy instruments'. *Economics Letters*, 154, 2017

Galizzi, M. 'Label, nudge or tax? A review of health policies for risky behaviours'. *Journal of Public Health Research*, 1(1), 2012

Ghesla, C, Grieder, M, and Schmitz, J. 'Nudge for good? Choice defaults and spillover effects', 2017

Gigerenzer, G, and Todd, PM, and the ABC Research Group. *Simple Heuristics That Make Us Smart*. OUP, 1999

Gold, A, and Lichtenberg, P. 'Don't call me "nudge": the ethical obligation to use effective interventions to promote public health'. *The American Journal of Bioethics*, 12(2), 2012

John, LK, Loewenstein, G, and Prelec, D. 'Measuring the prevalence of questionable research practices with incentives for truth telling'. *Psychological Science*, 23(5), 2012

Jones, JP. 'Advertising: strong force or weak force? Two views an ocean apart'. *International Journal of Advertising*, 9(3), 1990

Lindstrom, M. *Buy.ology: How everything we believe about why we buy is wrong*. Doubleday, 2008

Ly, K, et al. 'A practitioner's guide to nudging'. Rotman School of Management, University of Toronto, 2013

Macdonald, E, and Sharp, B. 'Brand awareness effects on consumer decision making for a common, repeat purchase product: a replication'. *Journal of Business Research*, 48(1), 2000

Nørnberg, TR, et al. 'Choice architecture interventions for increased vegetable intake and behaviour change in a school setting: a systematic review'. *Perspectives in Public Health*, 136(3), 2016

Roberts, K. *Lovemarks: The future beyond brands*. Murdoch Books, 2004

Selinger, E, and Whyte, K. 'Is there a right way to nudge? The practice and ethics of choice architecture'. *Sociology Compass*, 5(10), 2011

Sharp, B. 'How advertising really works'. In B Sharp (ed.), *How Brands Grow*, OUP, 2010

Simon, HA. 'Theories of bounded rationality'. In C McGuire and R Radner (eds), *Decision and Organization* (Volume 1), North-Holland Publishing Company, 1972

Skov, LR, et al. 'Choice architecture as a means to change eating behaviour in self-service settings: a systematic review'. *Obesity Reviews*, 14(3), 2013

Thaler, R, and Sunstein, C. *Nudge: Improving decisions about health, wealth, and happiness.* Yale University Press, 2008

Thorndike, AN, et al. 'A 2-phase labeling and choice architecture intervention to improve healthy food and beverage choices'. *American Journal of Public Health*, 102(4), 2012

Wilson, A. 'Can nudging principles encourage behaviours associated with obesity prevention?' (Masters by Research), University of South Australia, 2015

Wilson, A, et al. 'Nudging healthier food and beverage choices through salience and priming: a systematic review'. *Food Quality and Preference*, 51(16), 2016

Wilson, AL, Bogomolova, S, and Buckley, JD. 'Lack of efficacy of a salience nudge for substituting selection of lower-calorie for higher-calorie milk in the work place'. *Nutrients*, 7(6), 2015

Yong, E. 'Replication studies: bad copy'. *Nature*, 485(7398), 2012

Zajonc, RB. 'Attitudinal effects of mere exposure'. *Journal of Personality and Social Psychology*, 9(2), 1968

Zajonc, RB. 'Feeling and thinking: preferences need no inferences'. *American Psychologist*, 35(2), 1980

25

IS THERE ANY SUCH THING AS BRAND LOVE?

Written by **Helen Edwards**

Brand love is a contested concept. This chapter argues that it is an overstatement – but draws on remarkable new academic research to show the power of an 'emotional something' that exists between consumers and their favourite brands. If not love, what is it? A contribution to personal identity. Extrapolating from three decades of academic research into symbolic consumption, the chapter goes on to show why people use brands to bolster their sense of self, which kinds of brands tend to get disproportionately chosen, and how marketers and planners can use the theory to give a brand a 'tie-breaker' edge in prompting consumer choice.

'Brand love' is a concept routinely evoked in the PowerPoint charts of marketing teams, and the agencies who advise them. Scholarly papers have been devoted to it. At least seven books, two of them bestsellers, have evangelised for it. The industry journals *Campaign* and *The Drum* have published articles on the steps marketers need to take to achieve it. And why not? This is love we're talking about – why shouldn't every marketer want that for their brand?

Because, says the evidence-based school from its locus at the Ehrenberg-Bass Institute for Marketing Science, it doesn't exist. Citing data to advance the more transactional virtues of salience, easy availability and wide reach, its adherents pour scorn on the pursuit of brand love, and deride as baseless the commercial objective to which it is normally shackled: brand loyalty.

This isn't a well-mannered divergence of views on a trip down one of marketing's many arcane byways. It is a schism at the level of fundamentals. Is our discipline really so plastic as to be wide open to interpretation at the most vital interface of all, the one between consumers and brands?

Less than love, more than transaction

One of the problems here is looseness of language. 'Love' is a short word, but a huge one – a bare syllable that seeks to convey the profound emotions that give meaning to our closest human relationships. Perhaps it can be justifiably extended to the animals we welcome into our lives, and to religions and countries – but brands? Do we really think these mere commercial fragments are up to bearing its weight?

True, consumers themselves are apt to slip into declarations of seemingly amorous intent towards the brands or products that have captured their enthusiasm: 'I just love the new iPhone X'. 'We love the way First Direct doesn't feel like a bank'. 'How can you not love Oreos?'

But, as a 2012 academic study from Rajeev Batra et al has warned, there are 'numerous problems' in equating the concept of 'interpersonal love' with the feelings people have towards brands. It is one thing for consumers to launch into hyperbole in casual reference to the brands they most favour, quite another for marketers to appropriate that language in earnestness.

In the context of the marketplace, then, 'love' is an overstatement. Let's put the word to rest. But that still leaves a space where a quieter force holds sway. I will not be the only marketer who has over the years observed an 'emotional something' that exists somewhere along the spectrum between cold transaction at one end and full-on love at the other. A sense of closeness, of personal aptness, that some brands inspire.

What should we call it? How does it come about? Is there any evidence out there to support its existence and demonstrate its effect? As this is a book about evidence in marketing, let's take that last question first.

The 'Brand Aid' study

In a paper published in October 2017 in the *Journal of Consumer Research*, three authors demonstrated the remarkable effect that 'close brands' can have on people's sense of wellbeing.

Conducted by academics from the University of Arizona in the US, and Tecnológico de Monterrey in Mexico, the study aimed to explore whether 'close brand relationships' could mimic close interpersonal relationships in their ability to help people cope with pain.

Volunteers were asked upfront to name brands they felt particularly close to – a list that included BMW, Nike, Zara, Starbucks, Apple, Trader Joe's, Adidas, Guinness and Ford.

Across seven experiments, involving 1,511 participants, the authors showed that seeing, or even just contemplating, a favoured brand resulted in lower reported levels of pain induced in the experimental setting, and also in remembered pain from an accident or event in the past.

In the first experiment, volunteers placed their hands inside a 'cold compressor' ice chest – 'an established method of inducing pain'. While doing so, each was asked to look at an open laptop in front of them.

The group had been randomly divided into two. In one half, each volunteer saw on the screen the logo of a brand they had said that they felt particularly close to. The other half – the controls – just looked at a fixation cross in the centre of the screen.

When asked afterwards to assess on a six-point scale the pain they had felt, those who had seen their favourite brand reported much lower levels than the control group.

In other experiments, controls were given 'neutral' objects to focus on or imagine – such as a basket or chair – to discount the possibility that seeing or recalling a brand constitutes a distraction which could explain the findings. Those in the 'close brand' group still reported lower levels of pain.

'Across seven studies,' concluded the authors, 'the current research demonstrated that contemplating close brand relationships insulates against physical pain.'

Most marketers, of course, are not in the business of helping their

'Brand-Aid'

Martin Reimann, Sandra
Nuñez, Raquel Castaño

JCR, October 2017

RESEARCH (clockwise from top left): the October 2017 journal and the authors; the 'cold compressor test' ice tray that was used as part of an 'established method of inducing pain', and the screen on which favoured logos were shown; some of the brands that volunteers claimed to feel close to; one of the 'neutral' images viewed by the control group

customers deal with pain. Nevertheless, the findings illuminate the remarkable transference of feelings at the brand level to a more generalised positivity, in a situation where the brand's functional qualities are irrelevant.

That still leaves a vital question unanswered: the nature of the 'emotional something' that prompts this generalised enhancement in the first place.

The authors reach for the explanation of brands as 'relationship partners', echoing a much earlier concept from Susan Fournier. It's not so far from the typically vague notions the industry conjures to fill the void: brand engagement, emotional connection, attachment, bonding.

We can do better than that. We can be more specific. The place to look, in our search for the 'something', is the three decades' body of academic research into symbolic consumption and the role of brands as contributors to personal identity.

Symbolic consumption and the concept of 'brand for me'

The founder of the theory was Russell Belk, with his seminal 1988 paper 'Possessions and the extended self'. Since then, the interplay of consumption choice and personal identity has been the subject of intense scrutiny by a suite of behavioural and psychological academics.

Key to the flow of reasoning is the concept of 'self'. Socrates' admonition to 'know thyself' dates back to three centuries BCE, yet for almost the entire intervening period the freedom to 'be thyself' has been a privilege denied to all but a few. Even as recently as the mid-20th century, what a person really was at heart would be buried beneath the welter of circumstance: birth, gender, location, occupation and social class. For most of history, to know yourself was, in large part, simply to know your place.

This changed during the period social academics call the 'post-modern era', and what the rest of us would call the 1970s. With the dismantling of the barriers of social class, individuals began to enjoy a new freedom; to express who they really were, and to vary that expression over time, rather than accept the stable social roles society had hitherto mandated.

Not as easy as it sounds, as it turns out, since people now had to work out for themselves what their true identity was, and construct a narrative scaffolding to support it. In 1991, Anthony Giddens in his book *Modernity and Self-Identity* reduced the dilemma to three reflexive questions: What to do? How to act? Who to be?

The way that individuals went about answering these questions came to be known as 'The project of self' – summarised by John Thompson in 1990 as the process by which a person actively constructs an identity out of 'the available symbolic resources in order to weave a coherent account of who she or he is'.

The 'available symbolic resources' include brands, which are a potentially vivid means of self-endorsement: 'This is the person I am inside, and this brand helps me feel that'. Note that the point is not outward display – not 'badge values' signalling status to others – but rather the internal whispering of self to self. The upshot is that all kinds of brands are potentially involved – even those kept out of sight from others in cupboards, handbags or sports lockers.

Industry commentators have glibly paraphrased symbolic consumption as 'You are what you buy'. This is too passive and reverses the arrow of agency. The truth is more forceful, more actively self-determined: 'You buy what you are'.

A brand that makes it across the membrane of self is not there by accident; it survives the audit because it carries sufficient meaning to reflect an identity that a person not only feels profoundly, but has probably pondered at length too. It is a *brand for me*. The intimacy of that symbolism is why it is credible that the brand's mere contemplation could trigger a generalised sense of 'rightness', sufficient even to take the edge off perceived pain.

We have found our 'emotional something'. Now, which kinds of brands inspire it, and what commercial rewards might it bring?

Meaning, belief, culture and roots

Taken at the level of any single individual, of course, a 'brand for me' could be pretty much any brand out there, no matter how unremarkable, bland and listless – there's no accounting for taste.

Some brands, though (like the ones cited by the volunteers in the pain study), manage to pull off the trick of inspiring a strong appeal to self *at scale*. They induce stronger feelings of closeness, across more people, than their competitors, even where functional capability is at parity. Is there a common ingredient that helps them achieve this?

It is more like an amalgam than a solitary ingredient – a sense of authenticity, integrity and inner strength that some brands convey, which disproportionately suggests them to consumers as potential expressions of identity.

Underlying this, as the foundation of those constituents of meaning, you will often observe something else: a belief, a point of view about the world that is both related to and yet bigger than the category in which the brand operates.

The US retailer REI is a strong example of a brand with a belief-led point of view, not just because of the trenchant simplicity with which it is set down, but also because of the company-wide, totally integrated and sometimes commercially sacrificial intensity with which it is manifested (see overleaf).

REI: Big symbolic gesture

The US outdoor-wear retailer REI states its corporate belief as: 'A life outdoors is a life well lived'. It puts its money where its heart is. On Black Friday – the biggest shopping day of the year, worth upwards of $10bn in sales – it closes all its stores and suspends e-commerce, giving its 12,000-strong workforce a paid day off. The symbolic gesture, tagged #OptOutside, aims to encourage people away from screens and out of malls to embrace the great outdoors. Note the significance of symbolising this core ideology for employees, not just consumers.

Some brands, sensing an ideological vacuum that has led to brand drift across the years (or being made aware of it by consumers), turn to their roots for inspiration. Ford and Avon (see below) are examples of brands that have recently pored over the words and deeds of their long-dead founders, and reinterpreted them for consumers today, to foster the combination of authenticity and relevance that could encourage greater appeal to sense of self.

Avon: Reinterpreting roots

Avon was founded in 1886 by David H. McConnell, a travelling book salesman, after realising his female customers were far more interested in the free perfume samples he offered them than his books. He also noticed something deeper: that many women were isolated at home while their husbands went off to work. So he purposely recruited female sales representatives from this untapped labour pool, believing they had a natural ability to market to other women. At a time of limited employment options for women, the Avon earnings opportunity was a revolutionary concept.

David H. McConnell

Those roots have been reinterpreted for today by putting the ideal of 'female empowerment' at the core of the brand, under the banner 'Beauty for a purpose'. All Avon sub-brands must show how beauty is a contributor to empowerment. The global business styles itself, simply, 'The company for women'.

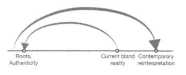

Roots, Authenticity   Current bland reality   Contemporary reinterpretation

Beauty for a Purpose

Meanwhile, the US academics Douglas Holt and Grant McCracken point to culture as another dimension on which brands can increase their traction in consumers' quests to express identity. McCracken has deconstructed breakthrough repositioning successes such as Dove's 'Real Beauty' and Persil's 'Dirt is Good' to show that they could not have been devised through either consumer understanding or internal values alone, but needed the alchemy of cultural insight. More recently, the fashion retailer Jigsaw has bravely used the UK's Brexit cultural backdrop as an amplifier for its 'Style and Truth' positioning, with its challenging paean to immigration.

Jigsaw: Cultural amplifier

Jigsaw's 'Immigration' campaign took a trenchant stance in the UK's febrile Brexit atmosphere, giving traction to the retailer's 'Style and Truth' positioning, and winning *Campaign's* 'Meaningful brand of the year' accolade for 2017.

Through overlapping means, centred on some kind of ideological firmness, certain brands offer customers more meaning for their money – making them greater units of utility in the expression of self. What commercial rewards do those customers offer in return?

Loyalty at parity

Here's what it isn't. It isn't biceps tattooed with the brand logo, nor Kevin Roberts' famously optimistic 'loyalty beyond reason'. The concept of brand loyalty has had a bad press of late, and the tendency of its advocates to overrate it may be part of the reason why. In the world of brands, where asymmetries lurk everywhere, loyalty can only ever be a relative concept.

Martin Weigel, head of planning at Wieden+Kennedy Amsterdam, has a nice way of urging marketers to curb their ambitions for customer loyalty. His counsel – paraphrasing the late Andrew Ehrenberg – is not to think about 'our consumers', but to regard them as 'consumers of other brands who sometimes happen to buy ours'. He is right. But what if we can improve on that 'sometimes' just a little?

It may be easier to come at this as a thought experiment. Imagine a routine sort of category where one brand happens to appeal more to your sense of personal identity than its competitors do – even though you're happy to buy them too.

Your preferred, brand-for-me option and one of those competitors are side by side in a supermarket aisle. Both tidily displayed, both easy to reach, both the same price. It's not hard to conclude that you would, almost intuitively, reach for your more favoured brand. Not through any perceived superiority at the product level, but because it just feels a bit more 'you'. This is *loyalty at parity*: the tendency to always choose one brand when everything else is equal.

But of course, it is very often not. If there were a promotion on the other brand, would you still choose your favoured brand as before? Unlikely. What if the other one commanded a more prominent position on the shelf? Probably not. What if your favoured one were not there at all, because it had a weaker distribution footprint, and you'd have to walk a couple of blocks to get it? Definitely not.

Loyalty at parity is worth having but is not a killer advantage. It is an all-things-being-equal tie-breaker. Its significance, in the industry's heated loyalty debate, is that it does not conflate 'loyal' with 'frequent purchaser' – since there can be many occasions when 'parity' does not come into play, and competitors get bought.

For marketers, it means there may be opportunity for a relative loyalty play in that long tail of occasional purchasers – a chance to persuade more people to make a positive choice when the playing field is level. If 'brand for me' status can achieve that, then it is an edge – no more. But, in today's oversupplied markets, where the functional attributes of brands tend towards high quality convergence, an edge is sometimes the best you can hope for.

Much of this chapter has been devoted to a diminution in the elevated status of much discussed industry concepts. Not the high peak of fierce brand love, but the lower plateau of brands as contributors to self-identity; not the marketer's nirvana of diehard brand loyalty, but the marketplace reality of a tie-breaker edge; not the single heroic virtue that all great brands embody, but a tangle of linked perceptual assets that tends to characterise a 'brand for me'.

And that 'diminution' motif, if I'm honest, applies at the level of evidence, too. The reader might have expected firm, quantitative, incontrovertible data to buttress the assertions I make. In their place I have offered an experimental academic study, a body of loosely connected interpretive research and empirical observation. In the messy, variable-rich, all-too-human domain of brand marketing, this is generally the kind of evidence I get to work with, and interpret.

It would be nice to offer instead a scientifically proven, one-size-fits-all framework to show marketers how to confidently build their brands. I'm just not sure it exists.

References

Batra, R, Ahuvia, A, and Bagozzi, RP. 'Brand love'. *Journal of Marketing*. 76(2), 2012

Belk, R. 'Possessions and the extended self'. *Journal of Consumer Research*, 15(2), 1988

Ehrenberg, et al. 'Brand advertising as creative publicity'. *Journal of Advertising Research*, 42(4), 2002

Fournier, S. 'Consumers and their brands: developing relationship theory in consumer research'. *Journal of Consumer Research*, 24(4), 1998

Giddens, A. *Modernity and Self-Identity: Self and society in the late modern age.* Stanford University Press, 1991

Holt, DB. *How Brands Become Icons: The principles of cultural branding.* Harvard Business Review Press, 2004

McCracken, G. *Chief Culture Officer: How to create a living, breathing corporation.* Basic Books, 2009

McCracken, G. *Culture and Consumption: New approaches to the symbolic character of consumer goods and activities.* Indiana University Press, 1990

Reimann, M, Nuñez, S, and Castaño, R. 'Brand-aid'. *Journal of Consumer Research,* 44(3), 2017

Roberts, K. *Lovemarks: The future beyond brands.* Murdoch Books, 2004

Sharp, B. *How Brands Grow: What marketers don't know.* OUP, 2010

Thompson, J. *Ideology and Modern Culture: Critical social theory in the era of mass communication.* Polity Press, 1990

Weigel, M. 'Why we should stop worrying so much about loyalty and relationships, and focus on getting a lot of penetration'. *Canalside View* blog. https://martinweigel.org/2010/09/07/why-we-could-do-with-a-little-less-talk-about-loyalty-and-relationships-and-a-little-more-about-conq/

26

SEDUCTION AND CAULIFLOWERS

Written by **Paul Feldwick**

What does trimming the leaves off a cauliflower have to do with seduction? This chapter considers this and other critical questions.

'There are no hidden persuaders', wrote Rosser Reeves in 1961. 'Advertising works openly, in the bare and pitiless sunlight.' It was never true, of course: even Reeves' own commercials made frequent use of men in white coats, which we now know are powerful subconscious symbols of authority. But ever since Vance Packard's 1957 book *The Hidden Persuaders*, the claim to be honest salesmen, offering nothing but transparent information, has been the ad industry's main line of defence – despite its serious inadequacy in describing how advertising really influences behaviour.

Given what we now know about implicit learning, low attention processing, the emotional roots of decision making, 'priming', the 'adaptive unconscious', biases and heuristics, and all those other findings from neuroscience and behavioural psychology that have recently become widely accessible, we can no longer pretend that Reeves' argument holds any merit. But if we accept that our decision-making processes are to a large extent unconscious, and that our decisions are influenced by signs and signals that we are frequently unaware of, where (if anywhere) can we draw an ethical line between what is acceptable in advertising, and what is not?

In considering this question, we should pay close attention to the power of the language we use. 'Brainwashing' clearly sounds quite evil, 'manipulation' is pretty bad too, and even 'seduction' is suspect (I'll come back to that word in a moment). All these, ironically enough, are metaphors; social constructions that come with their own powerful associations – biasing our responses without us noticing how they do so, in exactly the way that advertising itself could be accused of doing.

That might lead us to question the assumption that advertising is in some way a special case. Daniel Kahneman's 2011 book *Thinking, Fast and Slow* deals extensively with unconscious mental processes, but does not even mention 'advertising' in its index. What is true about how advertising influences us below conscious awareness is not only also true of packaging, of store design, and of product design, but also of the ways we dress, act and speak to each other every day – it pervades our lives. Timothy Wilson writes, in his 2002 book *Strangers to Ourselves,* that 'the causal role of conscious thought has been vastly overrated; instead, it is often a post-hoc explanation of responses that emanated from the adaptive unconscious', and he even cites evidence that we make more satisfying choices when we go with our intuition rather than analysis. The fundamental principles of subconscious decision making are not specific to advertising, and were not invented by sinister scientists – this is just part of the way our brains work, and how we make choices.

One of my first ad agency mentors liked to recall his first job on a market stall, cutting the leaves off the cauliflowers to make them look more attractive. You could argue that most of advertising and branding (not only packaging and design) is, like this, simply a way of making what you have for sale look more attractive. That aesthetic appeal is something people generally find hard to put into words; they may not notice the importance it plays in their choice, and indeed they may resist any suggestion that they didn't choose on more functional, 'rational' criteria. But traders soon find out from experience what makes the difference to sales, and respond accordingly. In the natural world, the peacock's tail evolved in order to attract a mate, as the bright colours and markings of flowers did to attract specific insects. Similarly, in the ecology of commerce, the presentation of the successful brand – including storefront, packaging, and advertising – has evolved because it effectively attracts more customers.

You could call this seduction (I dare say the peacock would, if he could talk). But the word is an ambiguous one. One primary connotation of 'seduction' is sexual, and in that context it *may* mean something close to rape, certainly something exploitative and damaging – think of *Tess of the d'Urbervilles*. On the other hand, it can be pleasant to be seduced, and ultimately the survival of the species may depend on it. Ethical and value judgements depend on many contextual factors: who is seducing whom, what happens afterwards, and so on.

I like the idea of the cauliflower removing its leaves in a seductive *déshabillé*. Alternatively, we could consider its trimming as a rhetorical device. Rhetoric – the use of language to make an argument more appealing – was the invention of the ancient Greeks, who also saw the ethical dilemma it posed: teachers of rhetoric were sometimes attacked for the crime of 'making the worse appear the better cause'. And many attacks on advertising are based on the argument that it makes the worse appear the better cauliflower. But this begs the question of how far an objective standard of 'better' or 'worse' exists, and who is to be the judge of that. Attempts to control the trimming of cauliflowers, in order to aid quality judgements, might be in the interest of the village produce show, but what if aesthetic appeal is part of the value that the customer is buying? What happens when you try to impose a similar uniformity on cars, or chocolate bars, or handbags?

There may be boundaries where techniques of display, presentation and rhetoric become unfair, exploitative or harmful. But our judgements of where these lie should not be biased by our own emotive use of language. Nor should we assume that subconscious decision processes are necessarily sinister, when we have increasing evidence that they are a universal, and even valuable, part of our human psychology. If the Rosser Reeves defence has been rendered untenable by modern science, then so, surely, has the Vance Packard attack.

References

Barden, P. *Decoded: The science behind why we buy*. Wiley, 2013

Crimmins, J. *7 Secrets of Persuasion: Leading-edge neuromarketing techniques to influence anyone*. Career Press, 2016

Feldwick, P. *The Anatomy of Humbug: How to think differently about advertising.* Matador, 2015

Heath, R. *Seducing the Subconscious: The psychology of emotional influence in advertising.* Wiley-Blackwell, 2012

Kahneman, D. *Thinking, Fast and Slow.* Farrar, Straus and Giroux, 2011

Packard, V. *The Hidden Persuaders: An introduction to the techniques of mass-persuasion through the unconscious.* Longmans, Green & Co, 1957

Reeves, R. (1961/1986). *Reality in Advertising* (16th printing). Alfred Knopf

Wilson, T. *Strangers to Ourselves: Discovering the adaptive unconscious.* The Harvard University Press, 2002

© marketoonist.com

27

MARKETING UTOPIA

Written by **Richard Shotton**

Brand purpose is one of the most influential theories in marketing. The main evidence for it has been supplied by Jim Stengel's 2011 book *Grow*. Stengel looked at the best-performing brands in the world, and claimed they were linked by a brand ideal or purpose: a shared intent by everyone in the business to improve people's lives. However, this chapter throws this evidence for brand purpose into question, querying the research on multiple fronts: the accuracy of the data, the circularity of the logic, the poor predictive power of the theory, and finally, the malleability of the definitions used.

What would marketing utopia look like?

How about this for a start? That we knew for certain how to create effective advertising and that it made such a difference to our clients that their share price skyrocketed.

Sound appealing?

Well, that is what Jim Stengel, ex-CMO of P&G, claims to have discovered. In his 2011 book *Grow*, he argues that brands which have an ideal, ie a purpose beyond profit, deliver a better stock market performance than those which don't.

Stengel came up with this finding after selecting the 50 brands with the highest loyalty or bonding scores from Millward Brown's 50,000-strong database. These star performers were termed the 'Stengel 50'. Stengel then searched for a link between the brands. This was found to be a 'Brand Ideal': a shared intent by everyone in the business to improve people's lives.

Next, he looked at the chosen brands' stock value growth between 2000 and 2011. Since the Stengel 50 had grown by 393% compared with a 7% loss for the S&P 500 benchmark, Stengel declared that ideals were driving business success. Ideals supposedly didn't just drive growth, they led to stratospheric success.

This theory has struck a chord in marketing. Planning and strategy presentations refer to the results in breathless tones. Sir Martin Sorrell declared he was 'utterly convinced'. Even the database of research papers, WARC, has succumbed to the excitement: it has over 7,000 articles on the topic.

The finding that companies which adopt an ideal outperform the stock market is extraordinary news. No one has ever found a simple, foolproof way of beating the stock market. Not Warren Buffett, not George Soros, not even John Maynard Keynes.

Yet Stengel claims he has cracked the stock market code and invented a means of generating untold wealth. All you need to do to make millions is to identify brands with ideals and then invest your life savings in those stocks. It makes you wonder why Stengel isn't keeping the idea to himself.

But before you sell your house to fund your investment, heed the words of Pierre-Simon Laplace, the influential French mathematician. He wrote: 'The weight of evidence for an extraordinary claim must be proportioned to its strangeness.' Or as Carl Sagan the astronomer put it more simply, 'Extraordinary claims require extraordinary evidence'.

So, are Stengel's extraordinary claims supported by evidence, let alone extraordinary evidence? If we're to have confidence in his findings, they need to pass four tests:

1. The experimental data must be accurate.
2. The theory predicts the future, not just the past.
3. The brands that outperform the stock market are linked by an ideal.
4. Those brands with ideals outperform those without.

Let's run through each of these tests and judge how his theory holds up.

1. Is the data accurate?

A basic requirement is that the data being analysed is accurate. Stengel's key piece of data is that his 50 stocks rose by 393%. But that's not quite the case. Some of the companies in question, such as Emirates and Wegmans, are privately held, which means they don't have a share price.

Nor do other brands in the Stengel 50 – like Stonyfield Farm, Innocent or Pampers – have a share price. They are parts of much larger publicly traded companies, respectively Danone, Coca-Cola and P&G. In Stonyfield Farm's case, its 2014 revenues were less than 1.5% of Danone's. Can you claim that Danone's share price rose because 1.5% of its holdings have a brand ideal?

Stengel also argues that the 393% increase in share price should be compared to the S&P 500, which declined by 7%. But it's an inappropriate metric as the Stengel 50 is an international group of companies and the S&P 500 comprises the largest American companies. You can't compare the performance of a company in Hong Kong or Brazil with an American benchmark. If you do, you're not capturing the effect of a brand ideal, you're measuring the relative economic health of those markets.

If you strip out private companies, brands which are part of a much larger entity and the non-American companies, then you are left with 14 brands to analyse. Is that a large enough sample to make a sweeping assertion about the effectiveness of brand purpose?

The most serious flaw, though, is how Stengel selected the 50 brands. He picked the best performers in Millward Brown's 50,000-strong database. That's the top 0.1% of brands. It's not surprising that those brands performed well in terms of their share price. If they hadn't performed well in the past, they wouldn't be in Millward Brown's top 0.1% of brands.

Stengel's finding, if you restate it at its most basic, is that the top 0.1% of brands have performed well in the stock market. That's circular logic.

2. Does the theory predict the future as well as the past?

Imagine, one night you're in a slightly dodgy pub. As you nurse your pint, a man in a tatty raincoat sidles up to you and offers you a once-in-a-lifetime offer: the chance to buy his method for winning at the racetrack. Being a cautious soul, you ask for a smidgen of proof. 'Fine,' he growls, in a voice ravaged by Rothmans, 'name a year and I'll tell you who won the Grand National.'

I hope at this stage you'd kindly take your leave, as it's obvious that being able to recount the past doesn't count as proof. The true test of a theory is how well it predicts the future.

For a more useful test, I examined the share price performance of Stengel's companies over the five years up to March 2017. Since this time period is before the publication of his book, it allows us to test the predictive ability of the theory. Bear in mind that I'm analysing 26 companies, as it's misleading to include brands which account for a small proportion of a larger company's incomes. That's 14 against the US benchmark and 12 against their respective benchmarks.

If ideals were the ultimate guide to performance, all 26 companies would outperform the market. In fact, a mere nine of the 26 stocks beat the S&P 500. Even if you cut the data differently and compared the non-American stocks to their own benchmark, only 10 beat the benchmark. Either way, it's fewer than the 13 you'd expect by chance alone.

3. Are the brands linked by an ideal?

For the theory to be valid, the brands in question must be linked by an ideal. Unfortunately, even this doesn't seem to be true.

My suspicions were first raised by the claim that all 50 brands exhibited an ideal. Not an above average likelihood of having an ideal, but every single one. That's strange isn't it? Theories rarely predict events quite so conveniently; reality is messier.

The reason Stengel can claim such widespread uptake of ideals becomes apparent when you examine his definitions. The term 'ideal' is tortured to such a degree that it's meaningless.

Have a look at the definition for three of the brands:

1. Moët & Chandon 'exists to transform occasions into celebrations'.
2. Mercedes-Benz 'exists to epitomise a life of achievement'.
3. BlackBerry 'exists to connect people with one another and the content that is most important in their lives, anytime, anywhere'.

Notice a problem? These ideals are just category descriptors – they could apply to any champagne, luxury brand or handset provider.

This isn't a subjective opinion. In 2015 Aidan O'Callaghan and I asked 1,000 consumers to match one of six brands to each of these ideals. If the ideals were a genuine fit, you'd expect consumers to recognise his brands. Yet only 6%, 10% and 21% of those questioned recognised BlackBerry, Mercedes and Moët respectively.

When the word 'ideal' means anything you want, then it is meaningless.

4. Do brands with ideals outperform those that don't have ideals?

To prove that ideals boost the odds of success, you need to compare successful brands with unsuccessful ones. In particular, you must demonstrate that successful companies are more likely to have taken ideals to their heart.

You can't make sweeping claims by looking at a single group in isolation. Otherwise you might come to the wrong conclusion and attribute growth to an inconsequential factor that occurred in all companies. For example, by just looking at high-performing companies you might notice that all of them have offices. However, before making any claims about the importance of offices, you must check whether underperforming companies have them too. If they do, then you haven't found anything of interest.

Unfortunately, Stengel makes no attempt to determine whether brands outside the top 50 have an absence of ideals. This alone means his case is unproven.

In the interests of trying to prove Stengel's theory, I examined some of the worst stock market performers of recent times. If they lacked ideals it would support his case.

First, Avon. Between March 2004 and March 2017 Avon's shares dropped by 91%. But you could plausibly argue that their brand ideal was 'to help everyone look as beautiful as they possibly can'.

You might object that this is my subjective opinion. Does my invention of an ideal have any merit? Surely, only the brand's marketing team know if they had an ideal? It's a fair criticism. But it's also one that can be levelled at Stengel's methodology. It was his team who defined the brands in the Stengel 50 had to have ideals – not the marketers who worked on them.

So, let's ignore Avon and instead turn our attention to Nokia, whose shares plummeted 95% between October 2007 and July 2012. You could claim that, like BlackBerry, Nokia existed 'to connect people with one another and the content that is most important in their lives, anytime, anywhere'. This time it isn't just my opinion. The consumers Aidan and I surveyed were 52% more likely to think Nokia fitted this ideal than BlackBerry.

It seems ideals apply as much to underperforming brands as successful ones.

So, how has Stengel's theory fared against our tests? For it to be valid it must pass all of them. Unfortunately, it has failed all four. Stengel has failed to prove that ideals drive superior profits.

But, perhaps, the hypothesis is true but inadequately articulated?

Can there be a formula for brand success?

There are two reasons why this is unlikely. First, brands operate in too varied a range of situations. What succeeds in one context might flop in another time or place. Hunting for a single guaranteed formula for success is a fool's errand. As Philip Rosenzweig, professor of strategy and international business at IMD, wrote in his book *The Halo Effect:* 'Anyone who claims to have found laws of business physics either understands little about business, little about physics or little about both.'

Secondly, success is not determined solely by a company's actions. Rosenzweig continues:

> *Following a given formula can't ensure high performance, and for a simple reason: in a competitive market economy, performance is fundamentally relative, not absolute. Success and failure depend not only on a company's actions but also on those of its rivals.*

Many well-managed companies fail, not for internal reasons, but because of a radical disruption from a competitor. Think of mainframe computers disrupted by PCs or video rental stores bankrupted by streaming services. The destruction of these companies was not due to a lack of purpose. If business performance is impacted by competitors (as surely it must be) then success can never be guaranteed by just sticking to an internal behaviour, like a brand ideal.

Marketing utopias do not exist

The appeal of *Grow* is that it offers straightforward, simple solutions to time-pressed managers. Simplicity is more reassuring than a realistic, but nuanced, explanation. Who wants to hear about improving the probability of success when a pundit is peddling certainties?

But reality is messy and muddled. Adopting an ideal might work for some brands but not others. If you take an ideological approach and apply brand ideals to all the problems you face, then sometimes you'll be force-fitting the solution onto an inappropriate problem. Far better to judge each situation on its merits. Take the time and effort to understand whether the benefits brand ideals offer are better than all the other approaches available.

The idea that there is one solution to solve all marketing problems is utopian. And like the term 'utopia' – which literally means 'no place' – it's a fiction.

References

Rosenzweig. P. *The Halo Effect.* Free Press, 2007

Stengel, J. *Grow: How ideals power growth and profit at the world's 50 greatest companies.* Crown Business, 2011

28

AUTHENTICITY, PURPOSE AND FAKERY – THE CHALLENGE FOR BRANDS

Written by **Kate Richardson**

The authenticity craze and 'Millennials' obsession has led brands to overplay their hand, and confuse the need to stand for something genuine with a desire to stand for something worthy. For some categories, perceived authenticity is an important driver of equity and preference. However, as this chapter argues, marketers should think carefully about the real role that their brands and products play in the lives of customers, and be wary of alignment with an inauthentic social purpose.

Much like disruption, authenticity is one of those overused and obfuscating words. It's an ideal that marketers have latched onto as they grapple with the challenges of unpredictable competition, diminished trust, social media chatter and rapid technological change. Bounced around the internet like a shiny new ball, authenticity has become a preoccupation for brands seeking to connect with a more informed and discerning consumer in the era of a socially charged internet. With online advertising becoming increasingly intrusive and progressively more disliked, authenticity is in hot demand. Companies are consistently told they need to be more real, human and transparent, and that credibility is the new currency.

However, authenticity is one of those terms which wriggles easily from our semantic grasp – it's difficult to keep hold of, and prone to being bandied about by well-intentioned hacks. In its simplest form, to be authentic is to live life in a way that's congruent with your values, regardless of external influence. In marketing terms, authenticity can be defined as 'a subjective evaluation of genuineness ascribed to a brand by consumers'. Given people's tendency to seek self-congruity, and the role of brands in self-identity construction, there is of course a link between personal and brand authenticity.

Against a backdrop of internet-fuelled fakery and conspicuous consumption, consumers are paying greater attention to this concept, particularly in self-identifying industries such as wine, food and fashion. The appeal of foundational factors of quality, heritage and sincerity has driven the rapid expansion of categories such as organics and craft beer, and the success of smaller independent producers alongside bigger brands with a story.

Attributes which contribute to brand authenticity include the original source of production, a sense of history, sincerity of purpose, timelessness, quality of production, traditions that have remained over time, and dismissal of commercial motivations.

While evidence shows that authenticity can influence brand equity and choice, there is a danger that brands are overplaying their care and responsibility card. A shift towards companies divining a higher social purpose has had the unintended consequence of homogenising identity and undermining credibility. In an effort to be more authentic, brands are stepping outside of the bounds of consumer expectation, and in the process, behaving disingenuously.

Brands are confusing the need to stand for something genuine with standing for something worthy. Part of the motivation for this is to increase appeal with the so-called Millennials – the 'authentic generation'.

It's all in a story

The Chobani success story is one that begins with authenticity. The company built its billion-dollar yoghurt business on 'an exotic name, a founder who embodied a rags-to-riches success, and buzz', as Charles Duhigg put it. The story of Turkish immigrant Hamdi Ulukaya's humble efforts to produce a Greek yoghurt with 'real ingredients' that tasted of his homeland has been told over and over again; initially on social media, and then in the mainstream. In recent years, the brand has explored more traditional avenues of marketing; however, it's never strayed from the 'real, authentic and simple' positioning, and its channels of choice, sampling and social.

Chobani is one independent brand whose success has come at the expense of more traditional and 'inauthentic' mass brands like Yoplait, a company that is now (to quote Duhigg again) scrambling to 'manufacture authenticity' to help arrest a significant drop in sales. In 2017, General Mills (owners of Yoplait) launched Oui, a cultured yoghurt made up of simpler ingredients and sold in a small glass jar, in an effort to stem the tide of decline.

That said, you don't have to be a small, humble farmer who threw in their corporate city job for a life hand-rearing happy chickens on the valley's finest organic grains to be perceived as the real deal. Brands such as 'Harley-Davidson, Mountain Dew, Nike and Corona' are deemed authentic by consumers, as Douglas Holt observed. Of course, what can be giveth, can be taketh away. Brands perceived to have been unfaithful to themselves, and therefore untrue to their consumers, face significant risks.

In 2009, iconic Australian beer brand Victoria Bitter (VB) changed both its formula and advertising agency. In an effort to move away from its working-class roots, the brand let go of its famous 'for a hard-earned thirst' tagline (with its heritage in hard work and reward) in favour of 'the drinking beer'. At the same time, amendments to taxation laws led to a decision to reduce its alcohol content and save costs.

VB's results went from bad to worse. A chorus of complaints on social media and in pubs was mirrored by a further drop in sales. People resented paying the same price for a beer with lower alcohol content, and this was confounded when their gripes were ignored for far too long. A few years later, the company issued a public letter of apology, noting they had got it wrong, and the old formula and traditional tagline were back.

As Matt Kirkegaard noted: 'Over the past three years they have told everyone that the beer that had always been about the Hard Earned Thirst was really just another Drinking Beer and, in very publicly f*#king around with the recipe to save a few bob, they said there was nothing special about that beer anyway.'

To VB drinkers, the brand had abandoned its heritage. It lost its foothold in authenticity, and carelessly discarded what was perhaps its greatest distinctive asset. Consumers were angry, and the company was accused of not being transparent, and reneging on its promise. What's more, it took three years and a financial belting for VB to actively listen, reinforcing the notion it was out of touch with traditional beer drinkers.

Authenticity and purpose – a mismatched union

Research in the field has sought to tidy up the morass of ideas about authenticity. Recent efforts have aimed to develop a sound definition and measure of brand authenticity, and establish a clearer link between its attributes and their relationship to brand choice, congruency, consistency and equity.

For example, Felicitas Morhart et al propose a clearer articulation of brand authenticity: 'The extent to which consumers perceive a brand to be faithful toward itself, true to its consumers, motivated by caring and responsibility, and able to support consumers in being true to themselves.'

The authors have also identified four dimensions: continuity, credibility, integrity and symbolism, each of which is underpinned by a set of core drivers.

In the case of symbolism, these are 'a brand that adds meaning to people's lives, a brand that reflects important values that people care about, a brand that connects people to their real selves, a brand that connects people to what is really important'.

The authors don't contend that all brands should strive for authenticity, but the idea of brands connecting people to bigger, more important themes of life and human existence is where organisations are messing up. It's one of the reasons why the notion of authenticity can be so problematic.

Too many brands are making the mistake of orienting themselves around a lofty, higher purpose that goes beyond the goal of profit, straying too far from their unique value and the realm of their category. Brands are getting distracted by standing for [insert important or worthy or socially conscious aspiration here] at the expense of standing for something relevant in the minds of their audience. In trying too hard to be responsible and caring, they're coming across as tediously homogenous and utterly disingenuous.

All the hoo-ha about authenticity, the hype around social media and prevailing discussion in the marketing community, instigated by leaders like Paul Polman and Jim Stengel, have created a false sense of the importance that (most) brands play in our lives. The fashionable discourse on beliefs and purpose has given rise to the idea that even the most innocuous of products need to create important meaning in our lives, and bring us closer to what really matters, regardless of the real role the product occupies in daily life.

As already noted in the 'Marketing utopia' chapter, in his book *Grow* Jim Stengel argues that companies that subscribe to a 'Brand Ideal' significantly outperform their competitors. For his research, he chose the 50 top brands from Millward Brown's database of 50,000. He then identified the common link in their superior share price growth as a purpose designed to improve the lives of others. While the methodology has been discredited, most notably by Byron Sharp and Richard Shotton, the mud has already stuck. And some of the top names in our industry have been evangelising the prosperity in purpose ever since.

Unilever's Paul Polman has built a popular narrative around 'Sustainable Living', a purpose which he credits as the unifying force behind the company's growth since it was first introduced in 2010. In May 2017, the company proudly announced that its 'Sustainable Living' brands grew 50% faster than the rest of the company, and were responsible for 60% of the growth – an increase from 2015 when they grew 46% faster and accounted for 30% of the growth.

However, it's difficult to determine whether the sustainable, purpose-driven nature of these brands was the only driving factor. For example, the company notes that, as of 2017, there are 18 Sustainable Living brands in the top 40 Unilever brands, up from 12 in 2015. With an additional six brands now counted in the numbers, there is a possibility that growth could have come, at least in part, by simply including more brands in the portfolio. In addition, it's unclear whether the brands that fall outside the portfolio are in slower growing categories, fewer or lower growth markets, lack innovation, have been disrupted by new entrants to market, or have been hurt by insufficient investment.

This is not to criticise Unilever (who should be commended for the work they are doing to be a better, more efficient and sustainable employer), but rather to highlight the somewhat unchallenged narrative that has developed around purpose. While it may be appropriate for some brands, there is an increasing tendency to confuse creating a socially responsible company with designing the locus of a brand around a socially responsible aspiration.

This is exactly where brands like Pepsi and McDonald's have made calamitous mistakes. Pepsi's widely observed, disastrous Kendall Jenner-fronted effort to deliver a message of 'unity, peace and understanding' was evidence of brand overreach, as the company clearly forgot not only what it stood for, but the teensy tiny role it plays in shaping people's lives (not to mention global harmony).

As Elle Hearns, executive director of the Marsha P. Johnson Institute (and formerly an organiser for Black Lives Matter), said, the ad 'plays down the sacrifices people have historically taken in utilising protest. No one is finding joy from Pepsi at a protest, that's just not the reality of our lives. That's not what it looks like to take bold action.'

Heineken's 'Worlds Apart' video brought together strangers with opposing views to discuss their differences over a drink (surprise surprise, it's a Heineken). The video garnered plenty of chatter, but as Mark Ritson noted, there was little that was unique about the ad; its rights advocacy-based subject matter was perhaps a long way from the brand, and the video lacked distinction, as it could have been done by any beer brand.

Brands are desperate to be seen as authentic, but in misinterpreting what this actually means, they risk damaging their credibility. One motivation for companies striving for authenticity (and purpose) is an attempt to appeal to the harder to reach, more discerning and much fawned over Millennial generation.

This mythical group is, by their own definition, a generation that sees through spin, doesn't respond to traditional advertising, and is all about transparency and authenticity. Brands like Pepsi have felt the online wrath of this audience in response to perceived mis-steps. Companies are right to be wary, and to consider what authenticity means for this audience.

What's interesting, though, is that this demographic is the first to grow up with reality TV, the internet and social media – all of which provide the murkiest of bacterial breeding grounds for trickery and fakery; two things considered marketing kryptonite by today's digital natives.

The likes of Facebook and Instagram have ushered in the era of the carefully crafted influencer. A declaration of war against the artificial makes the relationship to influencers being blatantly paid to tout sneakers, juices and everything in between both interesting, and at face value, completely contradictory. Particularly when the rules around the transparency of sponsored content are flaky at best.

While Millennials (apparently) don't trust advertising, they do put faith in their favourite Instagrammer wearing or sharing the very same product. This is regardless of the nature of the relationship between brand and tout, just as long as it feels real, with 'feels' being the operative word.

This is the crazy paradox of the real but not real, fake but not fake cultivated character of social media today. The kind of fake-real that has muddied modern-day marketing so things seem both more transparent and more obscured; more authentic and yet more disingenuous.

Brands are right to think about the drivers of authenticity relevant to their category, story and product; however, companies should carefully consider the pitfalls of hitching themselves to the social purpose wagon as they risk diluting a distinctive position and diminishing their credibility. In addition, while influencers have a role to play (as they always have), brands should be wise to the fact that the micro-influencer trend has resulted in the extreme proliferation of these endorsers potentially lessening their future impact and increasing consumer scepticism. And all at a time when the ubiquity of 'fake news' and its invasion of our media is undermining trust in what is real.

References

Associated Press. 'Yoplait's sales keep falling as Chobani targets non-Greek'. Available *The Seattle Times*, 28 June 2017: https://www.seattletimes.com/business/yoplaits-sales-keep-falling-as-chobani-targets-non-greek/

Duhigg, C. 'Yoplait learns to manufacture authenticity to go with its yoghurt', *The*

New York Times, 26 June 2017. https://www.nytimes.com/2017/06/26/business/yoplait-learns-to-manufacture-authenticity-to-go-with-its-yogurt.html

Escalas, J, and Bettman, J. 'Self-construal, reference groups, and brand meaning'. *Journal of Consumer Research* 32, 2005. https://faculty.fuqua.duke.edu/~jrb12/bio/Jim/escalasbettman.pdf

Fairfax Media. 'From strength to struth as Foster's cuts booze in VB'. Available *The Sydney Morning Herald*, 31 July 2009: http://www.smh.com.au/business/from-strength-to-struth-as-fosterx2019s-cuts-booze-in-vb-20090730-e30y.html

https://www.unilever.com/news/Press-releases/2017/unilevers-sustainable-living-brands-continue-to-drive-higher-rates-of-growth.html

Izadi, E. 'Pepsi pull Kendall Jenner protest ad after ridicule and backlash'. *Australian Financial Review*, 6 April 2017. http://www.afr.com/business/media-and-marketing/advertising/pepsi-pulls-kendall-jenner-protest-ad-after-ridicule-and-backlash-20170406-gvexks

Kirkegaard, M. 'Vic Bitter: for a try hard thirst?' *Australian Brews News*, 5 November 2012. http://www.brewsnews.com.au/2012/11/vic-bitter-for-a-try-hard-thirst/

Morhart, F, et al. 'Brand authenticity: an integrative framework and measurement scale'. *Journal of Consumer Psychology*, 25(2), 2015

Napoli, J, et al. 'Measuring consumer-based brand authenticity'. *Journal of Business Research*, 67(6), 2014

Newman, G, and Dhar, R. 'Authenticity is contagious: brand essence and the original source of production'. *Journal of Marketing Research*, 51(3), 2014

Ritson, M. 'Mark Ritson: Heineken should remember marketing is about profit, not purpose'. *Marketing Week*, 10 May 2017. https://www.marketingweek.com/2017/05/10/heineken-marketing-purpose-profit/

Roderick, L. 'Unilever's sustainable brands grow 50% faster than the rest of the business'. *Marketing Week*, 18 May 2017. https://www.marketingweek.com/2017/05/18/unilever-sustainable-brands-growth/

Sharp, B. 'Review of Jim Stengel's disappointing book "Grow"'. Marketing Science: Commentary by Byron Sharp, 30 December 2011. https://byronsharp.wordpress.com/2011/12/30/stengel/

Shotton, R. 'The problem with brand purpose'. *HuffPost UK*, 26 August 2016. http://www.huffingtonpost.co.uk/richard-shotton/brand-purpose_b_11679052.html

Stengel, J. *Grow: How ideals power growth and profit at the world's greatest companies.* Crown Business, 2011

Stotyn, A. 'VB back to full strength'. Available *The Age*, 4 September 2012. http://www.theage.com.au/victoria/vb-back-to-full-strength-20120904-25c72.html

© marketoonist.com

29

WHEN PURPOSE BECOMES A PROBLEM

Written by **Wiemer Snijders**

This chapter is critical of the role purpose plays in buying behaviour and its usefulness as a concept for the development of communications. The main critique is that purpose works against a large body of evidence on how the brains works, by reducing cognitive effort – the essence of branding.

There is a new buzz phrase in the boardroom, and it is 'purposeful positioning'.

Purposeful positioning is a perfect example of how some people just can't resist the temptation to flog a dead horse, which in this case is the idea that people need to care about brands.

Published in 1961, Rosser Reeves' book *Reality in Advertising* describes the concept of the Unique Selling Proposition (USP) – his main point being that you need to give people a reason to buy your brand.

In fact, Reeves made the whole thing up. There was no evidence to support the idea of the USP, and he himself applied the concept only loosely to his work. The book was simply an attempt to counter a potentially dangerous threat not only to Reeves' work but to the advertising industry as a whole, as Paul Feldwick explains in his 2015 book *The Anatomy of Humbug*.

Only a few years earlier, Vance Packard had published his famous book *The Hidden Persuaders*, which claimed that advertising – specifically the subliminal kind – was able to influence us and make us want stuff we didn't need.

Packard portrayed the practice as an evil art that should be stamped out.

Reeves' book countered this idea by stating: 'There are no hidden persuaders. Advertising works openly, in the bare and pitiless sunlight.' His argument prevailed, and continues to have a strong influence on marketing today.

For example, consider a typical briefing for an advertising campaign – at its core is usually something called 'the (value) proposition'. How do we position ourselves in the brain of our consumer? What is the message that needs to stick?

Or, as Jack Trout put it, 'differentiate or die'.

All this assumes we consume advertising in an engaged way, and that these messages do a good job of persuading us. However, decades of research into what is now called 'behavioural economics' has taught us that our brains don't like putting in the effort required to do all that. Given the chance, our brain will choose the path of least resistance, preferring simple 'tricks' or mechanisms to get through the task at hand.

In other words, we are lazy when it comes to thinking.

So, if we as marketers are able to make it easier for consumers to choose our brand, we are saving the brain from the hard work of having to weigh up options and make tough decisions.

It might even turn into a sale – think one-click (re)buying, on- and offline ordering, one-size-fits-all, home delivery or on-the-go packs. Or consider the purple chocolate bar, the car with the four rings, the ads with George Clooney, or the brand that keeps telling us to Just Do It.

Whether your product is bought from a shelf or a screen, you will benefit if your message is recognisable and distinct – for one thing, it will reduce the risk of you advertising for your competitor(s).

Shopping is quick, both online or offline, and decisions are usually made in a few seconds.

That doesn't mean people don't think at all about what they want from brands – it's just that they think rather little, and mostly very generally. The people who know a lot about your brand or category are greatly outnumbered by those who don't, not least because we don't need a lot of information to make satisfactory brand choices.

'Satisfactory', because optimising our choices would require a huge amount of work – would you really compare all the available television brands out there before making your purchase?

Our brain simply doesn't like to have to make a lot of choices.

Walk over to your fridge or kitchen cabinet and look at the brands in there. Look out the window and check out your car, bicycle or lawn mower. Go through your papers and check who offered you your mortgage or travel insurance. What brand are the jeans you're wearing?

Ask yourself what you actually know about these companies.

Do you know what drives them? Is it clear to you what they (read: the management) have defined as their company culture – probably at the end of a two-day session? What is *their raison d'être,* Big Hairy Audacious Goal, WHY or so-called purpose?

And most importantly, did it make you buy the brand?

Purposeful positioning assumes that we make the effort to understand and think about what a company stands for, that brands can differentiate themselves upon it, and that this is the reason we choose it over others. Richard Shotton's chapter, 'Marketing utopia', convincingly disproves the flaws in this reasoning. But it also goes against the whole idea of branding: to reduce cognitive effort, by making it easier for people to buy.

For most people, the main thing on their mind when they're in a supermarket is how to get out of there as quickly as possible. Retailers and brands that facilitate this will be favoured over those that don't – they've made it easier for people to shop and buy. So, people can get on with their lives.

Purpose is a notion that fits well in a time where we believe it is important to be transparent, sustainable, authentic and responsible. And who would dispute a company's desire to make the world a better place?

However, what people think and do are two very different things. Most people would be appalled by the working conditions under which most of our shoes and clothes are produced, yet we still buy cheap clothing by the truckload from the big chains. Most people would be horrified by the living conditions of the animals in our food industry, yet we continue to toss meat and dairy products into our shopping baskets each week.

Marketers can still learn a lot from their clients' buying behaviour – Keep It Simple Stupid.

References

Feldwick, P. *The Anatomy of Humbug: How to think differently about advertising.* Matador, 2015

Kahneman, D. *Thinking, Fast and Slow.* Farrar, Straus and Giroux, 2011

Packard, V. *The Hidden Persuaders: An introduction to the techniques of mass-persuasion through the unconscious.* Longmans, Green & Co, 1957

Reeves, R. *Reality in Advertising.* Alfred Knopf, 1961

Ries, A, and Trout, J. *Positioning: The battle for your mind.* McGraw-Hill, 1980

Romaniuk, J, and Sharp, B. *How Brands Grow: Part 2.* OUP, 2015

Schwartz, B. *The Paradox of Choice: Why more is less.* Harper Perennial, 2004

Sharp, B. *How Brands Grow: What marketers don't know.* OUP, 2010

Sorensen, H. *Inside the Mind of the Shopper: The science of retailing.* Prentice Hall, 2009

30

ALL YOU NEED IS EMOTION. REALLY?

'If we can't make people cry, we have lost. It's about emotion'
Lorraine Twohill, SVP Global Marketing, Google

Written by **Phil Barden**

This chapter takes a deeper look at the science of emotion, why emotional communication can help to sell, and how emotions really relate to actual purchase decisions.

Emotions have been the marketing hot topic in recent times, with increasing and exciting evidence that emotionally engaging communication correlates with positive impact on sales. This correlation is intuitively plausible, and creatively liberating, which is why this notion is heavily embraced by marketing and agencies. Moreover, it has rapidly given rise to a whole range of new tools designed to help marketers measure the emotional impact of their communication through, for example, facial expression, biometrics or an EEG (electroencephalogram).

As much as we may be excited by the correlation (and naturally inclined to believe in the 'emotion is everything' narrative), we also know many confounding cases where 'they love the ad, but it is just not selling...' Take, for example, the much-lauded Budweiser Puppies ad which ran in the 2015 Super Bowl. According to Jorn Socquet, the US vice president for marketing at A-B InBev, while everybody loved the puppies, 'they have zero impact on beer sales'.

Wherever there is something we want to believe, there is increasing risk of oversimplification and myth creation. How many times have you heard that '95% of decisions are driven by emotion' and that 'System 1 is all about emotion'? Science tells a very different (and much more helpful) story. Rigorous scientific analysis provides a more precise understanding of emotions, and of how exactly they relate to purchase decisions.

This level of precision is important because, if marketing is ultimately about shaping behaviour in favour of our brands, the winners will be those who best understand the true dynamics of behaviour, and how to use this to brief for effective communications.

What is this thing called emotion?

Most of us think we have a pretty good idea of what emotions are – it is 'good' to be 'in touch with your emotions', but bad to be 'too emotional'. Someone senior in the office 'lacks emotional intelligence', and on a weak day, we 'let our emotions get the better of us'. A dramatic week might be an 'emotional rollercoaster'. In everyday life we use the term emotion to express many different things. But to use emotions effectively in marketing we need a more precise understanding. So, what actually is this thing called emotion, from a scientific perspective?

First and foremost, emotions are a physiological response to something we experience or anticipate. Our brain continuously tries to make predictions about the world around us in order to survive. This helps us to prepare our bodies to cope with the upcoming situation by releasing neurotransmitters, adapting heartbeat, regulating blood pressure and muscle tension accordingly. Hence, the way emotions are measured in science is to measure these physiological responses, for example, heart rate, sweat and respiration. These affective physiological responses are automatic, fast and very basic – to prepare us for fight or flight.

There are two physical dimensions to emotion:

1. **Arousal** – intensity of the body's physiological response.
2. **Valence** – evaluation of whether something is positive or negative.

We like to try and make sense of these physiological sensations, and so we construct 'feelings' based on the emotional response. We attribute different

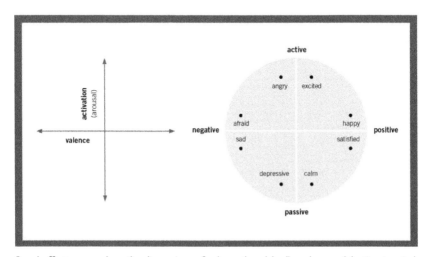

Basal affects occur along the dimensions of valence (good, bad) and arousal (active, passive)

feelings to the same emotional response based on the specific situation we are in, our experience, personality and our cultural background. The feelings are labels we attribute to the emotion experienced. We may frame and describe these feelings as 'love', 'hate', 'jealousy', 'anger' or other descriptors, but the underlying emotion is driven only by the two dimensions of arousal and valence.

So how does emotion drive communication effectiveness?

First, remember that emotional response evolved as a mechanism to prepare our body for fight or flight. If we are in a state of high arousal, our attention span increases and our senses are sharpened to be able to process deeply the object that triggers that arousal (known as 'orientation reaction'). However, sometimes an ad evokes high arousal, but no one remembers the brand – how come? To leverage the potential of the arousal, the brand/product needs to be the agent that triggers the response. If emotional response is not linked to the brand, the ad might be remembered but not the brand, because it is not instrumental in activating the emotional response.

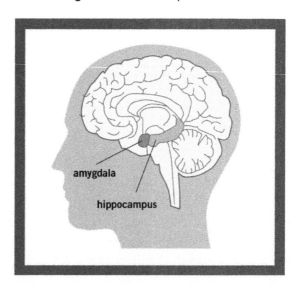

Secondly, due to its deeper processing, emotionally engaging communication is more likely to be remembered. To understand this positive impact on recall we need to look at the brain's geography. The hippocampus (named after its seahorse-like shape) is a brain structure that manages what we store, and where we store it. This structure is positioned right beside the amygdala (named after its almond-like shape) – our emotional centre. This shows the relationship between emotional response and memory formation: to survive, and to optimise future decisions and actions, it was especially important to store and remember those objects and situations that evoked a strong emotional response. This is why we are more likely to store episodes (eg TVCs) and objects (eg brands) if they are delivered with high arousal. So, if an ad is emotionally engaging, we are more likely to store it. This contributes to the recall of the ad, and also increases the mental availability of the brand (assuming the brand is correctly assigned to the ad).

Thirdly, research shows that arousal is a key predictor of sharing creative communication. The higher the arousal, the more likely people are to share. Hence, emotionally engaging ads are more likely to be shared, and this can greatly increase reach.

What about valence? The valence of our experiences with the brand – be it via usage or watching an ad – becomes part of the brand's associative network. Therefore, a communication that evokes a positive emotional response is helpful in building a positive attitude towards the brand. The research cited above also shows that communication creating positive valence is more likely to be shared than negative.

Conclusion: emotions drive advertising effectiveness by increasing depth of processing, memory formation (recall etc) and reach through sharing.

So, all I need is to be sure of emotional advertising, right?

Emotionally engaging communication can be more effective. However, despite the fact that emotions can help communications to be effective, the notion that 'emotion is all that matters' has significant limitations.

Scene from the Budweiser Super Bowl ad

Arousal and positive valence are fundamental, but also very basic dimensions. They do not help to differentiate our brands and products. Valence only provides a basal evaluation (good versus bad), and hence only provides basal differentiation between brands. Which brand doesn't want to be associated with positive emotion?! In any case, most products these days are of adequate quality to be considered 'good'. Indeed, the German consumer organisation Stiftung Warentest gives its quality seal of 'good' to 85% of products they test. As we all know, brand equity is the brand's associative network in consumers' brains, and valence can be a part of this network, but in itself, it's not sufficient to be distinctive or differentiating. Good versus bad does not go far enough in helping consumers to make decisions. So, emotion alone will not contribute to building a distinctive brand in the long run.

In addition, whilst emotionality is relatively easy to achieve in broadcast media, it does not lend itself so well to all brand touchpoints. Packaging and product development, in particular, need a more precise brief than 'make it positive and high arousal'. Emotion as the key guiding principle does not provide clear guardrails for execution across touchpoints, and hence emotion is not able to ensure a consistent brand experience across touchpoints. But what will the brand stand for, if there is no consistency across touchpoints and over time? The focus on emotional responses can result in generic briefings like 'make people love our brand' or 'bring back love'. But what does that look like? Emotionality does not provide sufficient guidelines for how to implement a coherent and consistent brand experience across touchpoints.

Conclusion: emotional communication helps to increase effectiveness of an ad, but is limited in building a distinctive brand equity, and does not provide sufficient guidance on how to create and implement the marketing mix.

Now for the greatest myth in the argument for emotion

Communication that evokes an emotional response helps us to process, remember and share the ad. So far, so good. But some emotional ads sell, others do not. And how does packaging or instore material influence choice when the emotional response looking at a product on-shelf is rather limited? The idea that consumers will experience the same emotional response in front of the shelf that they experienced while watching the ad is wishful thinking.

While there may be exceptional occasions when we react in a heightened state of emotion, such as hooting a car horn in annoyance, the vast majority of the multitude of decisions we make on a daily basis – getting dressed, having a cup of coffee, feeding the cat, popping out for the newspaper – are conducted at a routine level, with very low associated arousal. In fact, emotions generally do not cause behaviour! There is a link between emotion and behaviour, but correlation must not be mixed up with causality.

This is very counterintuitive, so let us have a deeper look at the science here. Renowned psychologist Roy Baumeister and his team at Florida State University have evaluated more than 3,000 scientific papers dealing with the question of 'Do emotions determine behaviour?' The result was astonishing, and certainly challenges the prevailing view: there is almost no indication in this vast body of scientific literature of a causal relationship between emotion and behaviour, except in extreme cases. Baumeister states that 'emotion is stimulated by actions and outcomes', and in another paper, that 'emotions [are] a feedback system whose influence on behaviour is typically indirect [by] providing feedback and stimulating retrospective appraisal of actions [to] alter guidelines for future behavior'. Emotions are a result of our actions – not the other way around. They provide feedback on whether we are on the right track or not.

But how does that fit with the insight that most decisions are determined by System 1? Doesn't the work of Daniel Kahneman prove that everything is about emotion? No! The notion that 'System 1 = emotion' is an inappropriate oversimplification and misses the point. Take one example: driving a car. In our first driving lesson, we needed to think and control everything we did. It was exhausting and effortful, and we were slow. We acted on System 2, because we had not yet developed intuition. Today, we drive without thinking. But do we drive based on emotion? Hopefully not. Our decisions today are based on intuition. This is what System 1 is about: intuitive, automatic, effortless and fast decision making based on associative processes. System 1 includes both affective and cognitive aspects and tasks.

Another myth is that Harvard Business School's Gerald Zaltman stated that '95% of our decisions are based on emotion'. He actually stated that '95% of thinking takes place in our unconscious minds'. Mixing up intuitive, implicit, unconscious processes with emotion is just wrong.

You might also have heard about 'Elliott', the famous patient of Professor Antonio Damasio. This patient suffered from a trauma in the frontal lobe, damaging an area called the OFC (Orbito-Frontal Cortex); this damage made it impossible for him to make decisions. However, Elliott could still experience emotions, but could no longer make decisions. As Damasio said, 'The machinery for his decision making was so flawed that he could no longer be an effective social being.' Damasio's main concept is 'somatic markers'. He used skin conductance during a gambling task as a measurement of somatic markers – hence he measured arousal. According to Damasio, these somatic markers are hypothesised as positive or negative input signals to decision making. Damasio's hypothesis has been interpreted by many as meaning that emotion is the basis of all decision making. However, Damasio himself later conceded, 'We caution against the idea that emotion-based signals "decide" for us, other than in extreme situations'.

Conclusion: emotional communication helps to make communication more effective as a vehicle to ensure processing of the content of an ad, but the emotional response when watching the ad as such does not drive the purchase decision, because emotions generally do not cause decisions and choice.

Let's now have a deeper look at what drives choice, and what the role of emotions in decision making really is.

If emotions don't drive our decisions, what does?

Let's look at some more concrete findings on how consumers make purchase decisions. In an article in *St. Gallen Review* in 2018, researchers wanted to understand which brain systems corresponded with actual sales. The visuals overleaf were used in store and sales were measured.

Which visual triggered more sales? Applying the notion of emotion, we might choose the 'couple' (Visual A). But, in fact, Visual B triggered the highest sales in store. Why? Brain scans showed which brain regions corresponded with actual in-market sales. The region that explained actual sales is the same part of the brain that was damaged in Damasio's patient Elliott, making him unable to make decisions: the OFC. Looking into this area, and what it does,

Visual A　　　　　　　　　　*Visual B*

shows us what actually drives brand choice. In a nutshell, this system assigns value to choices based on our current goals and needs, which is why the activation of this region determines choice, sales and willingness to pay. How does that work?

Imagine you are in a restaurant, you're hungry and you flip through the menu. You adore a good burger, so your emotional response to the burger on the menu is high and positive. However, the moment you decide, your emotional system shuts down and the OFC is activated. You could choose the burger, but maybe you are on a diet, and although you have a strong emotional connection with the burger, you opt instead for a salad. In both cases, the OFC will be the gatekeeper. The OFC assigned a goal value or reward value to the items on the menu based on their fit with your current goals. If your goal is to indulge yourself, then you'll have the burger, but if you want to lose weight, the OFC will assign a higher goal value to salad as a choice.

Behaviour is driven by the *expected value of a choice*. In very general terms, this value is a function of the experienced or expected discrepancy between the actual (current) state and the desired state. This discrepancy is what makes us do things, this is what motivates us (from the Latin verb 'movere' meaning 'to move'). If you feel hungry, you will start searching for food. If you have just eaten, then the best food in town will not motivate you to eat because there is no discrepancy between your desired state and your actual state. In other words, there is no need. It is the discrepancy from our desired state (goals) that determines the value of choices. You might love doughnuts, but you may have gained weight over the years, and this state increases the discrepancy with your desired goal state of self-esteem and feeling attractive.

So, you are motivated to go on a diet, and hence the reward system will assign a lower value to the doughnut. Once you have lost weight, your goal of feeling attractive is achieved, and so your goal of losing weight is deactivated because there is no discrepancy anymore. At this point, the doughnut gets a higher value again (unfortunately).

Motivation – unlike emotion – always has a target component, an outcome that we want to achieve. Behaviour in general, and consumer behaviour in particular, is 'goal-directed behaviour': we purchase brands and products to achieve the desired state, goals, needs or Job/s To Be Done (JTBD). Motivation actually determines what we purchase. Because it assigns value based on how rewarding the brain expects this choice to be, this system is referred to as the 'reward system', and it is the core of motivation. And this value expectation is based on the associations that we build with the choice over time. This explains why, in the Duplo example above, Visual B sold more. In this case, the distinctive reward of the brand is 'sharing', which is communicated more strongly in Visual B.

These motivating discrepancies between desired and actual state might be very basic (hunger), utilitarian (get from A to B), hedonistic (treat yourself with something sweet), social (get recognition), or we might want to change the mood we are in (pamper yourself with something warm). Regulating a mood state or feeling can of course motivate us to do something about it.

People who feel lonely use warmer water, and take longer, when they shower. People who are sad are more likely to help others. When we feel miserable we may turn to food or buy unnecessary luxuries. In this case, the experienced discrepancy activates the goal to change this bad mood. Therefore, products that are instrumental in lifting our mood get a high goal value. But a note of caution: the motivation to change our mood must not be mixed up with the emotional response while watching an ad.

This differentiation is important because it forces us to distinguish between, on the one hand, the emotional response evoked by an ad, and on the other, the message/value proposition of the brand as a means to reduce an expected or experienced discrepancy. Communication needs to dramatise that the brand is an effective means to close this gap, achieve the desired outcome, goal and JTBD – whether it be on a functional, social or mood level.

Conclusion: motivation is what makes us do things – not emotion. We choose the option with the highest goal value. The value is high if our product and brands are perceived to be an effective means to close the experienced or expected discrepancy between what we want to do, have, be or become (our goals) and our actual state.

So where does emotion fit in actual decision making?

Our current desires, needs, goals and JTBD drive our behaviour, and this is managed by the reward system in the brain. But in order to learn (and to guide future choices), we also need a feedback system that tells us if the choices we made were appropriate. This is where emotion fits in. Emotions are the feedback mechanism by which we gauge (via conscious 'feeling') the extent to which we are meeting our goals. So first we decide (or buy), then we experience an emotion that tells us if this was a good decision or not. As stated earlier, our brains are in a constant state of prediction, and these prediction errors (whether positive or negative) will result either in positive or negative affect.

When we achieve our desired goal, we experience happiness, joy, positive surprise or calm, whereas non-achievement causes us to experience anger, sadness and anxiety. In each case, the emotion is a *result of*, and not a *trigger for*, behaviour. This was largely discovered through the extensive work of Charles Carver and Michael Scheier, world-famous motivation psychologists, who identified that we experience emotions whenever the likelihood of achieving a goal changes. By way of example, when we are playing tennis with the goal of winning the match, and we are about to lose an important point, we feel emotions such as anger and frustration. When we turn it around and look set to win, we feel happy, proud and powerful. The intensity of the emotion depends on how important the goal is to us. If we really want to win the tennis game, we might get very angry when our partner misses a shot. If we don't mind so much, we will shrug our shoulders, smile and say 'never mind' or 'unlucky'.

Put simply, in the words of Roy Baumeister, 'Emotion serves as an inner mechanism to reward and punish behaviors'. If a behaviour leads to negative emotion, we can retrain ourselves and avoid this behaviour in the future. For example, if we go to a restaurant and have a bad meal, we feel disappointment (or even shame if we are entertaining others), and hence we 'learn' to avoid that restaurant in the future. If a behaviour leads to positive emotion, we learn to repeat the behaviour.

So how do I use all of this?

As we have seen, emotional communication is an effective vehicle, but it is not the message. To impact behaviour, we first need a message that increases the perceived goal value of our brand; a message that shows that the brand is instrumental in helping us to achieve our goals. In short, a message that positions the brand as an effective means to a desired end: if you use this brand, you can accomplish the desired state and achieve the desired outcome. These outcomes can be functional, social or mood states and feelings. A shampoo can repair the hair (functional), can make you admired (social), and so you treat yourself (mood) with the shampoo because it has these precious ingredients. The goal value will drive behaviour, and this message must be consistently landed across all touchpoints.

In order to increase the impact of communications, in appropriate media, the power of emotional response should be leveraged in order to optimise attention, recall and increase the likelihood of sharing. Let's look at some key points for how to do this. First, to make sure we maximise the impact of our communication, we need to get the WHAT and the HOW right:

The WHAT *Motivation*	Achieved? ✓ ✗	The HOW *emotionally engaging*	Achieved? ✓ ✗
Does the brief include a message that links the brand and relevant goals?		Does the communication evoke an emotional response?	
Is this message distinctive to your brand?		Does the brand/product play an instrumental role in the ad?	
Does the communication stage the brand as a means to this end? (with this brand you can do/have/be/become…)?		Does the brand play an instrumental role in evoking the emotion in a credible way?	
		Does it leverage the brand's iconic assets to ensure correct brand assignment?	

How do I know if I am landing this?

There are many tools around that measure emotion. It is important to remember that these are measuring 'affect' evoked by the communication (the HOW), but they do not capture whether the message (the WHAT) is motivating, and hence, if it will ultimately drive behaviour.

Consider the following: every year the John Lewis Christmas ad is eagerly awaited by a broad public (way beyond the marketing community) and is used as further evidence of the power of emotional advertising. What makes John Lewis advertising succeed is that both the message of the ad and the driver of the emotion are fundamentally and credibly rooted in unique truths of the John Lewis brand: their dedication to understanding their customers' needs and lives, and their ability to deliver a product range that perfectly meets these needs. Let's look at the 2017 ad using the checklist.

The WHAT *Motivation*	Comment	Achieved? ✓ ✗
Does the brief include a message that links the brand and relevant goals?	Ad links to the certainty that John Lewis provides of finding exactly the right gift for Christmas that will make your loved ones happy	✓
Is this message distinctive to your brand?	The message leverages the quality and breadth of the John Lewis range	✓
Does the communication stage the brand as a means to this end? (with this brand you can do/have/be/become…)?	The communication leverages JL's expert understanding of its customers' needs	✓

The HOW *emotionally engaging*	Comment	Achieved? ✓ ✗
Does the communication evoke an emotional response?	Yes, raises arousal with positive valence and is widely talked about	✓
Does the brand/product play an instrumental role in the ad?	Yes, the brand resolves the narrative tension of the exhaustion caused by the boy's nocturnal friendship with Moz the monster	✓
Does the brand play an instrumental role in evoking the emotion in a credible way?	Yes, Moz is a JL creation (available in store) and all the interaction between the boy, Moz and his parents involves JL products	✓
Does it leverage the brand's iconic assets to ensure correct brand assignment?	JL Xmas ad has become an iconic asset (through tone and narrative style). Distinctive font and logo appear at the end	✓

Conclusion

There is a common feeling that communication which triggers an emotional response increases its effectiveness because emotional response attracts attention and deepens processing of the communication. This leads to the 'emotion is everything' narrative in the marketing community. But acting on this oversimplification carries the risk of ending up creating an ad which people love, but which does not sell the product.

Science clearly shows that there is a gatekeeper that stands between an emotional ad and actual brand choice: motivation. Motivation, not the emotional response while watching the ad, is what makes people do something – and motivation is very different from emotion.

Motivation – our desires, needs, goals and JTBD – determines behaviour and choice. In fact, actual behaviour is *not* caused by emotion – emotion is a feedback mechanism that tells us if the decision we made brought us closer to our desired state or outcomes.

Motivation to buy a product develops if the ad stages the product as an effective means to get a 'job' done. A job can be functional and/or psychological or social. The desire to change our mood can also be a job that products help to accomplish.

An emotional response triggered by an ad can make the ad a more effective vehicle for the motivational message, but the emotional response while watching the ad is only a response – it is not the message in itself.

To impact sales, an ad needs to convey the right motivational message (the WHAT) in an emotionally engaging way (the HOW). Successful ads deliver on both.

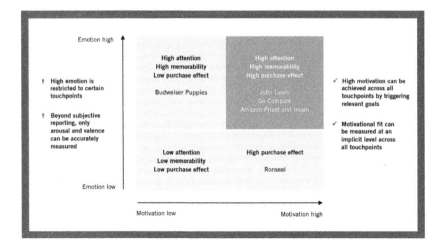

The two pillars of effective advertising: emotional response while watching the ad, and motivation

In briefs, agencies are often asked to create an emotional ad. While that is not wrong, if there is no motivating message, the impact on sales will be random.

In addition, the objective to evoke an emotional response does not guide implementation across touchpoints. What does emotionally engaging packaging look like? Which shapes and colours should be used? Which testimonial delivers the right message? And if every brand works to the brief of 'emotion', how can we create consistency across touchpoints and build a distinctive brand equity over time?

References

Bargh, JA, and Shalev, I. 'The substitutability of physical and social warmth in daily life'. *Emotion*, 12(1), 2012

Barrett, L Feldman. *How Emotions are Made: The secret life of the brain.* Macmillan, 2017

Baumeister, RF, et al. 'Does emotion cause behavior (apart from making people do stupid, destructive things)?' In Agnew et al, *Then a Miracle Occurs: Focusing on behavior in social psychological theory and research*, OUP, 2009

Baumeister RF, et al. 'How emotion shapes behavior: feedback, anticipation, and reflection, rather than direct causation'. *Personality and Social Psychology Review*, 11(2), 2007

Camerer, C, Loewenstein, G, and Prelec, D. 'Neuroeconomics: how neuroscience can inform economics'. *Journal of Economic Literature*, 43(1), 2005

Falk, E, et al. 'Creating buzz: the neural correlates of effective message propagation'. *Psychological Science.* 24(7), 2013

Letters to the editor. *Nature Neuroscience*, 5(11), 2002

Strelow, E, and Scheier, C. 'Uncovering the why of consumer behavior. From neuroscience to implementation'. *Marketing Review St. Gallen*, 1, 2018

Zaltman, G. *How Customers Think: Essential insights into the mind of the market.* Harvard Business School Press, 2003

3

MADVERTISING, BADVERTISING AND SADVERTISING FOR MAD, BAD AND SAD PEOPLE

Written by **Adam Ferrier**

'I've seen George Foreman shadow boxing and the shadow won'

Muhammad Ali

What is it about marketing that continues to scream inauthenticity? So much of it is so glossy and shiny. Well, as Batman once said to Robin, 'The brighter the picture the darker the negative'. This chapter explores an alternative to the high gloss approach.

The *Diagnostic and Statistical Manual of Mental Disorders*, 5th edition (*DSM-5*) is the latest edition of the American Psychiatric Association's bible, or 'classification and diagnostic tool'. This tool has previously wreaked havoc with its tendency to pathologise the normal (for example, homosexuality was in the earlier editions of the *DSM*), and make lay people neurotic, as just about everyone fits some disorder or other in this much abused tome. However, around the world the *DSM* is the universal authority for psychiatric and psychological diagnoses of all types.

In the middle of the book are what have always been my favourite bit of the *DSM*: the 10 personality disorders. A personality disorder, unlike a simple phobia or a time-limited mood disorder, is a persistent maladaptive set of behaviours that impact one's entire personality – to the point it causes harm to the self or others. These personality disorders come in three shades, or clusters:

- Cluster A – is the odd or eccentric cluster featuring Paranoid, Schizoid, Schizotypal PDs. They tend to be disorganised, erratic, unkempt, and have extreme difficulty staying on top of things.
- Cluster B – is the self-involved and emotional cluster, and includes Borderline, Narcissistic, Histrionic and Antisocial disorders. They tend to be self-serving and somewhat manipulative.
- Cluster C – is the anxious, fearful cluster, and includes Avoidant, Dependent and Obsessive Compulsive disorders. These people can be somewhat withdrawn, and have trouble coping.

Psychologists colloquially (and somewhat pejoratively) refer to these three personality clusters as 'Mad', 'Bad' and 'Sad'.

One of the reasons the personality disorders held such an interest to me (and other psychologists I hope) is their inherent relatability. All of us feel like we are at least a little bit mad, bad or sad from time to time. Further, when examining the diagnostic criteria within each of these PDs, it's more than normal to spot your own personality within each of them, and exclaim excitedly, 'I do that'. This is indeed an inevitable consequence of giving newly minted psychologists their first copies of the DSM.

The reason why we can so quickly spot various traits we have in ourselves is that the disorders, although presented as 'categorical' in the DSM, are indeed more aptly on a continuum. That is, we are all occasionally a little bit mad, bad or sad. Some of us may in fact be mad all the time – just not to the extent needed to meet the official cut-off score. This issue has vexed many clinicians, as again the DSM boxes people in, whereas it should ideally be talking about tendencies.

Approximately 15% of the population meet the criteria for a diagnosable personality disorder; however, it is closing in on all of us as many of us meet some (but not all) of the conditions of a personality disorder much of the time, ie we all have a touch of mad, bad and sad within us. As a very smart superhero once said, probably while channelling Jung, 'The brighter the picture the darker the negative'. That superhero was Batman, and he was giving a lesson in helping us understand that we all have a dark side; we all have impulses that drive us towards maladaptive behaviours – it's just a question of degree as to who gets a diagnosis and who doesn't.

Thanks for the lesson in the *DSM* – but what has all of this got to do with marketing?

As Rory Sutherland said in Amsterdam at a TEDx conference, 'The next revolution will be psychological not technological'. If this is true, then a good place to start wold be to examine the pre-existing frameworks that exist within the world of psychology – hence my turning to the *DSM*.

Another useful framework that psychologists largely agree upon is emotions, and primarily our tendency to be attracted towards the negative. Of our six primary emotions – joy, surprise, fear, disgust, sadness and anger – two-thirds (four) are negative, only one is positive (joy) and one is both, 'surprise'. This model, originally developed by Paul Eckman, has been studied widely and upheld across cultures; it basically says that our emotions were developed to react more negatively than positively. The reason for this was that being scared of the tiger in the tree, or spitting the poison out of our mouths with disgust, was more important for survival than admiring a lovely flower with joy.

Most emotions have cognitions built into them (I'm now on very shaking ground as this stuff is too complicated for a consumer psychologist like me), but suffice to say the cognitive mirror to our negative emotions is our inbuilt negativity bias. That is, we tune into negative stimuli more readily than the equivalent positive or neutral stimuli. Negative information requires us to spend more effort and resources to process, and therefore doesn't slip through our brain as quickly. We stop and notice, and process the negative.

So, we're all a little bit mad, bad and sad, and have more negative emotions than positive ones. We are also kind of 'hard wired' to pay attention to (and remember) negative information far quicker than positive or neutral information. This sounds like the kind of information those in the communications industry should be all over – and they are. However, it's not the marketing communications industry that's taking these findings up with abandon, it's other communications industries such as…

The media industry: clickbait is the result of media brands doing what they know works – appealing to the negative rather than the positive. This was researched by Mark Trussler and Stuart Soroka, who found that news stories were written in negative fashion with negative headlines because that's what (in controlled conditions) people chose to read over the equivalent positive stories. Their results suggested that behavioural results do not conform with people's attitudinal preferences, ie even if participants say they prefer to read positive stories, it's not true as they exhibit a preference for negative news content. Clickbait exists because we click it.

The entertainment industry: a classic forensic psychology book by Robert Simon called *Bad Men Do What Good Men Dream* posits that many people have the urge to commit crime, but we learn not to for fear of imagined and real consequences. However, what sticks is a fascination with criminal behaviour. From Netflix's *Making a Murderer* to HBO's *The Jinx*, and *Serial Season 1*, about the case of convicted murderer Adnan Syed, the universal popularity of crime is large.

Politics: negative advertising has been the hallmark of political advertising for many years. Political science has found merit in appealing to the negative. People will be more motivated to vote against a candidate if they receive negative information about them than they will vote for a candidate with the equal amount of positive information. People tend to be more motivated to vote against a candidate because of negative information than they are to vote for a candidate because of positive information.

There is obviously plenty of evidence through all forms of culture for the psychological embrace of the negativity effect. Indeed, I suspect the title of this chapter would make it much more likely to be read than an equivalent paper suggesting you market to the positives.

Why, then, has marketing communications for so long largely shunned such a large area of human motivation?

Probably for at least a couple of reasons. First, because marketing has never had to be that good – just advertising on broadcast communications was seemingly enough. Most marketers would rely on the category drivers for consumption occasions, and use advertising to create mental availability – thereby picking up a sizable slice of the market. What was important wasn't whether the advertising was good or not, but simply if you chose to advertise or not.

The second reason the darker themes mentioned above have not been embraced is because of the mistaken (or outdated) believe that brands are often used as psychological props to communicate to others who we want to be, rather than who we actually are. A consumer psychologist once said AS + B = IS (Actual Self + Brand = Ideal Self), therefore the role of the brand was to help fix the gap between who I am versus who I want to be.

However, in many developed markets (as opposed to developing markets) the role of brands and advertising has changed. Many brands in developing markets are full of cheesy smiles and fake characters. However, in developed markets the current paradigm is for more reality to be used. Real characters, real brands – 'real' is on every brand wheel in the country. Consumers are yearning for real, and are arguably looking for brands to reflect more of who they are, not who they want to be.

So, with this let's again consider the mad, bad and sad that lurks within each of us. If the next revolution is going to be psychological, then surely we are going to get better at creating brands that connect with people – and these brands may start taping into these themes. Even at a seemingly superficial level, the above data suggests that brands with a negative message will:

1. Generate more attention (according to our inbuilt negativity bias) and further this space (the mad, bad and sad).
2. Create more room for both distinctive and differentiated brands, as so many brands are still currently obsessed with portraying positive and unrealistic portrayals of life.
3. At a stretch, offer the opportunity to innovate at a category level, rather than a brand level. Creating a new category can be a shortcut to growth rather than eking out market share.

So, how to do it?

I'm now going to reverse-engineer this paper and give examples of brands tapping into negative themes by arbitrarily assigning them within the categories of Mad, Bad or Sad. But just like inter-rater reliability within each of the personality disorders is low, so too would be the attribution of these thoughts to these categories. It's more to just illustrate the idea.

Mad

First, here I'm talking about mad as in a little unhinged as opposed to angry. A little unhinged means we're talking about a brand which finds it difficult to present perfectly, and carries with it many errors. This is an area of behavioural economics referred to as 'blemishing', as coined by Baba Shiv and Zakary Tormala. Their research has found that desirability for brands increases when the brands are presented as slightly imperfect in some way. This research is also supported by the real-world case study of Monteith's Cider in NZ, where the ciders rolled off the production lines with twigs in the packaging. The perceived mistakes in the packaging led to consumers believing the cider was fresher and more natural.

Bad

Controversy is a sure-fire way to get attention. It's easy to outrage, and a hungry 24-hour news cycle needs to be fed. Hence being naughty, rude and risqué are all well-trodden strategies within marketing today. Ads that use a 'shock factor' have indeed been proven to evoke stronger feelings among consumers, to increase attention, and to be coded into memory more strongly; they even positively influence behaviour. Other studies have questioned the effectiveness of controversial tactics such as shock. As a personal anecdote, I've used it to great effect on several campaigns and ideas I've worked on, including an idea that created a fictitious marketing company on behalf of a streetwear brand called 'Golf Punk'. The fictitious marketing company was called 'Hypno-marketing', and promised to hypnotise people to fall in love with brands, and keep on loving that brand forever. You can see the fun case study here https://www.youtube.com/watch?v=USm2CZz9ERE.

Sad

Perhaps my favourite case study of recent years has been the Domino's turnaround in the United States. In around 2008, Domino's began doing focus groups with consumers who complained of their pizzas tasting like cardboard, and talking about all the things Domino's did wrong. Domino's then used the footage saying their pizzas tasted like shit in their TVCs, accompanied by an apology from their CEO. This 'apologising for everything' strategy has now been rolled out to other markets around the world. Domino's has significantly increased its market share, and its share price since 2008 has quadrupled.

Apologising, being sad, expressing negative emotion – again, all this is just another way to get people's attention.

Conclusion

In conclusion, our innate tendency to be mad, bad and sad has perhaps been underexploited by marketers to date. This is especially true when you see how fiercely other forms of communications (media, entertainment and politics) have pursued negativity. There is strong psychological evidence to suggest that the mad, bad and sad are fruitful areas of communications for marketers to consider, and as marketing sciences become more prominent in advertising, there will be increasing evidence to pursue these themes for brand growth.

'The unexamined life is not worth living', as Socrates would have it – perhaps brands will allow us to reveal our dark sides a little more often?

References

Dahl, DW, et al. 'Does it pay to shock? Reactions to shocking and nonshocking advertising content among university students'. *Journal of Advertising Research*, 43, 2003

Davis, JL. 'Personality disorders affect 15% of Americans'. 2004

Hamlin, JK, and Baron, A. 'Agency attribution in infancy: evidence for a negativity bias'. *PLoS ONE* 9(5), 2014

Handel, S. 'Classification of emotion', 2002

Klein, JG. 'Negativity effects in impression formation: a test in the political arena'. *Personality and Social Psychology Bulletin*, 17(4), 1991

Simon, R. *Bad Men Do What Good Men Dream: A forensic psychiatrist illuminates the darker side of human behaviour.* American Psychiatric Publishing, revised edition, 2008

Shiv, B, and Tormala, Z. 'When blemishing leads to blossoming: the positive effect of negative information'. *Journal of Consumer Research*, 38(5), 2012

Sutherland, R. 'Rory Sutherland: The next revolution will be psychological, not technological'. TEDx Conference, Amsterdam, 2012

Trussler, M, and Soroka, S. 'Consumer demand for cynical and negative news frames'. *The International Journal of Press/Politics*, 19(3), 2014

32

WHAT I LEARNT FROM JOHN WEBSTER

Written by **Paul Feldwick**

John Webster was a giant in advertising, but not one too lofty to impart his wisdom, as this chapter reveals.

I worked with John Webster at Boase Massimi Pollitt (BMP) in London mostly during the 1970s and '80s, when he was at the height of his powers. He was throughout that time the most awarded creative in the world – the Lions and Arrows crowded unceremoniously on the shelves in his modest office, gathering dust. I was, to start with at least, the most junior of account planners. Yet he treated me, as he treated all of us, with unfailing respect – more than that, he always seemed genuinely interested in what we had to say, whether we were reporting back from research or offering our own interpretations and opinions.

And I think that leads me to the first thing I learnt from working with John: that the best work emerges from keeping the conversation open, rather than closing it down. John's starting point would always come out of a dialogue with the account team, rather than the written brief (in the early days, we didn't even have a creative briefing form at BMP). And from that point on, John was always curious, always experimenting – the clay, so to speak, was always still wet. When stuck, he would go and talk to whoever happened to be around (after hours, that was often the security guard), and that conversation would give him the opening he needed to go on. Talking about the work was for John not a threat, but always an opportunity. After all, he didn't have to agree with what anyone else said. But as he didn't feel the need to be defensive, ideas were allowed to emerge from the conversation which John would not have arrived at in isolation.

John was especially interested in research, because it was more important for him to create work that would get talked about excitedly in the pub or the playground than it was to win yet another award (those kept coming anyway). If real people didn't enjoy what he'd written, or it rubbed them up the wrong way, he'd try and find a way to recast the ad so that it worked. In this way, the Honey Monster (for Sugar Puffs) became large and cuddly rather than small and annoying, or Arkwright (in the John Smith's campaign) was transformed from a lonely wife-beating alcoholic into a wily old philosopher. So, it was always a rewarding experience to sit in John's office, as he asked questions like 'Can you tell me a bit more about what you mean?' or 'How would it be if I tried it like this?' And then listened in deep thought as you answered.

The other big thing I learnt from John is the importance of craft. There's a universal fashion now to talk about the importance of 'creative ideas'. If that means that good campaigns always have some kind of internal logic and coherence to them (even if that's hard to put into words), I'll maybe agree. But very often it sounds as if having the 'idea' is the only difficult, 'creative' bit, and the rest is mere 'execution'. People respond to ads, however, not to abstract ideas: ads that exist in the full details of how they look, how they sound, the timing of the edit, the camera angles, the soundtrack, the lighting, every nuance of sets and propping and casting... and so on. If there's such a thing as a 'creative idea' (which I doubt, though I don't have room here to get too philosophical), we only know about it because of the execution that embodies it.

And John, it seems to me, never thought about ideas as separate from the details of execution. Unusually for an agency art director, he could write beautiful, hilarious, poetic copy; even more unusually, he could draw really rather well. From the outset, he would imagine a commercial as Mozart imagined a new symphony – in full detail – and would present it as a drawn storyboard in which each shot was already composed in his imagination, complete with dialogue and music. Often, much of this would change as the ad developed – either in response to research, or talking about it, or just because

John himself woke up one morning with a better idea. But in remarkably many cases, those very early storyboards would show an uncanny resemblance to the finished film. John's work was what it was because he approached it as Picasso would begin a painting: not as an abstract thought that he was trying to illustrate, but as a tangible creation that existed in the real world and in real time. The reason John's work still looks so fresh today, the reason we still admire so much of what he did, is not that he had better 'ideas' than anyone else. It's because he made better ads.

33

THE DEVALUATION OF CREATIVITY

Written by **Bob Hoffman**

The one thing every successful marketer needs – and the one thing agencies can provide better than anyone else – is imaginative ideas about brands. But we have lost our focus, asserts this article, and need to convince marketers once again that the most effective way to build brands is through the unique and unmatched power of great creative ideas.

Excerpted from a speech at the IAPI/ADFX awards in Dublin, Ireland, 2016

Thank you for inviting me here tonight.

I'm not usually invited to speak at high class affairs like this. I usually get invited to horrifying events like the 'The programmatic real-time digital insider summit', or some other majestically titled festival of horseshit.

But thankfully, tonight is different. Tonight, you are recognising the best of Irish advertising. And I am honoured to help you do that.

I love good advertising. I started my career as a copywriter. After a while I got myself promoted to creative director for a few agencies. And after proving myself to be an utter failure as a creative director, I was demoted to CEO.

But the one thing I always really wanted to be was a great copywriter. Sadly, my copywriting career consisted mostly of holiday weekend mattress sales and low, low financing on every Corolla in stock.

Despite my mediocrity, doing creative work was the only thing that really interested me about advertising. The rest was torture.

As far as I was concerned, the agency business worked like this: the creative people made the ads and everyone else made the arrangements.

What I could never understand was why it took five times as many people to make the arrangements.

I guess you could say I was a creative department chauvinist. And to be honest, I still am.

We are here tonight to celebrate effectiveness in advertising.

I know how hard you clients, and you account people, and planners, and data analysts, and media strategists worked for the awards you're getting tonight, and I congratulate you.

But I want you to know in advance, that I'm not going to be speaking about you. I am going to be focusing on the contribution that our creative people make to advertising effectiveness. And the peril they, and we, are facing.

Regardless of how brilliant the briefs we write are, and the strategies we develop are, and the plans we implement are, at the end of the line are the people who will take our plans and strategies and briefs and turn them into magic, or turn them into trash. They're our creatives.

For better or worse, the consumer never sees the briefing documents or the strategic rationale. All she ever sees are the ads. And if the ads stink, the whole thing stinks.

Over the past few years I have been doing a lot of travelling and speaking about advertising. Wherever I go in the world, I invariably hear the same two themes: first is that advertising has become less effective, and second is that advertising is less creative.

It is hard for me to believe that these two things are not related.

The problem we are facing today, I'm afraid, is that the creative side of our business is being devalued. Creativity is quickly and quietly becoming a support service.

The alarming thing about this is that I believe creativity is the agency business's only unique value to clients. Everything else agencies do clients can get somewhere else.

They can get business strategy from about a million different consulting firms. They can find media planners and buyers on every street corner. They can buy data by the truckload with two clicks of a mouse.

The one thing every successful marketer needs – and the one thing agencies can provide better than anyone else – is imaginative ideas about brands.

But apparently, the advertising industry has decided it can no longer support itself by focusing on creativity.

If you remember the aborted marriage between Omnicom and Publicis, the rationale for creating the biggest agency in the world had nothing at all to do with creativity. The primary reason given for the merger was their presumed ability to compete with Google and Facebook in the collection and utilisation of data.

It seems to me that the agency business is betting its future on playing the other guy's game. I think this is a mistake.

Over 25 years ago I left the agency business for the first time. Two years earlier we had sold our independent agency to a publicly traded 'global' network. And after the two worst years of my life, I decided it was not the life for me.

For three years thereafter, I did creative services on my own directly for clients. In that three-year period being outside of the agency business I learned a very important lesson. Clients, I want you to cover your ears and not listen to this. OK, agency people, here's what I learned: secretly, clients don't like agencies.

They put no value on 'account service' – or as one client told me, 'all it does is keep the agency from fucking up, it doesn't do a thing for me.'

Behind our backs, they chuckled about our 'strategic abilities'.

The value they saw in agencies was in creativity. They believed the only place they could get good ads was from an agency.

But creativity is in trouble.

There's a mantra I hear in agencies back in the States. I don't know if you hear it here, too. But it goes like this: 'We're all creative', or 'creative ideas can come from anywhere'. In my opinion, this is bullshit.

True creative talent is a rare and precious thing.

Have you ever wondered why there are so many shitty songs, and shitty TV shows, and shitty movies? I'll tell you why. Because it is really fucking hard to do a good one.

The same is true with advertising. No one sits down to write a crappy ad. Mostly they just turn out crappy. Why? Because it's really fucking hard to do a good one — and there are very few people who can do it.

If you really believe that we are all creative, then you have to believe that it's just a coincidence that Shakespeare wrote dozens of brilliant plays and Donald Trump didn't.

Now, I stipulate that when we talk about creativity, the word is confusing. It has two very different meanings. And the new bigwigs of advertising are trying their best to muddy the issue by confusing the meanings.

In the first meaning, creativity is seen as a method for accomplishing a practical goal. So, you can approach any task in a creative manner. In this meaning creativity is a way of thinking. So, you can fry an egg the traditional way, or you can be 'creative' and fry it in alligator oil or something.

In the second case, there is a special meaning for the word 'creativity' that is specific to the communication arts. This is the kind of creativity that makes music and art and literature, and yes, sometimes even advertising, extraordinary and delightful.

Sure, the guy who printed the tickets to *Hamlet*, or made the popcorn, or counted the proceeds, may have found creative ways to do so. But he didn't write the fucking play.

That's a whole different kind of creativity. And a whole different meaning of the word.

But the current generation of ad industry kingpins are trying very hard to dilute it into meaninglessness by asserting that we're all creative, and that creativity can come from anywhere.

If you think I am overstating my point, let me read you a quote from Martin Sorrell, the [former] CEO of WPP and the most powerful man in the history of the agency business (and by the way, an accountant by trade):

> *The snottiness of believing that creativity just resides in the creative department of traditional agencies, that media people can't be creative, or data people can't be or people who do healthcare or promotion or CRM can't be creative – it's a nonsense and it's insulting to the people who are in those areas.*

He's equating doing a practical job in a creative manner with creating something unique from scratch. He's saying they are the same thing.

Now, don't get me wrong. I have nothing against account people, or planners, or data people, or CRM people, or anyone else who thinks smartly and does a job in an imaginative way.

But I resent that the talents of our great creative people are being dismissed as the same thing.

This is not healthy for the ad business, nor is it healthy for the people who work in it.

Our industry has been hijacked by aristocrats with private jets. They have made the agency business leaner and meaner. They have made it more efficient. They have made it more productive. They have squeezed all the fat out of it. And in the process, they are also squeezing the life out of it.

They are money managers, and investors and financial wise guys. The one thing they are not is advertising people.

Advertising evolved as an industry of craftsmen and craftswomen. Account people, art directors, researchers, copywriters. People who actually worked on accounts would start their own agencies. There were hundreds of independent, entrepreneurial agencies in every country. When I started in the ad business 300 years ago, the largest agency in the US, Y&R, had about a 1.5% share of market. Today, four global giants control over 70% of US advertising spending.

A while back, Mr Sorrell gave a talk in London. According to press reports, he told the conference...

> ... 'media, has become "more important" than the message...'

This is unacceptable. Someone who believes media is more important than the message, believes the instruments are more important than the music, the canvas is more important than the painting, the bottle is more important than the beer.

It's unacceptable.

I'm worried.

Call me crazy, but I think ad agencies should be run by advertising people. I don't see airlines run by greengrocers. I don't see hospitals run by folk singers.

I am curious why the agency business is being run by bookkeepers.

In an industry led by people who now think delivery systems are more important than what they are delivering, creativity is floundering.

We need to convince marketers once again that the most effective way to build brands is through the unique and unmatched power of great advertising ideas.

In June 2016, the IPA released a report called 'Selling creativity short'. In it they reported that creativity by itself can make a marketing dollar ten times more effective.

We also have to stop deluding ourselves about what we are doing. You know, we talk a lot about our 'target audience'. As a former adman and recent Harvard faculty member Doc Searls says, there is no audience for advertising.

An audience is created by demand.

There is demand for music, so there's an audience for it. There is demand for movies, so there's an audience for them. There is demand for theatre, so there's an audience for it.

The demand for advertising is precisely zero. Nobody is demanding advertising. There is no audience for advertising.

Similarly, the idea that anyone wants to engage with advertising is equally delusional. We engage with people and things we enjoy.

We find books engaging. And music engaging, and dance engaging. And people engaging.

Who in their right mind wants to engage with advertising? On a rainy Sunday afternoon have you ever heard someone say, 'I'm going back to my flat to engage with some advertising'?

Advertising is at best a minor annoyance. Sadly, our obsession with online advertising has turned it into a major annoyance, in fact, a scourge.

It has been reported that over 600 million connected devices are armed with ad blockers. This is the opposite of engagement. This is disengagement on a monumental scale. This is the largest boycott of anything in the history of humanity.

We've got to stop bullshitting ourselves and come to terms with reality.

If we want there to be an audience for advertising, if we want people to be engaged with what we do, we have to do a lot better. We have to make advertising beautiful, and interesting, and entertaining. And I have bad news… algorithms, and data, and metrics can't do that. Only people can do that.

Let's not allow the devaluation of creativity to continue. I'm tired of hearing that advertising isn't as effective as it used to be, or as creative as it used to be. We have so many more amazing tools and amazing media options than we've ever had before for making wonderful advertising. We have much better data. We have much better ways to measure. We have no more excuses.

Let's stand up for what we are celebrating tonight.

Let's appreciate the unique gift of talent and creativity. And make it, once again, the centrepiece of the advertising industry.

Congratulations to tonight's winners. I know how difficult it is to create something really good. I know how hard you worked for what you're about to receive.

Down at the pub you may just be Jimmy or Mary. But to me, you're a hero.

Congratulations, and thank you all very much.

34

BITING THE HAND THAT FEEDS US? WHY ADVERTISING'S LOVE OF NOVELTY IS DOING BRANDS A DISSERVICE

Written by **Kate Waters**

There is good evidence that brands need to create distinctive assets – logos, endlines, visual identity elements etc – in order to strengthen memory structures in the brain and grow mental availability. However, the marketing and communications industry loves and rewards 'novelty'. This chapter argues that this love of original and new thinking, while intended to create more distinctive and cut-through communication for brands, may actually do brands a disservice. Finding new ways to reinforce or build existing assets through imaginative repetition is where our focus should be in order to build strong and resilient brands.

As mentioned in Phil Barden's chapter 'The science of effectiveness', in 2009 PepsiCo invested in a new pack design for its flagship orange juice brand, Tropicana. They hired a well-known design company and briefed them to create a new pack design and integrated marketing campaign that would 'reinforce the brand and product attributes' and 'rejuvenate the category'.

BEFORE AFTER

However, what followed was a disaster that saw Tropicana's sales collapse by 20%, with branded and private-label competitors all reporting significant share gains. As Mark Ritson memorably put it, the new pack's 'clean lines and empty aesthetics achieved something Tropicana's competitors had failed to in 20 years: a degradation of its brand equity and an undermining of its status as market leader. Devoid of its signature design of an orange and a straw, the package looked like a bland, private-label juice.' PepsiCo reverted to the old pack design within six weeks, as *Ad Age* reported. Quite apart from any subjective opinion about the merits or otherwise of the new pack versus the old, this is a cautionary tale that hints at a much wider problem within the advertising and communications world: our tendency to pay less attention than we should to what Byron Sharp and others have termed 'brand assets'.

A brief detour on brand assets

Brand assets are anything that consumers can use to help identify a brand, which are both unique to the brand and famous (check out Ehrenberg-Bass's 'Measure your distinctive assets'). Identifying elements might include colours, logos, pack shapes, endlines and characters, or ideas used in advertising. But to be of value to the brand, and therefore an 'asset', these elements have to be both unique to the brand – so that consumers don't attribute them to competitors – and famous, ie widely recognised as being representative of the brand in question. Good examples include Cadbury's purple, Nike's swoosh, Tesco's 'Every Little Helps' and Comparethemarket.com's meerkat.

Brand assets matter because consumers really don't care about brands anything like as much as we, in marketing, like to think (or hope) they do. When consumers choose one brand over another, the evidence suggests that they don't do so through an active and conscious choice, but because that brand has a strong memory structure in their brain that is, as Byron Sharp put it in his 2010 book *How Brands Grow*, 'easily accessible'. The network of neurons in the brain are connected and reinforced every time a brand is associated with a particular element or situation. Let's take Marmite as an example. If I see a black jar with a yellow lid, I know it's Marmite. This in turn is connected to my memories of its thick, treacle-like consistency, and the extreme reactions of my children to it: one loves it, the other avoids it passionately. It's this network of associations linking the brand's assets to situations, emotions, contexts and so on that makes the brand distinctive and memorable.

But these associations aren't built overnight. They take time, and regular, frequent repetition. Think back to when you were at school revising for exams. Sadly, it takes more than just a cursory glance through your notes for information to stick in your brain. Unless you're in the tiny minority with a photographic memory, usually hard work in the form of repetition of the key points is what's required to make the facts stick. And that's when you're actively trying to memorise information.

In the world of brands, not even the most ardent of brand fans will actively try to recall every aspect of a brand's message, advertising or packaging. The process is more passive, and as such we have to work harder to make it happen. This is why the likes of Byron Sharp and others at the Ehrenberg-Bass Institute argue that building assets is so important for brand growth. Strong assets make a brand distinctive, being distinctive creates mental availability, and it is mental availability that should be the primary objective of marketing communication.

Tropicana's relaunch with its new campaign and pack redesign failed because it rejected the 'straw in the orange' asset that was so distinctive for Tropicana. The new pack was virtually indistinguishable from private label. Consumers couldn't associate the new marketing with the brand, and then had trouble finding it in the supermarket. Tropicana's failure was arguably a failure to take its brand assets seriously.

The problem with advertising

Tropicana's was a spectacular failure, and that is what's made it infamous; but it is not an isolated case. Recent analysis from Les Binet and Peter Field demonstrates a significant decline in advertising effectiveness that is driven by lots of contributory factors. While the data demonstrates the worrying impact of underinvestment in brands and short-termism, I do wonder, however, whether another underlying issue is our failure as an industry to invest as much time and effort as we should in building the assets that our clients' brand need to grow.

In advertising, we love novelty. Award schemes (not just creative) reward new thinking and innovative thinking. There is kudos in being the first do something. Marketing directors, keen to make their mark on a brand, like novelty too – a new agency, a new positioning, a new idea. And of course, creating something new and original is the most obvious way for us to assert our ownership of it. If we have created something new, it's ours. And if it's ours, we can rightfully claim the glory if it results in a positive impact on the brand. Neither agencies nor clients like inheriting other people's ideas and having to use them – and of course, that's the problem with brand assets. They are, by definition, things that have been created by someone else. And so, it's not hard to see how there is a relentless pressure on planners, creative and clients to create something new.

But it would be wrong to assert that our love of novelty is driven only by our desire for awards recognition or the respect of our peers. One of the key motivations for original and novel thinking is the belief that a new way to say something or to position a brand is the best way to get the brand noticed. If a brand is losing share, or not growing as fast as it needs to, our first temptation is to think of a new way to attack the problem. As Einstein alleged, 'insanity is doing the same thing over and over again and expecting a different result'.

Our search for novelty, therefore, is also the quest to find a way to get the brand noticed, to make it stand out from the competition, and make it more relevant. Novelty and originality are, in our folk theory of advertising, what fuel brand growth.

But the danger is that this quest leads us to work that is both unusual and creative, *but that doesn't work as hard as it could or should for brands*. And this is because too often we equate novelty with being distinctive.

Creating novelty is not the same as being distinctive

There is a long-held assumption that the aim of brand marketing should be to differentiate a brand from competitors. But brands are almost never differentiated – brands in the same category meet the same needs, and the users of one brand rarely have significantly different attitudes to their brand than users of another. What matters for brands is 'distinctiveness'. And as we saw above, being distinctive is all about reinforcing memory structures in the brain and associating them with brand assets. Which is why the best definition of distinctiveness is very simply, to quote Byron Sharp, 'a brand looking like itself'.

If you understand what distinctiveness really is, you can see why a search for novelty and originality, while done with the best of intentions, can end up creating communication that actually does the brand a disservice. New positionings, new messaging, new designs, new endlines *only* work for brands if they are used consistently and in a way that strongly links them to other brand assets, thus strengthening the memory structures in the brain for that brand.

But too often this doesn't happen. Either good ideas fail to become real assets because they're not used for long enough or consistently enough (we all know the stories of campaigns that have been killed because the client and/or agency got bored and felt it was time to move on...), or we get excited about doing something new but fail to create a sufficiently strong link between the new idea and the brand's existing assets, so it fails to 'stick'.

The right type of originality

So, does this imply that originality and novelty are bad for brands? Not at all. In fact, let me be very clear: this is not an argument for staying still, for familiarity, for cliché, for generally poor advertising, or for resisting change when it's needed. But it *is* a plea for the *right* type of originality. John Bartle, one of the founders of BBH, puts it very well when he uses the term '*imaginative repetition*' to describe what he believes great advertising should be. Originality, creativity and novelty are absolutely critical to create successful advertising, but the originality is required in the way that the assets are used and reinforced, not in the unnecessary and recurring reinvention of brand assets themselves. And that's no easy task; arguably, it requires even *greater* creativity and imagination.

Imaginative repetition in action

There are some wonderful examples of imaginative repetition in practice, that are both effective and award-winning. This Cannes award-winning poster for Coca-Cola by Ogilvy uses three brand assets: colour, the Coke white swirl and the shape of the bottle to great effect:

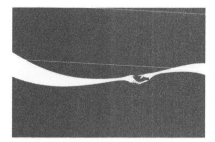

The recent campaign for Lloyds breathes new life into the black horse, the original logo for the bank that dates from 1677, but which was arguably an underutilised brand asset until adam&eveDDB gave it a starring role in the bank's recent advertising campaign.

The recent apology ad from KFC following the distribution problems that caused them to shut many outlets across the UK also demonstrates the power of building distinctive assets – in this case, to enable a tongue-in-cheek apology.

These are just three examples of the highly original and creative use of brand assets. There are many more.

But of course, sometimes brands do have to create new assets, and advertising is an extremely powerful way to do this. Brands might have a lack of existing powerful assets and need to create new ones (eg the meerkat of

273

Comparethemarket.com), or may need to replace assets that have ceased to have the impact they should. A good example of the latter is butter brand Lurpak. 'Douglas' was Lurpak's trombone-blowing buttery spokesman, whose job was to explain why Lurpak tasted better than other butter brands. The character was 'the brand's most distinctive asset', which had been built over many years, and was widely used in communications.

But by 2007, the brand was in decline, with falling share and penetration. Agency and client took the brave decision to 'retire' Douglas, replacing him with a more emotional, but also very distinctive, campaign, presenting Lurpak as 'the champion of good food', which has been used consistently ever since. Lurpak has recovered, growing volume and value share, to regain its market leader status. As this case demonstrates, when brand assets have ceased to work as hard as they need to, reinvention is needed. The trick of course is being able to spot when to take that risk and when not to.

The mindset for 'imaginative repetition'

So, what should agencies and clients do to do right by brands? I'd argue that, rather than a need for new talent or new processes, what's required is a change in mindset.

The industry's love of originality means that, quite understandably, our inherent bias will be to look for opportunities for change, reasons to move a campaign on, or excuses to create something new. But if we want to serve brands well, we would be wise to question these natural impulses. To ask ourselves, 'What assets does the brand already have that can be leveraged to good effect?' 'What assets have potential, but need reinforcement?' 'How best do we build mental availability for this brand?' And most importantly, 'How can we deploy our creative skill and imagination to these ends?' The key lesson is not to forget that when we create communications, however brilliant and creative, our first loyalty must always be to the brand. We are a service industry, but it is the brand to which we are in service.

References

Binet, L, and Field, P. *Media in Focus: Marketing effectiveness in a digital era.* IPA, 2017

http://adage.com/article/news/tropicana-line-s-sales-plunge-20-post-rebranding/
135735/

https://byronsharp.wordpress.com/2008/04/10/differentiation-vs-distinctiveness/

https://byronsharp.wordpress.com/2011/03/26/mental-availability-is-not-awareness-
brand-salience-is-not-awareness/

https://www.campaignlive.co.uk/article/mark-ritson-branding-freshly-squeezed/
898244

http://www.lloydsbankinggroup.com/Our-Group/our-heritage/the-black-horse/

https://www.marketingscience.info/wp-content/uploads/2015/08/Measure-Your-
Distinctive-Assets.pdf

John Bartle, personal communication, November 2017

Sharp, B. *How Brands Grow: What marketers don't know.* OUP, 2010

35

WHY INNOVATION ISN'T AS SEXY AS BUSINESS BOOKS PROMISE

Written by **Costas Papaikonomou**

As a rule of thumb, there are only two routes in innovation. One is about sleepless nights, pain and hardship. The other is about sleepless nights, pain and hardship – plus divorce and financial ruin. This is not what the business books are promising, says this chapter.

Unfairly, the word 'innovation' is mostly used to describe with hindsight what someone has already done, and done successfully enough to get noticed. Browse through any business book, TED talk or Twitter feed and this is exactly the picture that emerges. 'Winner's bias': attention is skewed to the few entrepreneurs who hit the jackpot, not to the many thousands of people in regular businesses who create new products and services every day. Nor the countless failed entrepreneurs whose ideas brought them nothing but ulcers.

The fancy chatter about disruption by start-ups with nothing to lose isn't much help either, when you're still at the front end of the journey wondering what to do next – with *everything* to lose. Besides, the chances of the world needing yet another digital platform Ponzi scheme that might succeed isn't very high. In all likelihood you need to create something new *within* the tightly confined space of your employer's business model and market.

Should you then copy the habits of the successful business people who smile at us from magazine covers and LinkedIn posts? Well, unsuccessful innovators show many of the same stubborn behaviours, so that probably won't work either.

Creativity gurus and facilitators tell you to get out of your comfort zone in order to achieve new things successfully. Edward de Bono's 'Hats' from the 1980s have been extrapolated into circus analogies and lining up in the colour of your underwear. What's more, they'll say further out of comfort, the better – blatantly ignoring that most people tasked with creating the next big thing already are deeply uncomfortable with that assignment. If anything, *more* comfort is what you need for good ideas – long car rides and hot showers to let your mind wander, rather than your boss's ambitious KPIs to stress over.

A simple (yet mostly overlooked) first step up and out of that place of discomfort is to move attention away from what the idea will *be*, to what it needs to *deliver*. Almost all innovation initiatives are commercially driven by someone wanting to make money with their new idea. From start-ups to corporate giants, that new idea's only purpose is to displace something else. Whether it's a small change to annoy a direct competitor, or a big one to overturn a whole industry, it starts with acknowledging what that new idea must *do* in order to be considered a success. Without that acknowledgement, it's simply impossible to adequately judge how radical an idea needs to be to make the impact you want.

Counter to business books arguing you to go 'Blue' or 'Bold', you're actually better off finding the *least* radical solution possible, because the less disruptive it is, the easier it will be to implement. A big reason so many innovations fail is not because the market won't accept them, but because they're too disruptive for the business itself to implement and sustain profitably. If the market wants a new flavour, don't bet the ranch by developing a whole new product with all the problems that come with it. And if you spot a very big unmet need that might overturn the whole industry, then you *still* need to find the simplest of solutions to answer it, ideally with a product or service very similar to what you're already making. The size of the unmet need being resolved is what makes innovation disruptive. Not the weirdness or originality of the solution.

If you're wondering what that means in practice, here's just one example from our history at Happen Group. Working with a cough syrups manufacturer, their ambition was no less than to completely revolutionise that market.

A very mature market, with established rules and dominant competitors. We knew we needed to find a *massive* unmet need in order to make such an impact, and the odds were clearly against us. But we realised quickly a weak spot in most of the market research floating around for the 'cough and cold' category. It was all based on quant surveys and focus groups amongst people who were asked to *remember* what it was like to have a cough. No wonder no one ever spotted something new to do.

Instead, we quickly drummed up a few friends and family members who were *actually ill* and convinced them it would be a good idea for a few of our team members to spend time with them. Our team tailed them for a couple of days, and found heaps of unmet needs. Small ones, like the nuisance of knowing the sore throat is coming but not *when*. Or figuring out what kind of cough a sick child has. And we found the big one too. Without exception, every sick individual struggled at the pharmacy when they needed to pick the right type of cough medicine. Was it a chesty cough, a tickly cough or a dry cough? We saw some cough in the face of the pharmacist, desperately asking 'What kind of cough do you think it is?'

Bingo! Big need identified. Now all we had to do was *not* come up with a fancy solution. Not an app to cough in for medical advice, not a shelf navigation system. Our client made cough syrups for OTC retail, we needed a solution that would fit them and disrupt the market, not disrupt their business model. A solution that would fully satisfy that unmet need of not knowing what kind of cough you have, was easy to manufacture for our client and hard to follow for competition. So, we created a cough syrup *for all coughs*. It went straight to number two in the market in the first cough season it was launched.

Based on many years at Happen Group, helping teams innovate successfully in very mature and crowded markets, there seem to be four distinct areas that dramatically affect success rates along the innovation journey.

**** *Spoiler alert: none are sexy* ****

1. Start with the right innovation objective, aka business objective

Clarity of what the business objective is, which the innovation is required to deliver in market. After a decade of taking thousands of NPD and innovation briefs, I dare say this is broadly misunderstood, or at least underestimated. All too often an innovation project within large corporate entities starts with defining the type of idea that is necessary, for example, 'We need the next [widget], with refill capsules like Nespresso'. *Wrong.* Consider innovation as a spectrum of activities, with a range of different outcomes – are you innovating to *protect, grow* or *transform* your business? By chunking it down to these three impact levels, each with its own definitions of success, restrictions and approaches to get there, clarity of thought comes much easier. For instance, you shouldn't try to create a revolutionary and expensive new product design if the business objective is merely to steal a little share. Equally, if the time has come to transform the business, you shouldn't be restricted by current factory capabilities. It might be that the historical overemphasis of disruptive innovation, combined with 'winner's bias', has made game changers all too much the benchmark for what good innovation looks like. The reality is different: managing innovation is less about spawning radical ideas and more about rigorous portfolio management. Businesses which maintain their portfolio durably over decades all judge well when it's time to create a new platform and when milking the old one will do.

2. Uncover frustrations you can resolve

Reveal real, unmet frustrations that will attract new customers to your innovative product or service. Too often innovation teams are distracted by industry truths, and chasing generic trends or even common human needs. While these are fun to investigate (and keep everyone busy), their value for creating innovative and relevant new products and services is limited. People will make a lasting switch to your product only if it removes a functional or emotional frustration. *C'est tout.* In mature, saturated markets people will already be using a competitive product, and only their unhappiness will make them switch to your less frustrating alternative. Even in the dullest, most gridlocked markets there will be frustrations to resolve. The depth of the frustration you need to find is directly related to the business objective, in other words, the innovation impact level you're looking to achieve. If it's merely snatching some customers away from your direct competition, resolving a small frustration will do. If you need to lure a whole new group of people away from another type of product and into your franchise, then you better find a big problem to solve for them – or a bundle of micro-frustrations – or they'll just stay put. Note, this isn't just about drawing attention for a purchase, or an 'activation' of your brand in a commoditised market ruled by boredom. This is about creating a new consumer behaviour that durably draws them your way for a better solution, product or service. *Packaging drives trial, product drives repeat.*

3. Create winners that make commercial sense

Leverage your capabilities across the marketing mix, without defaulting to the same types of solutions. You have to understand and acknowledge what the limiting factors will be to achieve success. Creating products that consumers love in tests is easy: just give them what they want. Creating products they love *and* make money for you is a different matter. Success is then defined by the degree to which you can use your current people, capabilities and assets. If you're looking to create a new product to launch next year to nudge a competing brand out of the way, then your current manufacturing assets will likely be the limiting factor. So, you need to find a way to answer the consumer frustration you found, with solutions that you can make in your factory now. If you're looking to create longer term 'grow level' innovations to open up a new audience of consumers in another aisle in the supermarket, then your sales team's capability to build new customer relationships will be the limiting factor you need to work within. Merely creating concepts that do well in consumer tests just won't cut it. Most large organisations have by now understood the importance of customer centricity. They've written it into their mission statements and KPI sheets. Sadly, it's only half of the solution. The truly innovative businesses are *insight-led* and *asset-out* in their work. They join up the demand and supply forces that make business work commercially. A key barrier to achieving this status is the often disturbed relationship between those responsible for innovation (eg marketing) and those responsible for materialising it (eg R&D and manufacturing). Both are to blame here. The former for not understanding the operational constraints behind how their products are made, the latter for considering their manufacturing systems like a highly optimised one-trick pony instead of the well-stocked kitchen that it is. Remarkably, in our experience at Happen Group, the area where most gains can be found is in stretching the 'asset-out' capabilities of an organisation, uncovering the countless new things that can be done within the current systems, at low CapEx. Immediate secondary benefits are not only saving the time of *not* building new assets, but also being able to scale up quickly at relatively low effort.

4. Energise the business into action

Keep the momentum through all layers of decision making, without letting 'risk aversion' get in the way. Engage internal and external stakeholders such that they will invest in turning your ideas into reality. Where protect-level innovation initiatives are often small improvements that can be planned by the calendar by a single team, the other two levels need a harmonious business ecosystem to survive. Grow-level innovation is truly opportunity led, and will require collaboration between disciplines to create new standards. Transformational-level innovation requires a bold vision and even bolder personality to push it through. But across all three, an energised business climate is required to keep innovative ideas intact through to the end – developing them positively, not compromising them and losing sight of the business objective that ignited the process in the first place. What appears often misunderstood is the entrepreneur's mindset when it comes to innovation in large organisations. You don't want entrepreneurs – they have different ambitions and motivations than people inside an organisation. Instead, you need the slightly rebellious team members involved. Contrary to the popular archetype, we found they have no interest in being an entrepreneur. They love their employer and their jobs, but they are eager to stretch the current operational straitjacket into a new shape. The more dramatic the change required, the more excited they get, not because they know what to do, but because they know they can *make it right*. They exist in every organisation, in every function, and are the polar opposites of the operational excellence people. They dislike structure and love ambiguity – just what you need to figure out how to get new things done successfully.

Successful innovation in popular business media looks sexy and aspirational. Thankfully, the ugly reality is that it isn't ugly either, maybe just a little less magical. More than anything, it's a skill you can learn and become good at, both on a personal and a business level.

There's no magic ingredient here, just lots of good cooking.

36

UNLEASHING THE POWER OF DISRUPTION – THRIVING IN THE POST-DIGITAL AGE

Written by **Tom Goodwin**

So, how would you build your business if you started it now? Knowing what you know about consumer behaviours, new expectations, the new possibilities that technology affords us and the accelerating pace of change? Many businesses would probably look rather different. Companies have good explanations for the way things are, and it's easy to see why start-ups have it easier, but do you think your customers care? Are explanations or excuses enough, or must you adapt, rebuild or die? Now not everything is changing, not all businesses face existential threats, but it's certainly wise to be open to all change. This chapter puts forward some guiding thoughts and questions to consider.

The power of digital disruption is transformative, not iterative

Electricity didn't change the world overnight, it took decades for industry and society to unleash its transformative power. Businesses made the mistake of adding electricity to existing processes, sprinkling change around the edges, and incrementally. Factories, for example, saw only marginal improvements by using electrical motors to drive the power belts that were previously steam powered. They saw further small gains by making each machine powered by smaller local motors as they were then able to alter factory layouts to be more efficient.

What is key is that at each and every stage businesses felt they'd understood the full potential of electricity. Yet only in retrospect was it clear they'd got it wrong – what electricity really changed was everything. Electricity should have been core to reimagining business from scratch. Factories could now be placed near ports, not near energy sources inland. Factories could be near large centres of population closer to workers and consumers. Factories could, by leveraging the full power of electricity, be shaped in entirely different ways, with totally new, smaller machines, and make entirely new products, in entirely new ways.

We are at the same point in the digital age as the marginally improved factories of the past: we have heads of digital, digital strategies, digital departments and tech companies; we've built on our accomplishments in small ways, we've garnished what we've got, and everywhere around us companies think they've done enough. They boast about Technology in annual reports; they've a digital department or an innovation laboratory. It's innovation as a gesture: they show they get omnichannel commerce because they've put iPads instore; it's innovation for PR, with a single plane using biofuel in one engine to get the headline.

From electrification to computerisation in the 1970s, we learn the transformative element is often spoken about the most, when it's not yet used. When a technology is really here it blends into the background; it's noticed only by its absence. It's merely unleashing the power of what's possible for an age of new consumer expectations, rather than something shiny at the side.

The companies that have unleashed the fastest growth and generated the greatest value creation in the shortest possible time have done so by building for the new world and with technology at the core. Digital isn't a thing, it's everything. From Uber to Facebook, Amazon to WeWork, Airbnb to Alibaba, Slack to Netflix, digital-first companies are here. Yet these aren't the final winners, they are not the only ones to succeed. From retail to governance, healthcare to democracy, banking to transportation, digitalisation, mobilisation and entirely new expectations and dynamics will transform business and destroy generations of incumbents. What role is a physical bank in a mobile-centric world of people who have never used (let alone seen) a cheque? What becomes of retailers when the fundamental unit of economics favours brands with no expensive real estate? What does insurance look like when cars drive themselves? What does healthcare become when our phones know more about us than anyone, ever? What replaces the smartphone?

We've many new opportunities and threats. What becomes of brands in the age of codified online trust or auto-replenishment? How can local business compete on scale with global? Who wants to own when they can just pay for access? Yet not everything changes.

Change is here; it's not entirely predictable or evenly distributed, but by looking at technology, society, and with the context of the past, it's possible to shine a light into the new; to be ready to adapt; to look to see what to ignore and what to embrace. One way to do this is to understand the thinking behind the 'paradigm leap'.

Unleashing the power of the paradigm leap

When the iPhone was launched in 2007, it was both the best phone the world had ever seen, and Apple's first phone. Tesla's first-ever car set the standard for the entire car industry. From Dyson's first vacuum cleaner to Nest Labs' first thermometer, to Uber's first taxi business to Amazon's first attempt at retail, it seems that the real step-changes in how things are done come from outside. So, have these companies succeeded changing the game despite a lack of experience, or because of it?

I believe what we witness is the leap from a world of possibilities to another – a leap from one paradigm to another; the notion of evolutionary funnels where optimal solutions suddenly jump.

Design follows a process: parameters are set; we establish the right combination of criteria that are fixed, and those that are flexible. Over time, investment, consumer behaviour and technology continually refine the process. The first personal cassette players were massive, expensive, had terrible sound quality, skipped badly, offered awful battery life, and best of all, didn't even have a rewind function. Over a period of years everything got better: we got Dolby, rechargeable batteries, rewind buttons. It got to a point where the improvements got smaller. It was easy to reduce the physical size of the player at first, but once the Walkman was not much bigger than a cassette tape, improvements were marginal. The very peak of Walkman design came as the worst personal CD player was made.

We'd made a paradigm leap; we'd gone from ever smaller, incremental design improvements towards an optimal goal to a whole new canvas for design. We now had new criteria to optimise, new design constraints and new problems to solve. We could now skip tracks, get digital sound, batteries lasted longer, and the device was far thinner; skipping, however, remained an issue until antishock was developed. Notably, all the criteria that once held back the cassette player were different; the problems were new, and the expertise needed to address them wildly different – laser engineers replaced electromagnetic sensor designers, and so on.

As Discmans became marvellously cheap, remarkably thin, far better than every music device ever made, music moved from physical discs to data; we jumped the paradigm of MP3 players, where once again all bets were off. And then again to streaming; we no longer needed a musical player, just an app on a phone. At every stage the new era demanded totally new assumptions, different thinking, and a step change in performance was noted. Often the dominant player changed, the incumbent built on the expertise of the past.

It's happened in many forms: the era of VHS, the era of DVD, the era of streaming on demand. The era of goods by horse, to goods by canal, to goods by railway and next largely by road. In high jumping, all records tended towards one optimal goal until the 'Fosbury Flop' changed everything. We have paradigms in other areas: we've architectural styles as fashions that all coexist, we've then reactionary movements against them where all rules change. We see them in science: we form theories to make sense of a current world, that all bind each other to existing thinking, until someone forces a leap forward where we accept the earth isn't the centre of the universe, or recognise the caloric theory of heat, and then together the world makes progress towards a new, better, more useful theory of thinking.

It's this process of design parameters, slower incremental improvements and a paradigm shift where everything changes that best describe the world around us; it just typically feels more complex.

So, some tips for your business based on this.

1. Work around people not technology; have technology at the heart

The reality of the modern world is that people don't consider competitive sets the same way businesses do. Uber doesn't compete with Fedex, but if I can see my car, my driver's name, rating, and when they will turn up, I now expect this of my logistics providers, my airlines and everyone. If Amazon can reply to my every email, I now expect my bank to. Modern times mean modern expectations; we're the most spoiled, flippant generation ever, we need to be very aware of what tools and possibilities are at our disposal, but relentlessly focus not on them as the product, but as the ordinance to serve people better than ever. Thrill people, manage their expectations, and they become our advertising.

2. Fix the right assumptions

What we've learned from paradigm shifts is that expertise and traditional thinking allow us to progress towards a marginally better solution, but ensure we can never make leaps. Ensure that the assumptions we make are based on reality, not guesswork – or more likely still, thinking from the past. Endless user testing at Nokia showed people didn't want an iPhone, until they did. Red Bull marketers made a product that no focus group ever wanted; *The New York Times* has a paywall despite 'nobody ever being willing to pay for news'. Ensure in all the work done that fixed assumptions about what is possible and what people want are tested to destruction daily.

3. Plan for new paradigms

Businesses in faster rates of change need to be beyond fast – they need to be anticipatory. It's hard to see all changes, but themes emerge. Despite new technology, humans end up being more predictable than expected. Selfies seem random unless you accept the human need to be validated, apps like HotelTonight show that people want ease more than choice. So, every business needs to focus on likely changes and what they mean, especially – and this is the hard part – where trends combine. What does your business look like in a world of self-driving cars, and blockchain, and mixed reality headsets, and AI, and many other factors at the same time? Even more, think of the role of your company and how it proliferates and evolves over time. Do you sell cars or mobility? Are you in the accommodation business or the leisure business? How does a wider platform allow you to succeed in new ways?

There are many other thoughts to consider, but this offers a cursory glance into the ways for businesses to be best prepared, most agile, most likely to succeed. The future doesn't care about why you failed. History is written by the winners. Not everyone has to change, not everything is changing, but to keep your eyes ahead, to study trend lines and dreams, to write your own obituary and imagine how things failed, these fast-moving times need people who can look down the road further ahead. And it's companies that do that which will make the most of the greatest time ever to work in business.

© marketoonist.com

37

WHY CHALLENGER BRANDS MATTER IN THE AGE OF DISRUPTION

Written by **Mark Barden**

This chapter looks at the differences between classic disruption theory, more everyday uses of the term 'disruption' in the business world, and challenger brand thinking. It examines how challenger brands succeed, and maps this to the findings of the Ehrenberg-Bass Institute. It considers how and why challenger brands create distinctiveness to drive salience and growth, how they use customer advocacy to create launch velocity, and fame to maintain that over time. It also looks at the role of having clear and strong beliefs to fuel the ongoing effort to maintain brand distinctiveness in the face of competitive response.

'Disruption' is the buzzword of the moment, pervading everything down to mayonnaise marketing. 'Challenger brand', too, is having a teenage growth spurt, with every Tom, Dick and Donald apparently seen as a challenger; 2016 was even the year of the 'challenger brand' according to some. The two are often conflated, but they are not the same, and understanding how they differ is essential to the modern marketer.

Disruption theory defined

Harvard Business School professor Clayton Christensen coined the term 'disruptive innovation', and is as responsible as anyone for creating the hype, albeit inadvertently. Steve Jobs and Jeff Bezos loved Christensen's 1997 book *The Innovator's Dilemma*, and such high praise from high places is catnip for Silicon Valley wags. As a result, 'disruption' has become the ubiquitous verbal tic we hear today.

But Christensen had something very specific in mind: business model disruption that comes from serving an overlooked segment with low cost, sometimes inferior product, and then migrating up the value chain over time, leveraging a superior cost structure. This is how Toyota gained a foothold in the US, for instance, and how Google captured a huge percentage of the advertising market with AdWords. This kind of business model disruption defines one end of the disruption spectrum (see Figure 1).

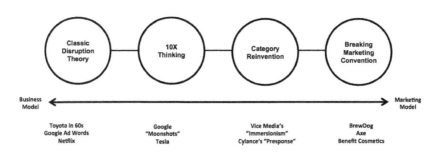

Figure 1: A disruption spectrum

Next to disruption theory is the kind of creative destruction that we see upending many industries these days. Less formally defined than disruption theory, it's exemplified by the kind of '10x thinking' of Google's Larry Page, where businesses aim to be not just 10% better, but 10 times better. Google's search algorithm might be 10 times better than the local library, for example. Amazon's ability to house and ship almost every book that exists is 10 times better than the neighbourhood bookstore. This may not be the kind of business model innovation required by disruption theory, but these products are clearly disrupting industries.

Next, we'll find the kind of disruption that Jean-Marie Dru, head of advertising agency TBWA, describes in his 1996 book *Disruption*. Here the emphasis is on breaking the codes and conventions of a category to change the way we experience it. Vice Media's 'immersionism' approach to journalism is a good example, as is cyber-security firm Cylance's approach to *predicting* cyber-attacks rather than simply *responding* to them after the fact. Both these businesses are growing fast.

And finally, there are the brands that people often call disruptive because of the very distinctive ways they market themselves, such as BrewDog in beer and Benefit in cosmetics. Such distinctiveness comes as much from the point of view and attitude of the brand as it does from the kind of distinctive packaging and iconography of which Ehrenberg-Bass data speaks.

Like all models, this disruption spectrum is an oversimplification, but it's a helpful one to guide our understanding of the kinds of disruption we need to think about in our pursuit of growth. If you don't see your favourite valet-parking app anywhere on the spectrum, it may be time to question how truly disruptive that really is.

Why Uber isn't disruptive, but Netflix is

Amusingly, the disruption theory gurus at Harvard are a little upset about what they consider to be the misuse of their term. Uber is *not* a disruptor, they say. Uber entered an existing market with a better service, but not one that is radically cheaper, or that brings new consumers into the market – they just move taxi riders elsewhere. Uber may be a 10 times improvement over traditional cabs, but it doesn't fit Christensen's definition.

On the other hand, Netflix does. Its initial mail order service of older movie titles was the poor relation to the Blockbuster experience of impulse shopping for new releases. Nevertheless, Netflix gained a toehold with movie buffs, and it later conquered all when it changed its offering to all-you-can-view deals in an on-demand format.

If you're scratching your head over the Uber and Netflix difference, it's because we've all been guilty of employing a more everyday definition of disruption than disruption theory allows (though ultimately, whether Uber is disruptive or not might be a question better asked of taxi drivers!)

If you're conducting a technical analysis of the long-term defensibility of a business model, Christensen's distinction is important. All those, 'We're the Uber of…' companies (Saucey for booze or Push For Pizza for pizza delivery) ought to think very hard about it. Take on-demand laundry start-up Washio, which was soon competing with Cleanly, FlyCleaners and other on-demand laundry apps with the same technology. With little else to differentiate it, Washio found it hard to stand out, and closed in August 2016, despite raising $16.8 million.

One way of thinking about Washio's failure is its inability to create the distinctiveness and salience that the Ehrenberg-Bass data shows is so important to customer acquisition and growth. And this is where challenger brand thinking comes in handy.

If your business model isn't capital D disruptive, your marketing had better be

Before 'disruption', 'best practice' was the religion. Everyone copied the procedures and practices deemed to be the most effective, including those in marketing. There is a logic to this, of course, but this is how conventions are created. Look at mass market hotel experiences, supermarket design, domestic beer marketing, much car advertising. All are expressions of best practice, which must fail to generate above average growth over time, because your brand can't be distinctive if it acts like all the rest.

So, all categories get stuck, until someone unsticks them. As described in *Eating the Big Fish*, my colleague Adam Morgan's book on how challenger brands compete, it's the ambitious challenger that has no choice but to try to do that. In addition to being out-resourced by the big fish, the little fish must fight inertia: an unwillingness to change on the part of the consumer (or the retailer), for whom the psychological rewards of safety and routine are so strong. We're all, as Byron Sharp says, 'cognitive misers', who won't pay attention long enough to evaluate whether it's worth changing, because frankly, we've got better things to do.

And yet, the challenger must make change happen. It does this by introducing new criteria of choice into the category; criteria on which it can win. These criteria need not be driven by conventional product differences (in fact, they seldom are), but must always drive brand 'fame', which (research from Les Binet and Peter Field shows) outperforms reason and emotion, and even a combination of the two, in driving sales.

Take craft beer pioneer BrewDog, launched in Scotland in 2007 with a £20,000 bank loan. Today, they're entering the US market with a valuation of $350 million, and have spent very little on conventional marketing. BrewDog makes very different beers with very distinctive stories. 'Tactical Nuclear Penguin' is the strongest beer on the planet, and must be sipped like scotch; 'The End of History' is packaged in roadkill and taxidermy; and 'Never Mind The Anabolics' contained banned substances and launched during the London Olympics. Each beer gleefully courts the outrage of the media, guaranteeing the kind of coverage that replaces the need to buy salience in more conventional ways. And this, of course, is how this case fits the Ehrenberg-Bass model of salience and emotional availability.

Despite the fun and games, the BrewDog founders are very serious about beer. Founder James Watt rails against the 'mainstream, industrial, monolithic, insipid, bland, tasteless, apathetic beers…', and is very clear that the controversy is there to both promote the rest of his line-up as well as the larger mission, 'To make other people as passionate about great craft beers as we are'. And in this he has been successful too. Unable to borrow money in the teeth of a recession, BrewDog turned to crowd-funding campaigns called 'Equity for Punks'. They recently announced their fifth round and have so far raised £61 million, from over 84,000 investor advocates.

While the long-term success of BrewDog and other challengers like them (American Giant, Impossible Foods, Everlane, Thinx) can't be built on such a small core of advocates, the importance of such a group in helping a brand gain traction in the early days – something all challengers struggle with – is essential. To Byron Sharp's assertion, 'The marketing consequences of these brand fanatics turns out to be very limited', we would simply add, '…in the long run'. Successful challenger brands must harness the enthusiasm of their fans to help them build momentum early on, and then create famous marketing thereafter to maintain it.

Countless founders have told us a story similar to the one Richard Reed of Innocent Drinks recounted. Surveying a wall of unsolicited fan mail from the first few years of business, he stopped to point out a piece of needlework on which an Innocent customer had embroidered the logo of a head with a halo over it. 'That's my mission,' he said, 'to inspire people to express themselves through the medium of needlework.' It was a joke, of course – and yet he wasn't smiling. That kind of loyalty is the lifeblood of a start-up. It ensures a new product stays on the shelf, and it serves to remind the staff that their long hours have an impact on people as well as sales.

And that's what matters about the conviction James Watt has about beer: its power to motivate the rest of the people who work at BrewDog. Much has been written about the power of purpose, and some of it debunked (by, for example, Richard Shotton inter alia). We share the scepticism. The kind of purpose pabulum we see on brand briefs these days won't cut it for the challenger. However, we've seen firsthand the power of strongly held beliefs to fuel the ongoing creation of distinctive marketing ideas over time. Working without the big budgets, or the tickets to the Grammies that go with them, is tough. Finding ever-more creative ways to do more with less seems to be fuelled by a strong sense of cause, whether that be trying to bring back American manufacturing by making the finest hoodie ever (American Giant), or convincing people to slow climate change by eating plant-based meat (Impossible Foods).

Leaders of challenger brands create heat in order to mobilise people. They provide a bold, ambitious vision of the world they're trying to create, while being equally clear-eyed about the 'monster' that threatens them. The tension between the two is what fuels their team, including their early advocates, to keep going despite the odds.

Engineering-led disruption versus challenger brand disruption

Let's take a simple, hypothetical look at the plumbing business to illustrate the differences we've teased out so far. An engineering mindset might see the opportunity to invent an entirely new device to snake the drains that is 10 times better than anything on the market today. This would be disruptive in the Dyson sense, doing for snaking what Dyson did for sucking. This kind of breakthrough would be differentiated enough to create the salience needed to drive sales growth. Even if it were copied, the disrupter might have built so much inertia (what Ehrenberg-Bass says marketers mistakenly call loyalty) that it could maintain its dominance – like Google has done in search.

A challenger, on the other hand, might start not with a clearly demonstrable technical advantage, but with a point of view. They might, for example, believe that the plumbing business is dominated by patronising men who seem to spend a good deal of their time alienating their mostly female customers – who loathe having to deal with them. They would recruit women-only plumbers and build a uniquely women-friendly customer experience around a more-or-less conventional plumbing offering. If they lean into this point of view, and express it with the kind of theatre and surprise of a BrewDog or Geek Squad, they could create a distinctive brand, and the kind of fame needed to fuel profitable growth. With genuine conviction around the need for a women-led plumbing company, and a culture built around it, this business could maintain its distinctiveness over time with a stream of innovative marketing ideas in line with its beliefs. This is how T-Mobile has grown with its Un-carrier releases in the United States, and how Tillamook succeeds in the highly commoditised dairy business.

So, while the disruptor might start with an insight about a technical possibility, the challenger starts with ideology. As Figure 2 illustrates, the further to the right of our disruption spectrum we go, the more important a set of beliefs becomes in driving distinctiveness. Because a good deal of a challenger's advantage may not be underpinned by a sustainable technical superiority, the work of challenging is never done. Belief-driven ideation sustains a challenger brand over time, and building that capability is the competitive advantage.

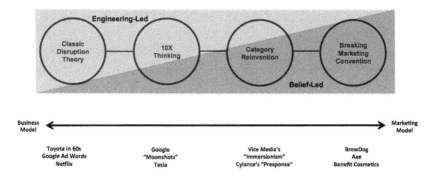

Figure 2: Engineering-led vs belief-led disruption spectrum

A full spectrum business

The gold standard, of course, would be a business that worked across every part of the disruption spectrum. Southwest Airlines might be such an example. It serviced second-tier markets, using only a single type of plane (Boeing 737) to keep costs down and servicing efficiencies up (the 30-minute turnaround), and forsook all frills (no food) – allowing it to hit price points no one had been able to hit before. This brought in bus passengers who'd previously not thought of flying as an option: classic disruption theory, and arguably a 10 times improvement over the bus.

Southwest was led by maverick Herb Kelleher, who built a culture of 'positively outrageous service' to further differentiate the experience beyond price, many illustrations of which became famous (eg see rapping flight attendant videos on YouTube) and continue to drive salience. Kelleher himself wrestled the CEO of a competitive airline – literally, in a ring, in public – over the rights to the name. Elements of the Southwest model have been copied, of course, but no one has done it as well across the entire spectrum. It's this complete approach that has led to Southwest's unprecedented record of profitability.

Warby Parker is the modern-day version of this story. It has a disruptive model in the Christensen sense: a limited selection of simple glasses frames, sold online only, for a price of just $99. Now we see them moving up the value chain, adding more expensive transitional lenses, and opening stores. But Warby has also been innovative in how it generates trial and awareness (eg home try-on), and how it maximises impact from owned media (a recent annual report 'went viral'). Their every action is animated by their socially conscious 'one-for-one' mission, and a belief that 'eye glasses shouldn't cost more than a smartphone'. Their charismatic founders are building a culture capable of furthering that cause for a long time to come, with the '5.15 report' (a report published at the end of every week, written in 15 minutes to be read in five minutes) that asks every staff member to come up with one idea to further improve the business.

Learning from challenger brands in a disruptive world

Amazon is now in the logistics business, challenging FedEx with Amazon Go. Tom's sells coffee now along with shoes. Restoration Hardware has opened a hotel. Apple may soon build a car. When big companies with established brands move into new categories, the incumbents would do well to learn from challenger brands.

Consider Toyota, one of disruption theory's lead examples. Their disruptive model of the 1960s was eventually copied, thanks in part to their generosity in sharing the insights of the Toyota Production System. Great cars at affordable prices are more prevalent than ever. And now there are new kinds of competitors on the horizon: the autonomous vehicles of Google and Tesla, and ride-sharing services like Uber; these are all threats (and possibly even opportunities) to the world's biggest car company. Can Toyota leverage their manufacturing prowess once again and hit more competitive price points than their powerful new adversaries? Will they embrace innovative new business models and new sales channels? Perhaps the bigger question, with so many possibilities, is how will Toyota decide? What strongly held point of view will animate their business for this new world? What driving belief will inspire the new Toyota, and guide innovation through the entire system, energising the culture for the next 50 years?

Google, too, could benefit from a more coherent point of view about what drives its engineering-led disruptions. Are its disparate (and so far largely unsuccessful) efforts to create new businesses driven more by engineering caprice than conviction? The consumer may not care as much about purpose as today's marketers would like to believe, but purpose is surely essential to determining the direction of a business when there are so many possibilities. Your employees will surely want to know, as will the top talent you'll need to hire to bring it to fruition. And without clarity, disruption becomes chaos quite quickly.

The challenger model is far more encompassing than the overly simplistic disruption we read about in the news. Challenger is a complete operating system to compete with the 'big fish', whether that's a powerful competitor or a market orthodoxy. It embraces mindset as well as method. Challenger brands must:

- Ruthlessly cut any idea that doesn't drive their core identity in order to commit fully to those that do.
- Design these ideas with a fame-first mindset to generate salience on limited budgets in a world of almost infinite choice.
- Develop a culture that values these kinds of bold ideas over the platitudes of being customer centric, and a capability to create and nurture these ideas that is world class.
- Know how to manage the conflict and tension that comes with being provocative, both internally and externally.

The way the challenger approaches marketing is largely consistent with the findings of the Ehrenberg-Bass Institute. Challengers prize brand distinctiveness above product differentiation alone, and use the fame it generates to reach as broad an audience as possible. That distinctiveness is derived from their ideology, as well as their iconography. This ideology drives the ongoing efforts to change the way consumers relate to a category, as the challenger can never stop challenging. The ideology is as much for the people who work at the company as it is for the consumer, as it brings both focus and energy to the ways the business needs to disrupt. In the words of Dave Hieatt, founder of Hiut Denim Co, 'Beware the person who believes in what they are doing'.

References

Binet, L, and Field, P. *Marketing in the Era of Accountability: Identifying the marketing practices and metrics that truly increase profitability.* WARC, 2007

Christensen, C. *The Innovator's Dilemma: When new technologies cause great firms to fail.* Harvard Business School Press, 1997

Dru, J. *Disruption: Overturning conventions and shaking up the marketplace.* Wiley, 1996

http://grist.org/food/disruptive-mayo-is-now-a-thing-and-its-spreading/

https://hbr.org/2015/12/what-is-disruptive-innovation

http://minutehack.com/opinions/2016-the-year-of-the-challenger-brand

http://www.huffingtonpost.co.uk/richard-shotton/brand-purpose_b_11679052.html

Morgan, A. *Eating the Big Fish: How challenger brands can compete against brand leaders.* Wiley, 1999

Sharp, B. *How Brands Grow: What marketers don't know.* OUP, 2010

38

MARKETS VERSUS MARKETING

Written by **Doc Searls**

Digital technology is changing us as human beings, and we in turn are changing markets – and humanising them in the process. This is a tall order, because the once benign business of marketing has taken advantage of absent personal privacy protections on the Internet to invade our lives and track us like marked animals. But we are about to make marketing as we've known it obsolete, asserts this chapter, because we'll have much better instruments for interacting with companies, and expressing demand, than surveillance-based marketing could ever guess at – and that will be better for everybody.

Bingo

When I ride subways in New York, I play a game with myself called 'Rectangle Bingo'. Here's how it works: if everybody I can see in a subway car is preoccupied with a mobile device, bingo!

I recorded the 'bingo' overleaf with my own rectangle in March 2017:

That was a pano: a panoramic photo you shoot by scanning the subject. It's a pretty obvious way to shoot, but nobody saw me shoot this one, because they were all heads down, looking at their rectangles.

Whatever else you might say about what's going on here, this much is clear: these people are not the same as they were 10 (or even five) years ago. And maybe not the same as they were five days or minutes ago. Nor are their jobs, their friends, their families, their churches, their sports teams, the businesses they work with, the government agencies that serve them. Nothing is the same.

Today, nearly everybody is pickled in digital technology and connected by the Internet. Soon many possessions will follow, as part of the 'Internet of Things'. As technology revolutions go, there are none like it in human history. Not fire, stone tools, wheels, speech, language, weaving, musical instruments, money, printing, sailing, steam, internal combustion, broadcast or sound and video recording. The Internet subsumes every one of those, putting all of them in an app anyone with a connection can use. The Internet also reduces nearly to zero the distance between everybody and everything in the world, at costs that want to be zero as well.

We are shaped

And we take all of it for granted, because every technology succeeds by making the miraculous mundane. If a replaced technology survives, it's both as itself and as a feature of the miracle that replaces it. That's why there is a sandal in every shoe, a bike in every car, a hammer in every nail gun. Technologies that die are preserved only in museums or in language. For example, almost nobody who talks today about having been 'through the wringer' has a working acquaintance with the real thing: a pair of rotating cylinders that squeezed water out of washed clothes in the days before washing machines with spin cycles…

Source: Library of Congress via Wikimedia Commons

In his 1967 book *The Medium is the Massage: An inventory of effects*, Marshall McLuhan unpacks the subtitle of his magnum opus, *Understanding Media: The extensions of man*:

> *All media are extensions of some human faculty – psychic or physical. The wheel is an extension of the foot. The book is an extension of the eye. Clothing, an extension of the skin. Electric circuitry, an extension of the central nervous system… The extension of any one sense alters the way we think and act – the way we perceive the world. When these things change, men change.*

The scientist and philosopher Michael Polanyi called this process *indwelling*. Our senses suffuse the tools we hold in our hands, the cars we drive, the planes we fly. The driver speaks of 'my engine' and the pilot of 'my wings', as if they were parts of their bodies. No other animal does this. Nor are other animals as altered as are humans by the tools they use.

> *'We shape our tools and then our tools shape us', Marshall McLuhan is said to have said (according to McLuhan Galaxy). In The Medium is the Massage, McLuhan adds, 'All media work us over completely. They are so pervasive... that they leave no part of us untouched unaffected, unaltered... Any understanding of social and cultural change is impossible without a knowledge of the way media work as environments.'*

He also wasn't just talking about communications media. As Eric McLuhan (Marshall's son and collaborator) explains in *Laws of Media: The new science*, 'media' meant 'everything mankind makes and does, every procedure, every style, every artefact, every poem, song, painting, gimmick, gadget, theory – every product of human effort.'

Marshall McLuhan died in 1980, so he didn't live to see the Internet appear, or how digital technology suffused and subsumed everything it could. But he saw in satellites the promise of instant worldwide communications: a miracle the Internet has made mundane. In his 1970 book *From Cliché to Archetype*, McLuhan wrote, 'Since Sputnik and the satellites, the planet is enclosed in a new man-made environment that ends "Nature" and turns the globe into a repertory theater to be programmed.' Borrowing Shakespeare's 'All the world's a stage' metaphor, McLuhan added, in *From Cliché to Archetype*:

> *The results of living inside a proscenium arch of satellites is that the young now accept the public spaces of the earth as roll-playing areas... A planet parenthesized by a man-made environment no longer offers any directions to a nation or an individual. The world itself has become a probe. 'Snooping with intent to creep', or 'casing everyone else's joint' has become a major activity. As the main business of the world becomes espionage, secrecy becomes the basis of wealth, as with magic in a tribal society...*

It is just when people are all engaged in snooping on themselves and one another that they become anesthetized to the whole process... As information itself becomes the largest business in the world, data banks know more about individual people than the people do themselves. The more data banks record about each one of us, the less we exist.

He wrote that almost half a century ago, and here we are, wide awake in a new world, yet still under self-administered anaesthesia.

Marketing's decline

Which brings us to marketing, which the Internet has shaped into a snooping business, hell-bent on diminishing our existence as independent human beings operating with full agency.

Go to a search engine and look up *marketing* + *'know people better than they know themselves'*. Dig though the thousands of results and you'll find this has been a preoccupation of marketing ever since it discovered all the cool stuff it could do with digital technology.

In technology, what can be done will be done – until the limits are found. Some of those limits are operational: what *can't* be done. Some are moral: what *shouldn't* be done. And some are morally compromised ones that fail. A textbook example is nuclear power. Once 'too cheap to meter', it's now too expensive to rationalise, if you take into account how long nuclear waste lasts, and how little anybody wants it near their backyard.

Time always passes between discovering all that *can* be done and the bad experiences that show convincingly what *shouldn't* be done. We are past the *shouldn't* threshold with surveillance by marketing today.

Proving Zuboff's laws

Shoshana Zuboff began pointing at that threshold in her 1988 classic *In the Age of the Smart Machine: The future of work and power*, when she was a professor at Harvard Business School. In 'Be the friction – our response to our New Lords of the Ring', an article published in the *Frankfurter Allgemeine* in 2013, she compressed to three laws the case she made in that book:

> *First, that everything that can be automated will be automated. Second, that everything that can be informated will be informated [a process that translates descriptions and measurements of activities, events and objects into information]. And most important to us now, the third law: In the absence of countervailing restrictions and sanctions, every digital application that can be used for surveillance and control will be used for surveillance and control, irrespective of its originating intention.*

Perhaps the best demonstration of Zuboff's third law is 'The Big Datastillery: Strategies to accelerate the return on digital data', produced by IBM and Aberdeen in 2013. It's a giant image of a copper-coloured vat, like the kind used to make whisky. Into the top go little ones and zeroes piped in from transactions, search engine optimisation, pay-per-click and other sources. Then, out of pipes at the bottom, marketing goop gets poured into empty beakers rolling by on a conveyor belt.

Those beakers are human beings – you and me. We're the 'right person' getting the 'right offer' through the 'right channel' at the 'right time'. At the far end of the moving belt, after each of our beaker-selves metabolises force-fed marketing goop, we fart flames upward into a funnel through which our exhaust gets piped back into the top of the hopper.

Why would a fantasy this appalling come so easily to marketing, and those selling to its appetites for more?

In a word, isolation. In a few more, here's a passage from my book *The Intention Economy: When customers take charge*:

> *Back in the early '90s, when I was making a good living as a marketing consultant, I asked my wife – a successful businesswoman and a retailing veteran – why it was that heads of corporate Sales & Marketing departments were always Sales people and not Marketing people. Her answer: 'Simple: Sales is real. Marketing is bullshit.'*

When I asked her to explain that, she said this wasn't marketing's fault. The problem was the role marketing was forced to play. 'See, sales touches the customer; but marketing can't, because that's sales' job. So marketing has to be "strategic".' She put air-quotes around 'strategic'. She acknowledged that this was an over-simplification, and not fair to all the good people in marketing (such as myself) who really were trying to do right by customers. But her remark spoke to the need to distinguish between what's real and what's not, and to dig deeper into why the latter has become such an enormous part of the way we do business.

What better way for marketing to be 'strategic' than by obeying Zuboff's third law? And what better way to sell surveillance than by telling CMOs that they need 'Big Data'? IBM did that too. To see how, start here:

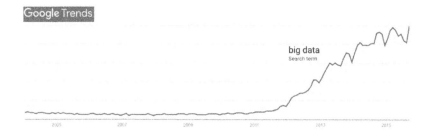

After searching at length through the history of all this, I am convinced that the craze began with a report called 'Big data: The next frontier for innovation, competition and productivity', published by McKinsey in May 2011. That report (and subsequent ones by McKinsey) drove publicity in *Forbes, The Economist, Financial Times* and many other publications. It also provided plenty of sales fodder for every big vendor selling Big Data products and services.

Starting with IBM. The first result in a Google search for *IBM + 'big data'* in calendar years 2010–2011 is 'Bringing big data to the enterprise', dated 16 May 2011, the same month as the McKinsey report (this item is gone from the Web, but it is referenced in a brochure-like web page at https://www-01.ibm.com/software/sg/data/bigdata/enterprise.html). The next, 'IBM Big Data – Where do I start?' is dated 23 November 2011 (this is also gone from the Web,

but referenced on this IBM page at https://www.ibm.com/developerworks/
community/blogs/ibm-big-data/entry/ibm_big_data_where_do_i_start).
Below is a Google Trends graph for McKinsey, IBM and 'big data' running
forward from 2004.

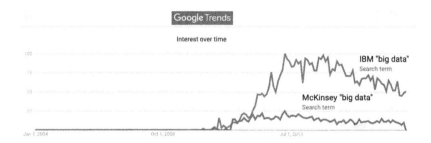

The first bump, in 2010, is for IBM 'big data'. I suspect that was due to a lot
of push on IBM's part, which you can see in a search for *IBM* + *'big data'* just in
2010, and a search just for *'big data'* in the same year.

So 'big data' was clearly in the water already when IBM and McKinsey lit
fires under 'big data'. But searches for 'big data', as we see, didn't pick up until
2011. That's when the craze hit the marketplace, as search trends for IBM and
four other big data vendors (SAP, HP, Oracle and Microsoft) clearly show:

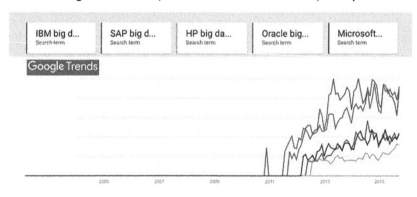

The target customer for all those companies was the CMO, or Chief
Marketing Officer – a title that didn't come into common use until the dotcom

boom, and grew as marketing's share of corporate overhead went up and up. On 8 February 2012, for example, *Forbes* ran a story by Lisa Arthur titled 'Five years from now, CMOs will spend more on IT than CIOs do'. It begins:

> *Marketing is now a fundamental driver of IT purchasing, and that trend shows no signs of stopping, or even slowing down, any time soon. In fact, Gartner analyst Laura McLellan recently predicted that by 2017, CMOs will spend more on IT than their counterpart CIOs.*

> *At first, that prediction may sound a bit over the top. (In just five years from now, CMOs are going to be spending more on IT than CIOs do?) But, consider this: 1) As we all know, marketing is becoming increasingly technology-based, 2) Harnessing and mastering Big Data is now key to achieving competitive advantage, and 3) Many marketing budgets already are larger – and faster growing – than IT budgets.*

So, how was a CMO supposed to understand a customer (again, better than the customer understood herself) through that big new budget?

IBM answered that in June of 2012, when its index page was headlined, 'Meet the new Chief Executive Customer. That's who's driving the new science of marketing', as noted in my blog. At a 'learn more' link, the headline reads, 'The new CMO and the science of giving people what they want'. From the copy there:

> *In this highly connected world of commerce and communication, you can no longer market broadly to a demographic. A consumer doesn't want to be a 'segment'. She's an individual. To capture and keep her business, she must be treated as one.*

> *The onus of this evolution has landed on the doorstep of the Chief Marketing Officer. And that means that the mind-set, as well as the skill set, of a CMO has to evolve right along with it. IBM has identified the three mandates for the new CMO.*

The first of those is 'Harness data to paint a predictive picture of each customer as an individual – on a massive scale'. The second is 'Create "systems of engagement" so you do more than shape desire – you predict it'. The third is 'Design your culture and brand so they are authentically one'. Above that last one it says this:

> Your brand is tested in every interaction. Today, the same transparency that allows you to understand each customer as an individual, conversely allows each customer to understand everything about your company. And gaps between what the brand promises and what it delivers are known – not just by those who experience them, but by others in their social network.

Note that it is the job of the company and the customer to *understand* each other, but *not* to connect, much less to talk. IBM continues (and I'm glad I quoted all this in my blog, as it's long since vanished from the Web):

> Today's abundance of data helps companies understand each customer in multiple dimensions. This leads to insights which, when combined, help build a clearer understanding of each customer as an individual. With that, marketers can make better decisions about the mix that will serve customers more completely – based on needs, desire, likely next action, opinions. Today's marketing practice requires building this capability of understanding customers as individuals across millions of interactions.

A sure sign of a relationship headed toward a break-up is when one partner says, 'We don't need to talk. I already know what you're going to say'. Or worse, 'I can also shape your desire'. But that's exactly what IBM is saying here, even though at this point it's only advising CMOs on how to flirt.

But CMOs bought it. According to Wikibon in February 2014, IBM was the top Big Data vendor by 2013, raking in $1.368 billion in revenue. In February of 2015, Reuters reported that IBM 'is targeting $40 billion in annual revenue from the cloud, big data, security and other growth areas by 2018', adding that this 'would represent about 44 percent of $90 billion in total revenue that analysts expect from IBM in 2018'.

The monster child of marketing's detachment from its human subjects and of its addiction to both Big Data and tendentious math is *adtech*: the surveillance side of advertising in the digital world, and the one that wants its human targets to 'interact' directly with ads. (Its powerful trade association is the IAB, or Interactive Advertising Bureau.)

Adtech today has become a giant four-dimensional shell game sustained entirely by small successes and a persistent belief by CMOs and their hired agents that the numbers they get are good enough (and the negative externalities small enough) to justify continued investment.

This will end.

The adtech bubble

One reason is that adtech is simply a bubble. In *The Big Short* (both the book and the movie), Wall Street guru Michael Burry says a sure sign of a bubble is high complexity and fraud. Adtech has an abundance of both.

But the bigger reason is that people are fighting back – massively. You can get one angle on that story with the below graph (Google Trends search for 'Ad blocker' and 'Do Not Track' from 2004).

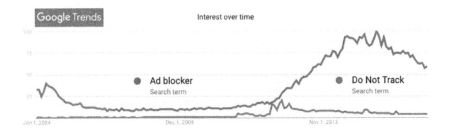

The graph shows two facts hardly noticed in coverage of either 'Do Not Track' or 'Ad blocker':

1. Ad blocking has been around a long time.
2. Interest in ad blocking didn't take off until interest in 'Do Not Track'

rose and fell in the 2012–2013 time frame, suggesting a correlation of some kind.

What happened in that time frame?

1. Big media got hip to how much tracking was actually going on. By far the best research and coverage of it was by the team of reporters, led by Julia Angwin (https://twitter.com/juliaangwin), who produced the 'What They Know' (http://wsj.com/wtk) series at *The Wall Street Journal*. The series ran from the summer of 2010 to mid-2012. The first piece was titled 'The web's new gold mine: your secrets', and subtitled 'A journal investigation finds that one of the fastest-growing businesses on the internet is the business of spying on consumers. First in a series'. I blogged, 'The tide turned today. Mark it: 31 July 2010.' But I was wrong. The tide was a tsunami of biblical dimensions that is only beginning to show signs of receding.

2. Do Not Track got awful help from the browser makers. In December 2010, Microsoft announced support as an opt-in feature, later turned it on by default, and reversed that decision in 2015. Apple followed in 2011, with a Do Not Track option in Safari, but didn't make a big thing about it. Google dragged its feet until November 2012, when, in the fifth paragraph of a Chrome blog, it mumbled (https://chrome. googleblog.com/2012/11/longer-battery-life-and-easier-website.html) about an opt-in setting. Mozilla gave mixed signals about supporting Do Not Track, but finally decided to attack surveillance by third party trackers directly in its Firefox browser in 2013. Meanwhile...

3. Google and Facebook both said in early 2013 that they would ignore Do Not Track requests (*Forbes*, 27 February 2013), which killed it right there. Yet death for Do Not Track was not severe enough for adtech's industry association, the IAB, which waged asymmetric PR warfare against Mozilla (the only browser maker not run by an industrial giant with an interest in the advertising business), saying it had lost its values. It even ran red herring ads like the following on its client publishers' websites.

SIGN THE PETITION

TELL MOZILLA NOT TO HARM
YOUR SMALL BUSINESS.
ADD YOUR NAME NOW!

In case you're not hip to the obvious, Mozilla was never out to harm 'your small business'. Nor were there any small businesses that gave a crap.

But it worked.

In early 2013, Mozilla caved in to pressure from the IAB. Worse, it started talking about getting into the ad business by doing personalisation itself, suggesting it supported tracking, even though that wasn't the plan. Users got hugely annoyed. I was too, and gently expressed that in a blog post titled 'Earth to Mozilla: come back home.' About a year after that, the new Content Services group at Mozilla hired me to help them (and yes, this was the assignment) 'give users superpowers' (https://www.slideshare.net/dsearls/2015-12-09amozlando). Specifically, two of those: 1) the power safely to advertise their intentions to buy certain products and services; and 2) to assert their own terms of engagement (more about both later). Alas, Content Services was killed off at the end of 2015, and neither of those superpowers were conferred. (But the work continues elsewhere. Read on.)

Still, killing Do Not Track was a pyrrhic victory for the IAB and adtech, because users took matters into their own hands, making ad blocking the biggest boycott in human history, as noted in my blog. According to PageFair's *2017 Adblock Report*, at least 11% of the world's population is now blocking ads on at least 615 million devices. According to GlobalWebIndex, 37% of all mobile users worldwide were blocking ads by January 2016, and another 42% would like to. With more than 4.77 billion mobile phone users in the world by 2017 (according to Statista), that meant more than 1.7 billion people are blocking ads already, a sum exceeding the population of the Western Hemisphere.

Nothing could send a clearer signal to marketers of what the market does not want. Yet the IAB would rather blame the messengers than hear the message. Search for *iab* + *'ad blockers'* + *Rothenberg* and see what comes up. (Randall Rothenberg is the IAB's CEO.)

But advertisers have started to wise up, led by the world's biggest advertiser, Procter & Gamble (as reported by Jack Neff). By now P&G, which pioneered and named branding in the 1930s, must surely realise that not a single brand known to the world has been made by adtech (after perhaps a $trillion or more has been spent on it), while some brands have surely been hurt by adtech.

Some publishers have been getting hip as well. These are led by Jason Kint of Digital Content Next, the online publishers' trade association. Jason (@Jason_Kint on Twitter) tweets relentlessly, and correctly, about how adtech hurts the publishing business.

Peak marketing

There are few signs marketing is picking up on any of these cues. Sure, there's lots of talk about improving the 'customer experience', but every company talking that talk has its own different 'customer journey', each starting with yet another login and password for the customer to forget, and yet another 'agreement' customers won't read because there's no point to it. Also, since the General Data Protection Regulation (GDPR) took effect in May 2018, adtech-supported commercial websites everywhere have been putting 'cookie notice' banners on their home pages asking for visitors to consent to the use of cookies by the site, without mentioning that some of those cookies are tracking ones.

There is also a broader trend of lack of interest in marketing by everyone who isn't in it.

That's what Google Books suggests. You can see *marketing* peak in the early 2000s, then fall off by 2008, when Google stopped scanning books.

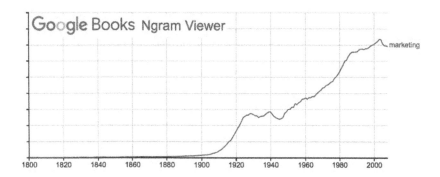

You see the same in Google search trends (which begin with 2004) for the same thing:

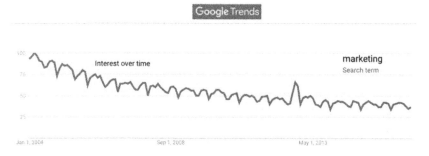

In Google Books, the word *consumer* looks post-peak too, right alongside marketing (shortlink, http://bit.ly/2ymGQhz):

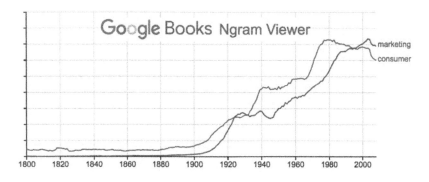

Same goes for Google search trends for *marketing* and *consumer* since 2004 (shortlink, http://bit.ly/2yIPfS6):

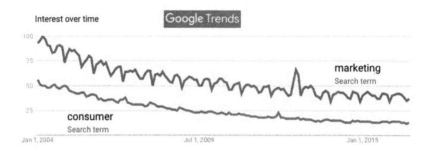

Searches dropped more, to less than half for both.

The main reason for a decline of interest in marketing is that we now live in a digital age when marketing no longer has the distance it used to have between performer and audience, and the audience is no longer captive – or even an audience.

As for advertising, while we might be entertained by some of it (for example, by a few Super Bowl ads), we wouldn't pay to come and see advertising in a cinema. This is why 'audience' is just one of marketing's long-held delusional conceits, now fully exposed.

But since marketing is accustomed to its remove from the actual marketplace, it has become insane. Seriously psychotic. Disconnected from reality. And here's a fun irony: *the bigger the data, the bigger the disconnect from the actual human beings who comprise a market.* To disbelieve that, you'd have to live in marketing, rather than in the marketplace. This is what advertising legend Bob Hoffman unpacks in his tweets (as @adcontrarian), in his blog http://adcontrarian.blogspot.com, and in his books *Marketers Are from Mars, Consumers are From New Jersey* and *BadMen: How advertising went from a minor annoyance to a major menace.*

Markets take over

Markets are made of customers and the companies that serve them. They aren't made by marketing, no matter how much marketing thinks that may be the case.

The Internet was designed for maximum participation by everybody. In a market led by customers, better marketing may not work, no matter how much marketers work to improve it. This is a simple fact that marketers will have to face.

People already have more choice than ever over how they spend their time and attention – and soon their intentions as well. Tools for expressing intention are not going to be marketing's. They will be the customer's.

Think about what will happen when people can signal exactly what they want better than marketing can ever guess at it. That's called *intentcasting*, and there are already dozens of companies building that business.

Think about what will happen when every person has a standard dashboard for managing all their business relationships as easily as they already manage their calendar and contacts (see my post 'Market intelligence that flows both ways'). So for example, a customer can tell every business she deals with that she has a new address, phone number or last name – in one move. With the same or similar tools, she can also supply good information about how she uses their products and services, and how and when they need servicing.

Think about what happens when customers have their own ways of managing their own data, and how it is shared and used by others. As with the last two things I asked you to think about, many solutions are brewing, and you can find a list of them at the ProjectVRM developments list (shortlink, http://j. mp/vrmdevwrk.)

Meanwhile, marketing can't contemplate anything I described in those three questions, because marketing works for companies, not for customers.

Now, let's go back to advertising for a minute.

Before we had the Internet, marketing could target advertising at whole populations, sending strong creative and economic signals (for more on this, read Don Marti's 'Team targeting, team signal'). In doing that, they could earn respect by sponsoring those publishers and broadcasters, while also delivering good branding results for advertisers. Even when people don't buy advertised products or services, they still hold strong brand associations in their minds, thanks to good advertising (I explain more about the difference between advertising and adtech in 'Separating advertising's wheat and chaff').

Today, people get extra annoyed at advertising because they know they ought to have the means for making it go away (this is the Internet, after all; the 'Land of Everything'). The means for making advertising disappear are now far more available than they ever were when the media's mainstream consisted of commercial print and broadcasting. Those media are also an ever-shrinking percentage of growing media options in the lives of Internet-connected people, who also have many more options about what to allow or block on their devices, and how they spend their time and attention. Are those people going to *want* advertising? Really?

It's no accident that Netflix now has more subscribers than all of cable TV, as reported by *Forbes*. The reason isn't content alone. Netflix also lacks advertising and other forms of interruptive promotion that have been the norm in broadcasting for so long that marketers take those interruptive moments for granted – which is a huge mistake. It also matters that a large percentage of the world's connected population blocks ads, tracking or both. Ask why they do it, and most people will simply say 'because I can' or 'why not?'

Think about it: if advertisers stopped all tracking and went back to simply sponsoring media the old-fashioned way – only now producing only the most creative, award-deserving and brand-supportive ads possible – would that stop people from blocking ads anyhow?

In a few cases it might. For example, in fashion, sports and tech publishing, the ads are almost like catalogue entries, and well matched to the publications they support and the markets they serve; there really is a symbiosis, an alignment of incentives. For sports on TV, there is no way to turn ads off if you want to watch games in real time.

But, at best, those will be exceptions to new rules written by customers and applied by their tech. When those rules are written, we can expect them to maximise useful signalling between demand and supply. Will marketing and advertising as we've known them make full sense in that world? Or will they be anachronisms, persisting only in specialised cases where they still make sense?

Like it or not, the Internet is turning the marketplace into a dance floor. If marketing isn't ready for customers to take the lead on that floor, those customers will find other corporate dance partners. Who will that be? Depends on who listens to signals coming from customers' own tools.

We can expect those tools to give customers full power over their data, their lives, and their experiences in the marketplace, as noted in my post 'Customertech will turn the online marketplace into a Marvel-like universe in which all of us are enhanced'. It's just a matter of time before customers are extended by their tools to a degree that they get exactly the kinds of superpowers Mozilla was looking for two years ago. And many more.

I hope for marketing's sake that it welcomes being shaped by those customers, and not just by big suppliers of marketing tech and BS. If marketing welcomes being truly led by customers, it will evolve. If it doesn't, it will become extinct.

References

Angwin, J. https://www.wsj.com/articles/SB10001424052748703940904575395073512989404

Cortland, M. *2017 Adblock Report*. PageFair, 1 February 2017

Google Trends for 'big data' searches. https://trends.google.com/trends/explore?date=all&q=big%20data

Hoffman, R. *BadMen: How advertising went from a minor annoyance to a major menace*. Type A Group, 2017

Hoffman, R. *Marketers Are from Mars, Consumers are From New Jersey*. CreateSpace, 2015

http://articles.latimes.com/2011/apr/14/business/la-fi-apple-do-not-track-20110414

http://www.ibmbigdatahub.com/infographic/big-datastillery-strategies-accelerate-return-digital-data

http://zgp.org/~dmarti/business/team-targeting-team-signal/#.W3mugOhKjIU

https://blogs.harvard.edu/doc/2014/04/12/earth-to-mozilla-come-back-to-us/

https://blogs.msdn.microsoft.com/ie/2010/12/07/ie9-and-privacy-introducing-tracking-protection/)

https://techcrunch.com%2F2015%2F04%2F03%2Fmicrosoft-disables-do-not-track-as-the-default-setting-in-internet-explorer

https://www.forbes.com/sites/eliseackerman/2013/02/27/big-internet-companies-struggle-over-proper-response-to-consumers-do-not-track-requests/#65a2967b22fc

https://www.iab.com/has-mozilla-lost-its-values/

Kelly, J. 'Big data vendor revenue and market forecast 2013–2017.' Wikibon, 12 February 2014

Lewis. M. *The Big Short: Inside the Doomsday Machine.* Norton, 2010

Mander, J. '37% of mobile users are blocking ads.' GlobalWebIndex, 25 January 2106. http://blog.globalwebindex.net/chart-of-the-day/37-of-mobile-users-are-blocking-ads/

Manyika, J, et al. 'Big data: the next frontier for innovation, competition and productivity.' McKinsey & Company, May 2011. https://www.mckinsey.com/business-functions/digital-mckinsey/our-insights/big-data-the-next-frontier-for-innovation

McLuhan Galaxy (https://mcluhangalaxy.wordpress.com/2013/04/01/we-shape-our-tools-and-thereafter-our-tools-shape-us/), 'the idea is McLuhan's', though the line was written by Father John Culkin, a friend of McLuhan's and a colleague when they were both at Fordham University

McLuhan, M. *Understanding Media: The extensions of man.* McGraw-Hill, 1964

McLuhan, M, and Fiore, Q. *The Medium is the Massage: An inventory of effect.* Gingko Press, 1967

McLuhan, M, with McLuhan, E. *Laws of Media: The new science.* University of Toronto Press, 1992

McLuhan, M, with Watson, W. *From Cliché to Archetype.* Viking Press, 1970

Morris, I. 'Netflix is now bigger than cable TV'. *Forbes,* 13 June 2017. https://www.forbes.com/sites/ianmorris/2017/06/13/netflix-is-now-bigger-than-cable-tv/#deab26f158bc

Neff, J. 'P&G tells digital to clean up, lays down new rules for agencies and ad tech to get paid.' *AdAge,* 29 January 2017. http://adage.com/article/media/p-g-s-pritchard-calls-digital-grow-up-new-rules/307742/

Reuters. 'IBM targets $40 billion in cloud, other growth areas by 2018'. 27 February 2015. http://www.reuters.com/article/us-ibm-investors/ibm-targets-40-billion-in-cloud-other-growth-areas-by-2018-idUSKBN0LU1LC20150227

Searls, D. 'Beyond ad blocking – the biggest boycott in human history'. *Doc Searls Weblog*, 28 September 2015. http://blogs.harvard.edu/doc/2015/09/28/beyond-ad-blocking-the-biggest-boycott-in-human-history/

Searls, D. 'Customertech will turn the online marketplace into a Marvel-like universe in which all of us are enhanced.' *Medium*, 29 May 2017. Shortlink, http://bit.ly/rallnhncd

Searls, D. 'Market intelligence that flows both ways.' *Medium*, 28 August 2016. Shortlink, http://bit.ly/2wayintel

Searls, D. 'Separating advertising's wheat and chaff.' *Doc Searls Weblog*, 12 August 2015

Searls, D. *The Intention Economy: When customers take charge*. Harvard Business Review Press, 2012

Searls, D. 'Yes, please meet the Chief Executive Customer.' *Doc Searls Weblog*, 19 June 2012

Statista. 'Number of mobile phone users worldwide from 2013 to 2019 (in billions).' 2017. https://www.statista.com/statistics/274774/forecast-of-mobile-phone-users-worldwide/

Zuboff, S. 'Be the friction – our response to the New Lords of the Ring.' *Frankfurter Allgemeine*, 25 June 2013

Zuboff. S. *In the Age of the Smart Machine: The future of work and power*. Basic Books, 1988

Note from Doc: The internet and World Wide Web were born as proper nouns, and to me deserve to stay that way, even if some authorities on usage have chosen to demote them to generic nouns. Thus, you will find both capitalised in this chapter.

© marketoonist.com

39

A SIMPLE WAY TO WIN

Written by **Sue Unerman**

This chapter reveals a simple way to make more profit. With evidence piling up that businesses with diverse senior management make better decisions, the chapter shows how to broaden the diversity of the leadership, and as a result produce better advertising that will truly resonate with women – 51% of the population, 80% of shoppers. There is clear guidance on how to avoid the all-too-common pitfalls of incremental change and plausible deniability. It may be challenging to drive real change, but it will deliver real competitive advantage.

'Is that even possible?'

'I never ask that question until after I've done it', Han Solo replies to Rey in *Star Wars: The Force Awakens*.

There's a very public debate going on about how much change we need (and how much is even possible).

Two tribes

There are overexcited neophiliacs out there who want to rip everything up and start again (with data analysed by robots). There are grumpy old-school resisters of change who are sure that the rules are the rules, and you mess with them at your peril.

There is one aspect of change in our industry where the evidence for change has been mounting. Where the talk about change is endless. Where actual change at scale seems, by current rates of progression, impossible – though like Hans Solo, I believe in rejecting that scenario.

This chapter doesn't advocate change in marketing or communications techniques – there is plenty of advice about that in the other chapters. This chapter isn't about what we do. It's about how we do it. Even *who* does it.

What needs changing?

We need an equal gender mix at every stage, from entry level to boardroom in our business. An equal share of voice in decision making. An equal share of feminine presence and status in marketing assets and advertising.

At least 70% of purchases worldwide are made by women. At entry level, 50% of most workplaces in our sector are already women. But most businesses overall are predominantly run by men. Most creative teams in agencies are run by men. Most agencies are run by men.

The most recent IPA diversity data (*Campaign*, January 2018) shows only marginal gains in terms of women in senior positions. Less than 1% improvement at C-suite level, with 30.9% of positions held by women in agencies (this has inched up from 30.3% the year before, but is down from the all-time high of 33% in 2015).

Australian screen director Gillian Armstrong called our industry to account at Cannes in 2017, saying that it was appalling that only 9% of ads were directed by women: 'The ad industry should be leaders in communication. There is such a thing as a woman's point of view, and it's not just feminine products', she said. 'It is not a level playing field.'

Armstrong's professional opinion aside, there is no shortage of global data that proves that businesses make better and more profitable decisions with a better gender balance at senior levels.

Companies run by diverse teams perform better

McKinsey has analysed gender diversity at executive level across 754 companies across the world.

Companies in the top quartile are 22% more likely to outperform the national industry average than bottom quartile companies in terms of profitability (earnings before interest and tax) or return on equity.

Twenty-two percent is substantial. But that's the conservative figure. Using 'economic profit' (ie the company's ability to create value in excess of weighted cost of capital), the difference between top and bottom quartiles is 67%.

A study by research agency Catalyst proved that firms with three or more women directors had *40%* better profit margin than average.

A study by Thomson Reuters ('Mining the metrics of board diversity', June 2013) shows that companies with mixed boards have a lower tracking of errors.

Grant Thornton analysis from 2015 (as reported by *The Guardian*) of businesses across the US, India and UK calculated that mixed gender boards were more profitable than men-only boards by £430bn.

It is not a huge deductive leap to conclude that an even balance of men and women in leadership across marketing decision making would improve marketing effectiveness, not just marginally but significantly – especially given the economic power of women and the fact that even where they lack economic independence, it is women who are buying more things, more of the time.

Outside of gaming, most purchasing decisions in most sectors are either totally made by women or are executed predominantly by women. (Most games are made for men and boys on consoles and PCs. Women play as much on smartphones as men do. Different kinds of games, of course. #GamerGate has been an important wake-up call for this sector, and the gaming industry is now taking steps to be more inclusive.)

More action is needed

Overall, there just isn't enough action.

Businesses sometimes sign up for change in principle, but do not follow through with accountable targets. In a business environment of uncertainty post-Brexit, excuses abound for lack of progress (there are other critical KPIs that come first), although it's very tempting to insert the following meme for any board worrying about profit:

I've developed some expertise in this debate over the last few years. My book *The Glass Wall: Success strategies for women at work – and businesses that mean business* was published in 2016, and myself and co-author Kathryn Jacob have been on tour since publication to over 100 businesses and networks for presentations and discussions. We've been at the heart of the debate about how to get business to change.

The truth is that, in too many businesses, there just isn't any fairness, real fairness, about how the workplace functions for women.

Why do we talk about a 'Wall' instead of a 'Ceiling'? The 'Glass Ceiling' implies that everything is fine until you reach a certain level of seniority. The truth, that has been revealed by our research (both qualitative interviews and quantitative analysis across the UK, US and Russia), is that women may hit a 'Glass Wall' at any stage of their careers.

Women and men can see through this wall, but often they don't speak the same language, or have the same cultural expectations. Women can see the meetings they should have been invited to, but somehow have not been; or the casual conversations that accelerate careers, but from which they are excluded.

The problem is a cultural one, and it exists across our sector. Even if there are lots of women around in the workplace, if there is no tradition of senior women, if the last CEO or the one before isn't a woman, there's probably some change needed. Or if the board is all middle-aged white men in suits, it may just be too homogenous to allow outliers to join them. There are cultural problems that arise from managers' nervousness around maternity leave (whatever the official company policy), or the inability to understand that not everyone finds the same jokes or boys' locker room humour funny. As the #metoo debate continues, there is increasing evidence of sexual harassment. The 'timeTo' research published in June 2018 by the Advertising Association, NABS and WACL (and backed by the IPA and ISBA) revealed that one in four people working in the industry have been sexually harassed. The new code of conduct is therefore overdue, and welcome. Many businesses still need to fix their culture.

It is undeniable, however, that some of the inequality in the workplace issues result from how women are brought up; how we're expected to behave by schools, our friendship groups, our parents.

Men and women have different motivations. They can respond differently to incentives, and challenges.

This is a good thing. This is what diversity is all about, of course. This is why professional decisions in our sector that are made by a balanced gender team will be better decisions.

The stats show that there aren't enough women at the top of our industry, with key decision-making influence.

There is a continuing failure of businesses to allow women to be different, and still to succeed, relative to men

The foreword for *The Glass Wall* was written by top civil rights lawyer Baroness Helena Kennedy. Kennedy said:

I have been involved in women's rights in the workplace for over 35 years. When I started out, there were very few senior women, and those who had made it were usually from privileged backgrounds and had often committed exclusively to their careers. In the years since then we've seen some change – but not at the highest levels, and not in enough numbers. We've been told that it is just a matter of women coming through the system; that it is just about evolution, just a matter of time. We are still waiting. Let's be clear that it's the system that is at fault, not women. We're perfectly smart, perfectly able and often better at management because of the need to run a family as well as a professional life. So, what's the problem, and what can we do about it? It is still the case that senior men tend to nurture and promote younger men. Women often underrate their own talent, when their peers who are men are doing the opposite. And when women talk about equality in the workplace, it can crowd out some important truths about difference. We've been so cagey about special pleading for special treatment that we have focused on equal treatment. Yet equalisation has almost always been to a masculine norm.

A masculine norm. A masculine idea of what is fair. And I would add, often, a toxic alpha masculine norm. A norm that prevents all kinds of talented people who don't comply with it from reaching top positions – some of whom are men; many of whom are women. This norm means that pushing for promotion means you're more likely to be promoted. Yet being good at self-promotion, being 'promotable' and 'the right kind of chap for the top table' does not necessarily mean being the best at the job that actually needs to be done.

Women need to take action, and so does business

Leaders must wake up to the fact that they will need to change their approach to succession management, and recruitment, significantly if they are to retain and benefit from talented women. It is not enough to maintain that you have created a 'level playing field' if that same 'level playing field' does not take into account the differences between men and women – whether that is around the approach to the care of young children or elderly dependants (which often falls to women), an ambivalence about self-promotion and ambition, or an attitude to banter in the office. If there isn't gender equality in senior management – and very few businesses currently do have this – then our research shows that the workplace culture must change to allow it.

Talent wastage

There is so much wastage of talent in our industry. Too many women face what seem like impossible hurdles to progression. As Hans Solo put it, let's not worry about 'impossible' until after we've done it.

It's very clear that rhetoric about diversity, an awayday, a spoken commitment or a few speeches are not enough.

Plausible deniability

At the 2017 FT 'Women on Top' conference, psychologist John Amaechi talked about the concept of 'plausible deniability' as a crucial factor in holding back real change.

Plausible deniability is specifically a legal term. At its most serious it is a term used for the ability of people to deny knowledge of (or responsibility for) any damnable actions committed by others in an organisational hierarchy because of a lack of evidence that can confirm their participation, even if they were personally involved in (or at least willfully ignorant of) the actions.

On the broader spectrum of plausible deniability, we may all have witnessed some version of it. People who witnessed and remained a bystander to behaviour that they could have challenged, but found easier, less fearful or politically expedient to ignore.

Amaechi thinks that it's one of the core reasons that things stay the same. Without diagnosing this in an organisation, calling it out and dealing with it, there is a real danger that any amount of training, coaching and KPI setting will be in vain, and generations of managers will go on a training day, commit to do things differently, and then carry on with exactly the same behaviour as before.

Some of the issues preventing talent from rising to the top of business that appeared in my research certainly have a whiff of this. Team leaders who don't spot (or spot but don't care) that there is someone in the team who is unhappy with the tone of the banter that *supposedly* is crucial for bonding. Keeping up the tradition that the Christmas outing is *still bound* to end up at a strip club because everyone always has gone along with it. Assuming that everyone will acquire the same ability to clamour for promotion when there is clear evidence that there is a gender divide.

Amaechi didn't mince his words that this kind of behaviour needs to be eliminated. Unconscious bias training might make the business feel like it is doing something, but it is no more effective than taking antibiotics for the flu virus. You're taking some action, certainly, but it's going to have absolutely no effect on the problem if the problem is rooted elsewhere.

Targets for diversity in senior management must be set, monitored and delivered. Why wouldn't you if it is going to deliver real competitive advantage?

"Describe what you can bring to this company."

We don't have equality for women at work. We don't have equality in how we treat women in advertising

The evidence suggests that we have only recently allowed women to be either funny or to have a sense of humour.

WARC's 2011 best practice marketing to women paper actually stated that 'men are more likely to enjoy humorous ads', and suggested that using humour to target women was higher risk.

As I wrote in my 2017 updated best practice paper, if you actually spend any time at all hanging out with women, they are of course frequently very funny. Yet if you spent time analysing ads targeting women, as opposed to ads targeting men, you might assume that women didn't have a sense of humour.

Millward Brown research (of course) states that humorous ads *can* appeal to women as well. So, get the humour right and your advertising will absolutely stand out from the crowd.

How do you get it right? Women must be a part of the decision-making creative team. They must be involved in the advertising creation at a senior level – a situation that still cannot be taken for granted.

Men and women tend to find different things funny. Here's diversity in play again. To swerve the powerful use of humour for fear of getting it wrong is surely a missed opportunity. Good use of funny women is going to give you cut-through, as Vicki Maguire, Grey's creative chief wrote in *Campaign*, January 2018.

Women don't even show up that much in ads relatively, based on a trawl of the Cannes Lions archive (the work the industry is most proud of); or if they do, they're 'humourless, mute and in the kitchen', according to data from the Geena Davis Institute and JWT. As Nicola Kemp reported in *Campaign* in June 2017: 'Men were 62% more likely to be shown as smart and one in three men was shown to have an occupation compared to one in four women. A quarter (25%) of ads feature only men, while only 5% of ads only depict women. Men get four times as much screen time as women and speak seven times more than women.'

Women don't feature behind the camera either. Less than 10% of commercial photographers are women.

Enough talk. More action.

The 2017 *Star Wars* movie, *The Last Jedi*, has been called a beacon of feminism. Finally, a movie that passes the Bechdel test (a method for evaluating the portrayal of women in fiction) with flying colours.

The movie launch was accompanied by outcries from the fanboy community, however, including a fan edit (BBC news) that chopped any women characters out (cutting 106 minutes of footage). Imagine that happening the other way around?

Impossible.

References

Harvard Business Review evidence that women don't apply for jobs unless they are 100% qualified, August 2014. https://hbr.org/2014/08/why-women-dont-apply-for-jobs-unless-theyre-100-qualified

http://share.thomsonreuters.com/general/Unica/pdf/Mining_the_Metrics_of_Board_Diversity_Thomson_Reuters_White_Paper.pdf

http://www.bbc.co.uk/newsbeat/article/42719084/star-wars-the-last-jedi-cast-mock-men-only-fan-edit

http://www.catalyst.org/media/companies-more-women-board-directors-experience-higher-financial-performance-according-latest

https://live-t.ft.com/Events/2017/FT-Women-At-The-Top

https://www.amaechiperformance.com/

https://www.campaignlive.co.uk/article/gillian-armstrong-lack-female-directors-appalling/1436863?bulletin=campaign_agencies_bulletin

https://www.campaignlive.co.uk/article/timeto-calls-timesup-sexual-harassment-ad-industry/1486271

https://www.campaignlive.co.uk/article/truth-behind-ipas-diversity-survey/1454468

https://www.theguardian.com/business/2015/sep/29/companies-with-women-on-the-board-perform-better-report-finds

https://www.theguardian.com/film/2017/dec/18/star-wars-the-last-jedi-women-bechdel-test

https://www.warc.com/SubscriberContent/Article/How_to_market_to_women/77092

Kemp, N. https://www.campaignlive.co.uk/article/women-advertising-humourless-mute-kitchen/1437171

Maguire, V. https://www.campaignlive.co.uk/article/why-funny-women-lead-advertising-year/1453221

Unerman, S. https://www.warc.com/content/article/bestprac/how_to_market_effectively_to_women/111603

Unerman, S. Opinion piece on McKinsey data about profitability from more diverse boards http://sueunerman.com/2017/10/want-to-boost-your-bottom-line/

Unerman, S, and Jacob, K. *The Glass Wall: Success strategies for women at work – and businesses that mean business.* Profile, 2016

40

MARKETING IN THE AGE OF UNREASON – THE RISE OF EMOTIONAL EXPERIENCE DESIGN

Written by **Patricia McDonald**

This chapter discusses the role of emotion and of the unconscious brain in communications. The evidence presented here draws on both seminal research from the IPA Effectiveness database and academic studies on persuasion, social proof and the power of aesthetics to shape behaviour. The chapter examines the rational fallacy that persists in how we design online experiences, and makes the case for 'Emotional Experience Design', identifying four parameters: Cause, Context, Community and Craft.

It's often said that we live in an age of perfect information. Yet 'post-truth' was the *Oxford English Dictionary*'s word of 2016.

It is undoubtedly true that search marketing and social media have created a new era of transparency for brands. More information than ever before is available, on everything from product performance to corporate ethics. The beauty blogger can elevate a cheap and cheerful pot of moisturiser with a single tweet, the unhappy consumer trigger a boycott.

It is easy to assume that an age of infinitely available information should generate more rational decision making and more considered purchasing. We can, after all, interrogate products on a host of dimensions, from functional specifications to environmental impact to peer and expert reviews, at the mere click of a keyboard.

But to make rational decisions, first we would have to actively engage in (and consider) our purchases. Secondly, we would have to evaluate impartially the information available, free of existing biases. Those two conditions are extraordinarily unlikely, for a number of reasons.

Most brand decisions involve very low levels of active consideration

Back in 1999, Robert Heath developed the theory of 'Low Involvement Processing': the idea that most communications are processed at a relatively passive (but nonetheless powerful) level, and that most purchases tap into a set of deeply ingrained brand associations rather than engaging our rational brains. In partnership with Jon Howard-Spink, Heath wrote:

> Low Involvement Processing uses very little working memory… it collects input and stores it pretty much exactly as it comes in, without 'thinking' about it very much at all. On this basis, Low Involvement Processing seems to be the poor cousin of High Involvement Processing. In fact, Low Involvement Processing is an immensely powerful tool. Indeed, it is the glue that holds the whole world of brands together.

Likewise, Byron Sharp in *How Brands Grow* emphasises the importance of creating and working with brand memories in order to make brands as easy as possible to buy:

> The dominant way that advertising works is by refreshing and building memory structures. These structures improve the chance of a brand being recalled and/or noticed in buying situations; this in turn increases the chance of a brand being bought.

On a day-to-day basis we draw on these deeply entrenched memories, thinking very little about the brand decisions we make – we would otherwise be completely unable to function. There are relatively few occasions on which we actively research, compare and consider our purchases. Categories such as automotive, travel or consumer electronics are obvious exceptions, but account for relatively few of our purchases.

Most brand decisions are much less rational than we believe

Even the more considered purchases we make are seldom entirely rational – research from Antonio Damasio shows that patients with injuries affecting the emotional areas of their brain struggle to make decisions, even when their rational capabilities are otherwise unaffected. While we perceive ourselves as rational beings, making autonomous and considered decisions, a host of unconscious biases (and increasingly, psychological 'nudges') shape our every decision.

In a world of emotional and irrational decisions, we might assume that facts are our friends; that we can change hearts and minds with data. Studies have shown, however, that confronting individuals with strong beliefs with evidence to the contrary can actually have a negative effect. In 2011, professors Brendan Nyhan and Jason Reifler of Dartmouth College surveyed parents about the misreported link between vaccinations and autism. Respondents were shown video evidence debunking the myth. Despite this, those with an existing bias against vaccinations were *less* likely (having seen the evidence) to vaccinate their children than before. This is known as the 'backfire' effect.

In our own industry of course, we've seen time and again that emotional campaigns outperform rational ones. Les Binet and Peter Field's seminal 2007 book *Marketing in the Age of Accountability* demonstrated significantly higher business results from emotionally driven campaigns over the longer term. Subsequent (2013) analysis by Binet and Field showed that the most profitable campaigns have a ratio of 60:40 in favour of emotive, brand-building media versus rational, sales activation media. Yet Binet and Field's most recent findings (in 2016) show that most brands now spend a disproportionate share of budget on short-term sales activation activities, up from 31% in 2014 to 47% in 2016. This will of course reflect the rise of online marketing and e-commerce, and we may find over time that these categories become less clear as the boundaries between brand experiences and transactional experiences become increasingly blurred.

Nevertheless, it is clear that campaigns that engage emotionally are more likely to succeed than those that adopt a more rational approach, not least because of the limited amounts of active attention we pay to brand messages.

Infusing every touchpoint with emotion

As marketers, it is tempting, then, to default to what we know best, using TV (or video) to drive an emotional response, and relying on digital or direct channels to do the slightly grubbier task of converting, or of carrying the weight of information we couldn't find a home for elsewhere.

Yet the boundaries between tasks and channels is no longer so clear cut. We spend ever-increasing amounts of time online. The average Briton, for example, spent three hours and nine minutes online in 2016, of which 45% was spent on a smartphone – arguably the most personal and emotionally significant device we own; the first thing many of us touch in the morning, and the last thing we touch at night.

A host of technologies – from shoppable content to connected stores to social commerce – is blurring the boundaries between an emotional, or brand-led experience, and a more functional or transactional one. Consider the scenario in which a favourite fashion magazine or blogger posts a highly engaging (yet fully shoppable) photo story: is that an emotional experience, a transactional one, or both? The boundaries between content and commerce, social experiences and shopping experiences are being eroded, yet many online experiences still assume a highly rational and linear journey from A to B.

As these boundaries blur, we will need to learn to infuse every touchpoint with emotion. Yet this requires us to think about emotion in a very different way. For decades our default response has been to generate emotion through narrative – through evocative audio visual or print advertising. Yet we know that outside the narrow realm of communications there are a host of other ways in which brands evoke an emotional response.

It has often been observed that there is emotion in utility, but there is also emotion in elegance: emotion in the weight of a fabric or the clink of a glass. Emotional cues in the sound of a luxury car door closing (and teams dedicated to perfecting the sound). Emotional cues in how a space is lit, how its acoustics are designed. Emotion in the sense of recognition we may get from store personnel or fellow customers.

In his 2003 book *Emotional Design: Why we love (or hate) everyday things*, Donald Norman explains that, all things being equal, aesthetically pleasing design seems to work better. Norman highlights the critical role emotions play in decision making, and in driving usability:

> We now have evidence that aesthetically pleasing objects enable you to work better. As I shall demonstrate, products and systems that make you feel good are easier to deal with and produce more harmonious results.

Offline, successful marketers think long and hard about every aspect of the brand's body language: the sound, smell, pace and rhythm of the brand. They consider how design cues can be used to hurry users along or slow them down, to relax or excite. Online, our focus on reducing friction means that we focus less on the distinctive body language or ergonomics of brands than on the most efficient path to purchase.

A frictionless experience can undoubtedly be a delightful one, but as Norman's research highlights, aesthetically pleasing or emotionally satisfying experiences can also enhance usability, while building a more distinctive set of brand associations. By now we should have moved beyond simply asking 'Does it work?' towards asking 'How does it feel?'

This will become increasingly important as we enter a new era in user experience, as a combination of new data and new interfaces changes the way we interact with digital experiences of all kinds. Technology will become increasingly invisible, and paradoxically, increasingly human. The entire language of interaction design will be transformed.

The rise of invisible technology

One of the founding principles of technology is Zuboff's Law: 'Everything that can be automated will be automated'. One of the most beloved principles of technology is Clarke's Law: 'Any sufficiently advanced technology is indistinguishable from magic'.

We are seeing both these principles at play in the world of modern experience design: the more advanced technology becomes the more invisible and intuitive it becomes.

Much has been written on how interface brands (Uber, Airbnb, Zipcar) are the winners in the digital age. The most successful interfaces, however, will ultimately become the least intrusive – metrics such as dwell time and visibility will become obsolete as experiences become seamless, effortless and automated to invisibility. As Matthew Panzarino puts it, writing in *TechCrunch*:

> You've probably heard the argument that for an app to be truly successful it needs to earn a place on your home screen. We could see another whole class of apps that not only don't need to fight for a home screen slot, they don't need to be opened at all to add value. And that's interesting.

Ever smarter algorithms are building more dynamic, contextual understanding of where we are, what we're doing, and what we might do next. Today my phone knows where I am, and where I need to be. It knows the weather and the traffic conditions. How long before, without asking, it hails me a cab exactly when I need it without any need to interact with the cab company's app or interface? If we consider the rise of the chatbot, how long before an increasing number of brand interactions are conducted via messenger app? In these scenarios, the brand experience as we know it today recedes to the point of invisibility, unless we find new ways to brand and enhance these interactions.

The human touch

Going a stage further, and thinking beyond the home screen (or indeed any screen), technologies such as voice recognition, augmented reality, haptic feedback, gesture and voice recognition are moving us beyond a screen-based interface towards a world where our bodies, lightweight wearables and smart environments will be our primary means of interacting with content and commerce experiences of all kinds.

Brands from banks to fashion are experimenting with the potential of biometric interfaces to improve security or transform the path the purchase. Everything from a selfie to a heartbeat can become a password. Voice recognition, linked to shopping baskets via properties such as Amazon's Alexa, is becoming a new way of ordering, or of controlling our environment.

A team at Saarland University in Germany are experimenting with temporary electronic tattoos that can turn the contours of the skin into smartphone controls, while Levi's® has pioneered a smart jacket sleeve to similar effect. Meanwhile, Sony has patented a contact lens that records video.

So in this new world of interface, where I can unlock an account with my thumbprint, make a payment with a selfie, or receive notifications at a glance, how do we make these interactions tangible, branded and rewarding?

Critically, how can we build (or draw on) the deeply ingrained brand memories and associations that Robert Heath and Byron Sharp tell us are so critical in driving brand choices when we are designing with a very different and much less obvious toolkit? This is largely unchartered territory today, but the potential is significant. Research conducted jointly by J. Walter Thompson and Mindshare UK explored the impact of voice interactions on users' brains. It showed that voice interactions used consistently lower levels of brain activity than touch interactions. Yet it also demonstrated that users who mentioned a brand name had a stronger emotional response than those who simply typed the name. Low Involvement Processing indeed.

I believe the combination of increasingly invisible and increasingly human technology calls for a new way of thinking about how we design experiences. An approach that moves beyond services that deliver towards services that delight.

We may not be able to predict today what the digital artefacts of tomorrow will be. Today, the building blocks of our digital experiences are web pages, apps and display ads; tomorrow they will be something very different. Yet whatever formats we find ourselves working with – bots, skills, filters – fundamentally we will remain in the business of 'experience design'. Experience design as a term is often used to describe a relatively narrow set of activities. What I mean by the term here is a much broader definition: identifying and designing moments where brands can make emotional connections with their users. I think of it as Emotional Experience Design.

It's worth noting here that (for an exciting moment) I thought I had coined the term. Unfortunately, a quick Google search revealed that Forrester has been using the term Emotional Experience Design for a while. Nevertheless, I hope this is a fresh take on what it means in practice.

As mentioned at the start of this chapter, there are four key aspects to Emotional Experience Design as I see it: Cause, Context, Community and Craft.

Emotional Experience Design

Cause

In a world where emotion is more important than ever, but needs to manifest through a host of new interfaces and experiences, a sense of brand purpose is more important than ever.

Purpose is an overused word in our industry. Too often we assume that for a brand to have purpose it must have an altruistic social mission, confusing brand purpose with CSR and forgetting the role of product. Not every brand can exist to connect the world, break down barriers or champion individuality.

It is undoubtedly true that consumers have heightened expectations of corporate transparency. Hitherto private debates around ethics, diversity and sustainability are now played out in public, impacting share price and brand reputation.

To me, however, purpose (or cause) is very simple: what does your brand exist to do in the world? This may be altruistic, or it may be something much less lofty. An outdoor clothing brand may exist to champion exploration, a pasta sauce to bring the family together, a toy company to ignite imaginations.

With that in place, it becomes much easier to establish a set of experience design principles that shape distinctive interactions at every touchpoint. A brand that champions exploration and celebrates those who venture off the beaten track should behave very differently from a brand that promises the ultimate in efficiency. That difference should be palpable at every turn, from where the brand is discovered to how the browsing and transaction processes are designed. Just as in the offline space, those two brands should have a different rhythm, pace and movement.

Context

One of the early victims of automation (via adtech) has been context: the ability to know when and where our advertising is being displayed. The irony is that, used correctly, adtech should offer us a greater and more sophisticated ability to understand and respond to context than ever before, not simply knowing where our messages are placed, but understanding how our users are feeling and which messages are most relevant in that moment.

There is nothing more human or more emotionally powerful than feeling heard and understood. This is what a true understanding of context can achieve.

In the offline world, relevance is a question of serendipity: we may or may not see a poster or TV spot at a moment in time that connects powerfully with what we need then and there. Proximity targeting is based on the hope of maximising these moments of serendipity.

Online, a host of real-time data signals — mood, weather, location — enable us to design for serendipity; to ensure we are delivering the right message at the right moment. This is the opportunity adtech should offer us, of precision targeting delivered at scale. Not targeting a niche, but targeting a moment in time when we are particularly responsive to a particular message — hungry, happy, sad or bored.

Carat UK, for example, developed a strategy for Arla Food's Lurpak butter brand based on targeting moments when the mood of the nation was low, and consumers would be most responsive to the brand's focus on delicious buttery comfort food. Using a combination of IPA TouchPoints data and the agency's bespoke 'Spirit Level' tool (which tracked and forecast social sentiment), the agency were able to forecast in advance those weeks when morale would be lowest, and activate media in response.

Digital OOH also enabled the agency to respond in real time to key events impacting mood, such as weather or sporting events. The campaign delivered a 9% sales uplift on previous years, and a cost saving of 50% compared to a standard campaign planning approach.

In a similar vein, Pantene US partnered with The Weather Channel to develop the 'Haircast', recommending relevant hair products to women tailored in real time to their location and the day's weather. The ads linked to mobile coupons redeemable at Walgreens, and drove a sales increase of 24% in July and August versus the previous year.

Long term, the opportunity will be to make these messages resonant at an individual level, not simply to respond to more macro events. Ultimately, context is about three Rs: the ability to make our message *relevant* and *responsive* in *real time*.

Going forward, of course, we will not be serving messages up in the formats we recognise today, such as banners or pop ups. The interventions we make may be more like a haptic nudge, or a sound cue. Yet as they become less literal and more intimate, the requirement for interactions to be supremely relevant will only increase.

Community

The influence of the crowd has been one of the dominant themes in marketing theory for the last decade, sparked by the advent of social media. Much has been written on the extent to which our actions are shaped by social learning, or as Mark Earls and his co-authors put it, our tendency to 'have what she's having'. Social learning is our ability to learn, at speed, from the wealth of social cues that surround us every day. As Earls et al put it:

> We are wired to copy... Other animal species are able to learn, and a
> good number of them on occasion practice social leaning, but humans are

more accurate social imitators than any other animal yet tested. Other animals don't come close to our speed of learning by imitation.

Social learning is of course at the heart of many of the all-consuming online platforms we use today, from Amazon's recommendation engine to eBay's seller ratings system. Facebook has built an entire revenue model on delivering social proof at scale. As consumers, we have developed an ability to read and process these social cues in an almost unconscious (or *low level*) way online as well as offline.

In 2013, the Dentsu Aegis Network conducted a social experiment in partnership with the University of Cambridge to test the impact of the size of a brand's social community on brand perceptions.

To create a controlled experiment, users were asked to evaluate a fictitious brand, Ashwood Furnishings, using a series of 12 different brand visuals. The only difference was the size of the brand's social following. Respondents were asked to rank the brand in terms of interest, trust, consideration, preference, advocacy and value. There was a significant correlation between brand 'likes' and positive brand perceptions on all key metrics.

The study concluded that:

> *This suggests that Likes generate an unconscious and immediate effect, similar to any number of cues in the 'real' world... The results demonstrate that the phenomenon of herding, described in behavioural economics for offline behaviour, also applies in the case of Facebook Likes to online behaviour.*

Other studies have also identified a similar cumulative advantage effect, sometimes referred to as the 'Matthew effect:' 'to he that has much, much shall be given'. Sociologist Duncan J Watts investigated this phenomenon by exploring the impact of social cues on the popularity of music.

In a controlled experiment, Watts and his team invited users to download and rate 45 unknown music tracks. Unsurprisingly, feedback was mixed, as users' tastes in music diverged. In subsequent trials, however, they showed users the number of downloads the tracks had received. The performance of individual tracks differed significantly once these social cues were introduced: the popular tracks became more popular and the unpopular tracks became less popular still.

The social cues we take for granted online (likes, star ratings, rankings) are actually surprisingly powerful emotional nudges in building brand perceptions and driving brand choice. An interesting challenge will be how we reinvent those cues for a world which is significantly less text driven; which brings us to the question of Craft.

Craft

Embracing emotion has important implications for every aspect of how we craft online experiences.

On the one hand, this means understanding how even the smallest design elements can transform user engagement. Airbnb users were once able to save properties to a list using a star icon. In 2011, they changed the star to a heart and saw engagement levels increase by 30%. Exploring the difference between the two icons, and what they might mean in terms of a user experience, led to a wholesale redesign of the site, based on the understanding that browsing attractive properties is not purely a rational exercise, but a compelling content stream in its own right. Users are not simply shortlisting, they are daydreaming, imagining an incredible holiday or a different lifestyle.

On the other hand, as interfaces evolve, Emotional Experience Design will require learning very new craft skills. The new world of invisible and intuitive interfaces opens up new dimensions in how we think about branding. It prompts us to think not just about tone of voice or look and feel, but about an entirely new language for brands in the digital space. How do our brands feel, sound, swipe and gesture?

Developing new brand cues for new kinds of interfaces will require us to draw learnings from a host of new sectors, from sound design to choreography to industrial design. Just as the smallest interaction in the offline world provides an infinite number of brand cues, so too will the smallest interactions in the online world. These hybrid craft skills will remain critical, both in shaping emotional responses and in helping users navigate new interfaces.

It is not surprising in that context that, in 2017, Visa spent considerable time aligning on its 'signature sound': a less-than-a-second sound made at the point of transaction that aims to communicate speed and convenience. The company also introduced a bespoke vibration and animation, all designed to ensure the brand remains resonant in an increasingly cardless world. As Lynne Biggar, Visa's chief marketing and communications officer, puts it:

> With the launch of different kinds of payment experiences, it became obvious to me and us at Visa that we needed to ensure that the Visa brand mark is as prevalent in these new ways to pay as it has been in the old ways to pay.

In a similar vein, Amazon is attempting to trademark the ring of blue light that characterises its Echo devices. This points to new parameters in branding, where interactions as subtle as the ways a light pulses or a transaction is processed are interrogated as rigorously as logo design or typeface in the 'old' world of brand identity. Interestingly, in both these cases the aim is to brand what might historically have been considered very functional interactions – something which poses its own set of challenges.

Conclusion

While we have never had more access to information, our preferences and decisions remain overwhelmingly driven by instinct and emotion. Indeed, we might argue that as the volume of information we are confronted with every day increases exponentially, and our ability to verify it declines (the 'fake news' phenomenon), our decisions will become ever more instinctive as a coping mechanism.

In our own industry we have seen time and again that emotional campaigns, over the long term, outperform more functional ones. Yet too often in the online space we assume a highly rational and linear user journey. As, however, we have shifted from search to discovery, and from destination sites to distributed experiences, the boundaries between emotional and functional experiences have blurred. To succeed, we must begin to infuse every touchpoint with emotion, not only those channels we have historically perceived as 'brand' channels.

This will become increasingly important, and increasingly challenging, as the world of interface design evolves, moving us away from screens and keyboards towards a world where our bodies, lightweight wearables and connected environments become our primary means of interacting with content of all kinds.

To thrive in this new world, we will need to think about everything we do as Emotional Experience Design; designing emotionally resonant experiences that engage across the path to purchase.

As discussed, I see four key principles underpinning Emotional Experience Design: Cause, Context, Community and Craft. These principles marry our industry's historic strengths – the ability to infuse brands with purpose and meaning – with an entirely new creative toolkit.

The fusion of skills we will need to design emotional experiences going forward makes it a phenomenally exciting time to be in our business.

References

Aegis Media. 'The science of social – an experiment in influence'. 2013

Binet, L, and Field, P. *The Long and the Short of It: Balancing short and long-term marketing strategies*. IPA, 2013

Bruell, A. 'Visa spent a year developing a "signature sound"'. *The Wall Street Journal*, 2017

Carat Lurpak, IPA TouchPoints case study, 2015

Damasio, A. *Descartes' Error: Emotion, reason and the human brain*. Putnam Publishing, 1994

Earls, M, Bentley, A, and O'Brien, M. *I'll Have What She's Having: Mapping social behavior*. Wiley, 2011

Fast Company. 'How Airbnb evolved to focus on social not searches'. 2012

Heath, R, and Howard-Spink, J. '"And Now for Something Completely Different": Current thinking about the brain means we need to change the way brands are researched'. UK, Market Research Society, 2000

Internet Advertising Bureau, Time Spent Online, January–June 2016

JWT London, Mindshare UK, Mindshare Futures SpeakEasy, 2017

Norman, D. *Emotional Design: Why we love (or hate) everyday things*. Basic Books, 2004

Nyhan, B, and Reifler, J. 'Why corrections fail: the persistence of political misperceptions'. *Political Behavior*, 32(2), 2010

'Pantene Weather Program'. 2014 MMA case study

Panzarino, M. 'Foursquare's Swarm and the rise of the invisible app'. *TechCrunch*, 2014

Rogowski, R. 'Introducing Emotional Experience Design'. Forrester, 2009

Sharp, B. *How Brands Grow: What marketers don't know*. OUP, 2010

Watts, DJ. *Everything is Obvious: once you know the answer*. Atlantic Books, 2011

41

SWALLOWING THE LITTLE FISH – HOW BIG BRANDS STAY BIG

Written by **Gareth Price**

Strong brands make choosing and buying as simple as possible. To achieve this, they must establish collective meaning and be consistent in the associations they communicate. This requires both their positioning and product portfolio to be tight, ensuring that the shared connotations that circulate about them are accepted as truths. All of which is at odds with personalisation and one-to-one marketing, which sacrifice shared cultural meaning to establish unique relevance through targeted messaging. This chapter explains why many companies are going too far in their veneration of the individual, and describes how a 'Simple-Collective-Tight' framework is critical to brand building.

How brands died

In 2040, following mass media's demise, big brands were in rapid decline. Without mass marketing as a barrier to entry, companies created more and more products designed to appeal to each consumer's unique tastes, with ever-shortening lifecycles.

New technology enabled personalised messages to be beamed directly into an individual's brain at the precise moment they displayed a relevant need-state. However, AI rapidly became so adept at identifying those moments, people began to receive 8.6 million targeted messages a day, with an average of 100 micro-brands competing each second for their attention.

Despite the initial reduction in information asymmetry arising from aggregated reviews, the number of choices became too great to cope with, so algorithms were developed to receive all communications and automate every purchase based on the relevance of the message to the individual.

As culture further fragmented, the opportunity to create shared meaning dissolved, with the collective associations held around the few remaining products with a market penetration above 1% collapsing. By 2048, mass market brands had disappeared entirely. And with new product variants being continually invented, repeat purchase became the exception. The notion of living up to a promise of performance vanished as a result.

Without big brands, the public discovered that they had less power over companies than ever before.

Why brands must resist the cult of the individual

I believe many companies are inadvertently embracing this dystopian scenario, propelled by a veneration of the individual – the driving force behind Western society in recent decades. Encouraged by management consultants, marketers are increasingly adopting personalised approaches through targeted media at the expense of broad reach.

McKinsey describes 'digital personalisation at scale' as 'marketing's Holy Grail', while Bain & Company states that the 'segment-of-one is disrupting the conventional marketing and sales funnel'. In a study sponsored by PwC, Forrester concludes: 'Personalisation is critical for marketers seeking to enhance customer centricity and engagement'. Experian, meanwhile, reports that 'to be effective, marketing communications should be tailored to individuals, regardless of channel'.

Exploring this approach through the context of 'cultural syndromes', however, helps to illustrate why putting individual relevance before collective meaning does not work for larger brands.

Psychology professor Harry Triandis describes cultural syndromes as the pattern of shared attitudes, beliefs and norms organised around a theme. In any culture, he demonstrates that complexity (in economic, political or social standards), individualism (prioritising autonomy and personal goals) and looseness (in rules and values) are always intertwined. Conversely, Triandis shows simplicity, collectivism and tightness are equally connected. Any move towards one entails a corresponding shift towards the related syndromes.

We often forget, when talking about brands finding a place in culture, that they can never escape being part of it in the first place. Coca-Cola is a quintessential American brand that shapes our view of the United States as much as it is shaped by our view of the country and its people. Mass market brands form an integral part of objective culture, and as such, can be the organising theme to which Triandis's theory is applied.

The reason why emerging trends such as personalisation are risky for larger brands to adopt then becomes clearer. Targeting individuals requires greater complexity in the approach, and a looser range of contextual messaging. To be relevant to the individual, the brand must relinquish control of a unifying idea to establish unique meaning. Prioritising the individual inevitably means adopting a more complex and looser communications plan.

However, mass market brands must always be:

1. **Simple** in making decision making easier.
2. **Collective** in creating shared associations and meaning.
3. **Tight** in their portfolio and positioning.

In this chapter, I will explain why these three principles are so important to building brands, before introducing a framework to help marketers apply them.

The three pillars of successful brands

1. Simple

The speed of technological change disrupts society in ways increasingly impossible to predict. Even across millions of years, *Sapiens* author and historian Yuval Noah Harari recognises that societal change is happening faster than at any point in history.

In contrast, human beings remain unchanged. Underpinning all decision making, an important aspect of our unchanging behaviour is the fact we evolved to be 'cognitive misers'. In the words of Daniel Kahneman, 'thinking is to humans as swimming is to cats; they can do it but they'd prefer not to'.

As such, the brand's primary role is to reduce the cognitive burden. Whether it's simplifying choice, signalling an identity or communicating a position everyone can grasp, the brand is a tool for simplification.

Risk expert Gerald Ashley describes a watch as 'complicated but not complex': 'When we open it up there's a whole heap of complicated gears and springs, but its outcome or objective is simplicity itself – it just tells the time.'

Similarly, the brand conveys the veneer of simplicity, masking the complexity underneath. As Steve Jobs highlighted, simplicity comes from conquering, not ignoring, complexity: 'It takes a lot of work to make something simple.'

Brands make life simpler

Economist Herbert Simon contends that we have evolved to 'satisfice'. Rather than maximising our benefit from a particular course of action, in most situations we merely seek a satisfactory solution.

If we make a terrible choice in what to eat, we may never eat another meal again. However, if we pick a bad one, although we may get a dodgy stomach, we will live to see another day. Similarly, when picking a product or service, it's rarely worth investing much time finding the optimal choice. A good one is good enough. So, a brand invested in maintaining its long-term reputation – as implicitly indicated by communicating its name to lots of people – must be a sensible purchase.

Beyond making the purchase decision easier, brands can also have symbolic value, enabling people to express their identity to others. Across every age and culture, we've hunted for ways to acquire social cachet – consumption has always been social, never private.

Former University of Oxford professor Douglas Holt demonstrates how even Vitaminwater enabled people to address class anxieties and signal their social status simply by buying a bottle of flavoured water. Social cachet is not restricted to luxury brands.

The placebo effect

Brands can also frame the experience we have with them. In a study by Dan Ariely, subjects read out 84 unrelated words while wearing sunglasses. Everyone received the same pair, except half were labelled Ray-Ban and half with a cheaper brand, Mango. Those wearing Ray-Bans made half the errors made by those wearing Mangos, and completed the task faster. The expensive brand created a placebo effect, convincing people they had superior mental abilities simply by wearing them.

This self-fulfilling belief has a positive effect on our experience with products and services. Like the Ancient Romans, who branded livestock with mystic symbols protecting them from harm, we still experience the magic of the brand.

In each instance, the brand provides a simple way of:

- Choosing what to buy.
- Conveying an identity.
- Creating perceived value.

To achieve this, the brand must establish collective meaning and ensure the shared associations people hold remain tight.

2. Collective

The individual can never escape 'the Other'. It's virtually impossible to opt out of collective knowledge of a brand and assign it entirely personal meaning. As Mark Earls highlights, brands are 'in the business of anticipating and shaping mass behaviour'. Despite this, media fragmentation and the increasing amount of behavioural data collected though digital channels encourages companies to appeal directly to individuals in tailored ways.

The Law of Double Jeopardy explains why brands must increase penetration to grow: those with a smaller market share have fewer buyers, who are slightly less loyal. If purchase frequency always reflects market size and category norms, it's not something that can be readily affected by marketing.

The largest financial payback comes from communicating with light and potential future buyers who know and think less about the brand. As such, broad reach is more effective than targeting heavier buyers the company invariably holds more data on.

Our understanding of how brands are built from a psychological perspective further demonstrates why the individual is less important than the collective in establishing meaning too.

Brands offer a social dimension

Paul Feldwick states that 'an attitude towards a certain behaviour is not simply determined by my own beliefs or experiences, but also by what I imagine other (relevant) people might think of the same thing'.

In the same way humans have always created hierarchies to ensure we don't waste time and energy learning how to treat each other, so we rely on brands as buying shortcuts based on shared knowledge and understanding. Brands are no different to the intersubjective order Harari believes binds us all, existing within the communication network connecting the shared imagination and 'subjective consciousness of many individuals'.

Creating intersubjective meaning requires the brand to reach and affect people who may never consider buying it. If it fails to demonstrate what it stands for amongst non-buyers, it risks losing the social dimension. There's no point buying Vitaminwater to signal your social status, if no one else knows what Vitaminwater stands for.

Part of the additional value of 'wasting' money advertising to non-buyers comes from signalling the brand's superior quality to rivals who spend less on it. People have never trusted advertising, but they have always trusted brands that advertise through mass media.

Brands are myth-making machines

Neuroscientist Antonio Damasio proposes that somatic markers are the feelings within the body that guide decision making. Although these emotional processes happen within the individual, they are never developed in isolation. Built through our encounters with the world, they guide behaviour through the associated positive and negative outcomes.

Holt states that, 'products acquire meanings – connotations – as they circulate in society. Over time, these meanings become conventional, widely accepted as "truths" about the product.'

Since all brands are imagined, however, these truths are inherently fragile. Therefore, the larger the brand, the more fragile it is, and the harder it must work to sustain the intersubjective myth through shared experiences – including advertising.

A study of 3,500 companies found that brands which maintain or increase marketing spend during a recession experience double the growth in share compared with those who reduce expenditure. Even long-established brands with widespread recognition must maintain collective meaning to retain market share. Awareness is not a task to be completed.

3. Tight

How brands shape perceptions

On his blog *Slate Star Codex*, psychologist Scott Alexander discusses a research paper which views perception as 'a handshake between top-down and bottom-up processing'. Top-down models predict what we'll see, while bottom-up ones perceive the real world. The two meet in the middle to calculate a prediction error. Low enough, and it's smoothed into a consensus view of the world. Too high, and it registers surprise, causing us to reconcile the two and adjust our priors.

Brands also act as a top-down processing model, guiding perceptions by predicting the experience we will have with the product or service based on our existing knowledge of it.

If a bottle of Coca-Cola in a Majorcan restaurant didn't taste right, you'd ask for another. If the same thing happened at two other restaurants in the area, you might suspect something was wrong with the local bottling plant. If it happened on a return trip to Spain, you'd question whether there was something wrong with Coca-Cola's local operations, but it would be unlikely to impact your purchase behaviour back home. The same story for an unknown local drink would have ended at the first restaurant.

The brand widens the confidence intervals, smoothing over any minor differences in our actual experiences with products and services. To achieve this, it must create a tight model of reality to anchor the brand. This requires the shared associations and meanings around the brand to remain consistent across groups of people.

Nike's Phil Knight believes that once you hit critical mass, 'you can't push it much further... otherwise the meaning gets fuzzy and confused, and before long, the brand is on the way out'.

To remain effective, advertising must find new ways to repeat itself.

Keep the portfolio tight

In 2006, Ford reported a loss of $12.7 billion – the largest in its history. The following year it sold Aston Martin, with its Jaguar and Land Rover operations divested in 2008. By 2009, focusing on the core brand saw car sales fall 44%. However, the company returned to profit ($2.7 billion) for the first time in four years.

As marketing professor Nirmalya Kumar highlights, the most effective way of boosting company profits is to sell or 'delete loss-making brands' and even 'declining, weak, and marginally profitable brands'.

Freeing up resources to focus on the remaining brands ensures the stronger ones receive the necessary time and investment to enable them to thrive. Creating a new brand can be all too easy, killing one painful; but a tighter portfolio is more profitable in the long term.

Further demonstrating the importance of tightness from a product perspective, Apple's Steve Jobs warned Google's Larry Page: 'What are the five products you want to focus on? Get rid of the rest, because they're dragging you down.'

Strategy requires sacrifice.

The 'Simple-Collective-Tight' brand-building framework

Applying these three principles has implications across the marketing discipline.

Communications

Media fragmentation means consumers are increasingly difficult to reach simultaneously. However, whatever channel used, the brand must create shared cultural meaning and establish common knowledge. As Nick Kendall highlights, the planner's job is to identify 'what makes people and their brands similar, not different; to find what unifies us, not what fragments us'.

This requires big ideas, transcending media types and building in creative publicity from the start of a campaign to ensure maximum exposure. The type of PR conceived by Edward Bernays – who embraced media-neutral campaigns to dramatise the brand – once again has a critical role to play in the communications mix. Of all the marketing disciplines, the biggest opportunity is for creative agencies who have always excelled in delivering ideas that redefine the future of brands.

Innovation

Instead of battling complexity by encouraging the engaged minority to download apps, the focus should be on reducing the cognitive burden amongst the indifferent majority.

For an FMCG brand, the approach to e-commerce should be to make repeat purchase as habitual and frictionless as possible through a single action. With direct-to-consumer sales accounting for just 0.3% of P&G's revenue, marketers in this category should always be wary of click-to-purchase activity.

Dollar Shave Club shook up the market through a subscription model that sends grooming products to customers for as little as $1 a month. It did so by *reducing* the need for repeated interaction with the brand at the point of purchase, not increasing it.

Marketers must also consider the level of interaction with the product, and how influential it is in driving perceptions and choice. In contrast to FMCG, in more involved categories seamlessness may not be a contingent condition for success when designing user experience.

Measurement

Prioritising shared ways of measuring marketing effectiveness will improve evaluation. First, that means putting models before metrics. The rise in data available to marketers makes it increasingly easy to find metrics demonstrating 'success'. Instead, we should question anything contradicting what established models, like the NBD-Dirichlet, explain about how marketing works.

Secondly, we should aim to use simple shared models that work under a range of conditions. As Andrew Ehrenberg and Byron Sharp highlighted: 'For a model to have scientific value it will have had to be validated in many very different situations; this may be impossible to achieve for regression-style models that make causal inferences.'

As the pair have demonstrated, single-source data remains the only effective way of judging the ability of a specific ad to maintain or increase sales versus competitors. Advances in its collection, such as the partnership between Facebook and dunnhumby, point the way forward.

Research

If the associations attached to a brand are less about what the individual thinks, and more what they think others think, many of our current research methodologies appear outdated.

For inspiration, we should look to the Iowa Electronic Market. Instead of asking voters about their own voting intentions, they buy and sell shares in whom they believe others will vote for. It's proved to be more accurate than polls three-quarters of the time.

If we're better at predicting what others will do than we are at predicting our own future behaviour, we should instead focus on asking people what others will think and do.

A 'Simple-Collective-Tight' marketing framework

	Simple-Collective-Tight	Complex-Individual-Loose
Communications	Shared associations	Personalised messaging
Consumers	Cognitive misers	Engaged audiences
Innovation	Aims to simplify choosing/buying	Aims to increase involvement with the brand
Measurement	Single source data	Market mix modelling
Media Planning	Media neutral	Channel first thinking
Performance	Simple, shared models	Real time data
Portfolio	Narrow range	Wide range
Research	What the individual thinks others think	What the individual thinks
Targeting	Mass reach	Target individuals

Conclusion

In the face of rising complexity, the immediate future becomes less predictable. Rather than attempt to look forward, we should first look back, focusing on what we know won't change.

Human beings will not evolve in our lifetimes. And so, what a brand must do (simplify the complex), and how it achieves this (collectively and tightly), will not fundamentally change either.

In fact, as the pace of technological change quickens, and more routes to market lead to a proliferation of choice, a brand's primary role of reducing the cognitive burden will become even more important.

Mass market brands must:

- Make buying as *simple* as possible.
- Establish *collective* meaning.
- Be *tight* in both their portfolio and positioning.

Recognising how entwined these three pillars are, and putting them into action, will always be critical to the long-term success of brands.

References

Alexander, S. 'It's Bayes all the way up'. *Slate Star Codex*, 2016. http://slatestarcodex.com/2016/09/12/its-bayes-all-the-way-up

Ambler. T, and Hollier, EA. 'The waste in advertising is the part that works'. *Journal of Advertising Research* 44(4), 2005

Ashley, G. 'Thoughts on decision making and risk'. 2016. https://geraldashley.blog/2016/10/17/finance-complex-not-complicated

Bockemuehl, M, et al. 'Avoiding the pitfalls of personalized marketing and sales'. Bain & Co, 2016

Clary, M, and Dyson, P. 'The case for long-term advertising'. *Admap*, February 2014

Corlett, PR, Frith, CD, and Fletcher, PC. 'From drugs to deprivation: a Bayesian framework for understanding models of psychosis'. *Psychopharmacology*, 206(4), 2009

Damasio, A. *Descartes' Error: Emotion, reason and the human brain*. Putnam Publishing, 1994

Dhalla, NK. 'Assessing the long-term value of advertising'. *Harvard Business Review*, January 1978

Earls, M. *Herd: How to change mass behaviour by harnessing our true nature.* Wiley, 2009

Ehrenberg, A, and Sharp, B. 'Problems with marketing's "decisions" models'. Australian New Zealand Marketing Academy Conference, 2000

Experian. 'Why customer profiling and segments of one aren't the same thing – are you treating your customers as individuals?' 2016. https://www.experian. co.uk/blogs/latest-thinking/marketing/segments-of-one/

Dunnhumby. 'dunnhumby and Facebook partner to measure marketing effectiveness'. 2016. https://dunnhumby.com/dunnhumby-and-facebook-partner-measure-marketing-effectiveness

Feldwick, P. 'Understanding brands: defining a brand'. In D Cowley (ed.), *Understanding Brands: By 10 people who do,* Kogan Page, 1991

Feldwick, P. *What is Brand Equity, Anyway?* WARC, 2002

Forrester Consulting. 'The power of personalization in the age of the customer'. PwC. https://www.pwc.com/us/en/services/consulting/technology/forrester-customer-personalization-power.html

Franzen, G. *Brands & Advertising: How advertising effectiveness influences brand equity.* WARC, 1999

Gino, F, Norton, MI, and Ariely, D. 'The counterfeit self: the deceptive costs of faking it'. *Psychological Science,* 21(5), 2010

Gregg, B, et al. 'Marketing's Holy Grail: digital personalization at scale'. McKinsey & Company, 2016. https://mckinsey.com/business-functions/digital-mckinsey/our-insights/marketings-holy-grail-digital-personalization-at-scale

Harari, Y. *Sapiens: A brief history of humankind.* Harper, 2015

Holt, DB. *Brands and Branding.* Harvard Business School Press, 2003

Holt, DB. *How Brands Become Icons: The principles of cultural branding.* Harvard Business Review Press, 2004

Holt, DB, and Cameron, D. *Cultural Strategy: Using innovative ideologies to build breakthrough brands.* OUP, 2010

Isaacson, W. 'The real leadership lessons of Steve Jobs'. *Harvard Business Review,* 90(4), 2012

Kahneman, D. *Thinking, Fast and Slow.* Farrar, Straus and Giroux, 2011

Kendall, N. 'How to develop an effective global brand strategy'. WARC, 2016

Kennedy, R, McDonald, C, and Sharp, B. 'Pure single-source data and take-off time for Project Apollo'. *Admap,* February 2008

Kumar, N. 'Kill a brand, keep a customer'. *Harvard Business Review,* 81(12), 2003

Price, G. 'Thinklong'. *Campaign,* November 2017, IPA supplement

Sharp, B. *How Brands Grow: What marketers don't know.* OUP, 2010

Stamp, J. 'Decoding the range: the secret language of cattle branding'. *Smithsonian* magazine, 2013. https://www.smithsonianmag.com/arts-culture/decoding-the-range-the-secret-language-of-cattle-branding-45246620/

Sutherland, R. 'This thing for which we have no name: a conversation with Rory Sutherland'. *Edge*, 2014. https://www.edge.org/conversation/rory_sutherland-this-thing-for-which-we-have-no-name

The Economist. 'Who's wearing the trousers?' 13 September 2001

Triandis, HC. 'The psychological measurement of cultural syndromes'. *American Psychologist*, 51(4), 1996

Willigan, G. 'High-performance marketing: an interview with Nike's Phil Knight'. *Harvard Business Review*, July 1992

Zahavi, A, and A. *The Handicap Principle: A missing piece of Darwin's puzzle.* OUP, 1997

42

RISING FROM THE ASH [ART, SCIENCE, HUMANITY] – THE PERSONAL AND THE PROVABLE

Written by **Faris** and **Rosie Yakob**

Is advertising art or science? The Renaissance cleaved art from science, creating a naive binary that rendered them oppositional; but of course, they are not. What is art? Is more creativity more effective, and how could that be measured? What are the creative dimensions of advertising? What is science? Does evidence-based marketing remove the magic? What about people? Where does commerce and culture come between the art and science? What's the new story advertising should be telling about itself? This chapter discusses.

Part 1: Art

> 'Advertising is fundamentally persuasion and persuasion happens to be not a science, but an art.'
>
> Bill Bernbach, *Bill Bernbach Said...*

Bill Bernbach wrote this in a memo at Grey Advertising in 1947, and it is echoed to this day by creatives everywhere (despite what 'Big Data' evangelists and adtech salesmen might lead you to believe). 'Ads are not art, but creating good ads is' proclaimed 'copyranter' Mark Duffy.

The debate as to whether advertising is art or science can perhaps be traced all the way back to the Renaissance, when art and science were still intrinsically linked. The rebirth of knowledge was an age of observation, where art was used to help people make sense of the world around them.

There were so many discoveries to be had that the great minds pursued them all. The notebooks of Italian polymath and artist Leonardo da Vinci embraced philosophy, astronomy and engineering, and his art was informed by the same. In fact, one of the oft-cited reasons of his exceptionalness is the incorporation of science – the precise detail and scale in anatomy, for example.

The division of science and art is a relatively recent phenomenon – separation by specialisation. During the Industrial Revolution, specialisation was seen as one of the key ways to organise society – from business to education. It was then we decided that art's definition, unlike science, was profoundly personal.

Art and science became the balances to each other: yin and yang, the creative based and the fact based, the personal and the provable.

In his book *What Is Art?*, Leo Tolstoy said, 'To evoke in oneself a feeling one has experienced, and… then, by means of movements, lines, colours, sounds or forms expressed in words, so to transmit that feeling – this is the activity of art.'

Today, we define art similarly, as (in the words of the *Oxford English Dictionary*) 'the expression or application of human creative skill and imagination, typically in a visual form such as painting or sculpture, producing works to be appreciated primarily for their beauty or emotional power' or 'the various branches of creative activity, such as painting, music, literature, and dance.'

Art, while sometimes inspiring others to change their perception (or even take action) is not always designed to do so. (But to say art doesn't have a commercial intent would be silly; it's a commercial endeavour for itself and its creator.)

If we agree that self-expression is a key to art, and that interpretation of self-expression by viewers is equally a tenet, it seems unlikely that advertising could be art. Advertising, after all, always has commercial intent; it is always ghostwritten in the company's voice. It is intended to change perceptions and behaviour in a required way, and there is therefore a designed limit on any interpretation other than which was intended.

Bernbach was (consciously or not) quoting Aristotle, whose treatise on persuasion was called (in Latin) *Ars Rhetorica* ('The art of rhetoric'). Art here, however, meant something worthy of systematic study, which is more akin to what we now think of as science, or at least technique, as in Sun Tzu's ancient classic *The Art of War*. In fact, the ancient Greek word for art was 'techne', from which technique and technology are derived. Aristotle was trying to codify the linguistic tools that made discourse persuasive. For example, he suggested that 'lexis' (that's 'reading level' to you and me) will be appropriate if it expresses emotion and character, and is proportional to the subject matter. So, the language must suit the speaker and the topic, not just the audience.

Research codifying the 'art' of creativity in advertising has been conspicuous by its absence. Anecdotes and aphorisms are easy to come by, but empirical research tying creativity to sales is not. 'Because product and brand managers – and the agencies pitching to them – have lacked a systematic way to assess the effectiveness of their ads, creative advertising has been a crapshoot', as a June 2013 *Harvard Business Review* article noted.

One of the only robust studies analysed 437 TV campaigns for 90 FMCG brands in Germany from 2005 to 2010. Using the definition of creativity as 'the extent to which an ad contains brand or executional elements that are different, novel, unusual, original, unique' they developed five dimensions – originality, flexibility, elaboration, synthesis and artistic value – and tied those elements (and combinations thereof) to sales.

They found that 'more creative campaigns were more effective – considerably so.' Specifically, 'A euro invested in a highly creative ad campaign had, on average, nearly double the sales impact of a euro spent on a non-creative campaign', but that not all forms of creativity were equally effective. It also showed that more creative advertising works better in some categories than others – the body lotion and face care categories were actively harmed by additional creativity; the sales impact fell by nearly 2%.

Bernbach's art argument was itself, of course, a selling tool for his agency and his ideas. To this day, creatives leverage it to give subjective opinion the weight of fact, without need for substantiation. A copywriter expressed this succinctly to us in a conversation on Twitter: 'No clever research is going to convince me to doubt my gut feeling, I'm afraid.'

Persuasion, if it is an art, is not like any other in that it has a primary objective beyond its own consumption. We can argue that art historically always did – that royal portraiture was propaganda, for example – and, of course, this is true, but it's not what we mean when we say art today.

Part 2: Science

> 'The time has come when advertising has in some hands reached the status of a science.'
>
> Claude Hopkins, *Scientifc Advertising*

> 'I warn you against believing that advertising is a science.'
>
> Bill Bernbach, *Bill Bernbach Said...*

In 1620, the English philosopher Francis Bacon published a book called *Novum Organum Scientiarum* ('new instrument of science'). The title is a reference to Aristotle's *Organon*, because nothing 'new' comes from nothing: all culture, art or science is accretive, building upon that which came before.

In his book, Bacon rejects Aristotelian deductive logic and syllogism as mechanisms for getting to useful truths about the world, since they essentially require you to somehow just 'know' things *a priori* before you can learn anything else.

Bacon instead posits the idea of inductive reasoning, which is to infer general laws through the observation of particular instances. He then outlines a complicated system for doing this, which is considered an Ur-text for what we now know as the 'Scientific Method'. It is predicated on methodical observation, the formulation of hypotheses which produce testable predictions, and experimentation to support or disprove them.

It is also an inflection point at which the domains we call 'art' and 'science' were split in two and began their spiraling arcs apart. Before that, the distinction made no sense. When painting discovered perspective, the gap between geometry and drawing was non-existent. It took hundreds of years for them to end up as apparent opposites. As late as 1949, in *Art and Scientific Thought*, critic Martin Johnson wrote: 'Nowadays between Science and this poetic experience there is danger of a definite divorce. An increasing cleavage between them is rapidly becoming an abyss.'

It is important to understand that science makes no claims to absolute truths. Experiments can only falsify hypotheses. As Karl Popper pointed out, in a quote far more famous than he is, 'No matter how many instances of white swans we may have observed, this does not justify the conclusion that all swans are white.'

Rather, science is an endlessly iterative process, based upon using experimentation to derive principles that can be used to make predictions, until we find new conditions in which they cease to work, and thus new principles and experiments must be developed.

> *'The value of science is in prediction',*
>
> General Valery Gersimov

In 1923, Claude Hopkins published his book *Scientific Advertising*, which made the grand claim that advertising had achieved 'the status of science':

> *It is based on fixed principles and is reasonably exact. The causes and effects have been analyzed until they are well understood. The correct methods of procedure have been proved and established. We know what is most effective, and we act on basic law. Advertising, once a gamble, has thus become, under able direction, one of the safest business ventures.*

He goes on to say that 'this book deals, not with theories and opinions, but with well-proven principles and facts', which perhaps should have been a clue. You see, this is an old copywriting trick, deflecting criticism for weaknesses that follow; because Hopkins was no scientist – he was a copywriter, trying to convince the reader of his ideas.

That's not to say that the book doesn't contain some cogent ideas. It suggests that you should measure and optimise the response rate of coupons and direct mail, which is no doubt sensible. It also recommends running massive A/B tests on copy, in different markets and media. But beyond that, it provides not a single datum of evidence for any of his points. It only alludes to a few conceptual examples, along with some vague and anonymised anecdata.

Scientifically inspired in its experimental approach it may be, science it is not.

More recently, Byron Sharp's meticulously researched and evidence-laden books show how brands grow marketing share in their category, which has brought evidence back to the forefront of consideration for marketers, as indeed it should be. One of his most important points is the fallacy of targeting the heavy buyer. Loyalty does not (indeed cannot) drive growth – it is market penetration and new customer acquisition. This is remarkably close to proving one of Hopkins' aphorisms: 'Your object in all advertising is to buy new customers at a price which pays a profit.'

Hopkins' science argument (like Bernbach's art argument) was itself also a selling tool for his agency and ideas. It offered the possibility of prediction, the guarantee of results, as do the programmatic promises of adtech today.

The endless debate as to whether advertising is art or science, like so many binaries that are increasingly applied to the complexity of the real world, is naive, facile and almost always self-serving. Advertising is, of course, both.

Let's consider architecture, a field in which the same useless debate has raged. ('Architecture is art, nothing else' the American architect Philip Johnson opined.)

The *Oxford English Dictionary* once defined architecture as 'the art *and* science of designing buildings', and indeed it must be. Buildings must obey the laws of physics so they don't fall down. When someone imagines a planet-destroying space station [The Death Star] that cannot be constructed, this is art and not architecture. Equally, designing a building isn't following a set of rules that then guarantee a building's success. The Bilbao Guggenheim, which put both the city and Frank Gehry on the map, both contains (and is often hailed as) modern art.

With advertising, just as with architecture, both art and science are *necessary but not sufficient.*

Part 3: Humanity

The problem with dividing the world into the personal and provable is that many things are neither.

Several years before Gehry's Guggenheim made him the most famous architect alive, he was spotted by another creative visionary – Jay Chiat, founder of legendary advertising agency Chiat/Day. Chiat hired Gehry to reinvent the nature of the office for their LA outpost, transforming it into a creative space – one suitable for the agency that had smashed the grey authoritarian face of corporate America with the classic Apple spot, '1984'.

It was arguably the first hotdesking office, allowing workers to sit anywhere. To encourage the flow of creativity, all private offices were replaced with clusters of couches in common areas. There were 'Tilt-A-Whirl' cars taken from old amusement parks, a four-storey high sculpture of a pair of binoculars, and a sign in/out system for PowerBooks and phones. Staff were given small lockers where they could, as Chiat said, 'put their dog pictures, or whatever'.

In order to encourage employees not to lapse back into antiquated office behaviours, Chiat banned 'nesting', and would walk around making sure people weren't in the same seats as the day before.

This was the pinnacle of art and science, designed by two notable visionaries. It was also an unmitigated disaster.

Since people had no real storage space, they took to using the boots of their cars as filing cabinets. No one knew where anyone else would be, and could never find the right person when inspiration did strike. And worst of all, to quote the delightful *Wired* article about the fiasco, 'there was no damn place to sit'.

Despite Chiat/Day being the darling of design magazines (at one point they were even giving paid tours of the office), it didn't work for people. Beyond the impracticalities, the experiment attempted to impose one man's vision onto the behaviour of the whole agency – and if there's one thing people hate more than anything else, it's having their own agency taken away.

Art and science alone aren't enough when we have to factor in humanity in all its glorious complexity.

Complexity 'describes the behaviour of a system whose components interact in multiple ways and follow local rules', to quote Wikipedia. While often misused as such, it is not a synonym for complicated. Complex systems – which include any that involve groups of people – have emergent properties, and are inherently stochastic. It is impossible to make accurate predictions about human behaviour in the real world – just look at the news.

Worse, humans don't act in ways that make sense, even to other humans. This was the realisation that overturned decades of economic theory, which had been predicated on the absurd myth of 'homo economicus': the rational person who somehow had perfect information and made perfect decisions to maximise their own utility.

The insights of behavioural economics give us more clarity than the normative fictions that preceded them, but they still don't provide guarantees. Instead, we can use them as a model of behaviour that we can apply to the arts and sciences of advertising, to give ideas the best chance to create commercial effects. We can experiment and observe and improve iteratively, as science does. Then we can support creative leaps that may multiply the impact of our media and justify the vast sums spent.

The current obsession with collecting data is a worse than useless drain on budgets and resource without a model of understanding, a hypothesis to be disproved. Indeed this, and only this, turns data into evidence.

We've come to a time where thinking has become a lost art. Employees are expected to get to the answer as quickly as possible. Especially at advertising agencies, employees keep long hours and calendars filled with meetings. To apply data in a meaningful way, you must first have a hypothesis. And having a hypothesis is not the same as simply searching for statistics that shore up the work you want to sell in.

Bernbach's and Hopkins' contrapuntal claims were used by both men to sell their work to their colleagues, employees and clients. Which brings us to the most important point: it doesn't matter what the evidence is, if you can't sell the story.

In a world of fake news and alternative facts, there are plenty of people who, despite all the evidence presented, continue to believe whatever tickles their fancy. And while you might think that we're only talking about the poorly educated, don't be fooled: 90% of American Trump and Clinton supporters believe in at least one political conspiracy theory (according to a Public Mind poll conducted by Fairleigh Dickinson University). In 2016, the United States elected a man to preside over the country with no political experience, despite him saying innumerable things that are demonstrably untrue – or perhaps *because of* that.

It's a natural human tendency to absorb information that already fits our own perspective of the world, whether about politics or a new product. Confirmation bias drives how we parse evidence. 'No clever research is going to convince me to doubt my gut feeling, I'm afraid' has become the unfortunate aphorism of the age.

Viren Swami, professor of social psychology at Anglia Ruskin University in Cambridge, explained on National Public Radio: 'We look for information; we look for evidence that fits what we already know or what we already believe, and we try to avoid information or evidence that we either disagree with or that we know doesn't fit with our perspective. And if someone comes along and says, here's the evidence, your natural tendency's actually to rehearse arguments against that evidence.'

This is known as the 'backfire effect', which describes how in the face of contradictory evidence, well-established beliefs don't change but *rather get stronger.*

So instead of pointlessly debating art or science, best to embrace both, and beyond. But as Seth Godin says:

> *Here's the conversation that needs to happen before we invest a lot of time in evidence-based marketing in the face of skepticism: 'What evidence would you need to see in order to change your mind?'*

If the honest answer is, 'Well, actually, there's nothing you could show me that would change my mind', you've just saved everyone a lot of time.

References

Bernbach, W. *Bill Bernbach Said...* DDB publication, 2003

Fairleigh Dickinson University poll. http://view2.fdu.edu/publicmind/2016/161011/

Hopkins, C. *Scientific Advertising,* New Line Publishing, 1923

http://digiday.com/marketing/copyranter-advertising-not-science-never-will/

https://hbr.org/2013/06/creativity-in-advertising-when-it-works-and-when-it-doesnt

https://seths.blog/2011/03/the-limits-of-evidence-based-marketing/

https://wired.com/1999/02/chiat-3/

Johnson, M. *Art and Scientific Thought.* AMS Press, 1949

Popper, K. *The Logic of Scientific Discovery.* Hutchinson, 1959

Tolstoy, L. *What is Art?* Penguin Classics, 1995

Tzu, S. *The Art of War.* Capstone, 2010

EPILOGUE AND ACKNOWLEDGEMENTS

Around September 2008, someone sent me a cover from *The Economist*. It was black with (in white) 'OH ****!' inscribed on it. Faced with one of the world's largest financial crises, there was indeed not much more to say about the mess we were in. But the cover never actually ran. A designer had created and placed it on his own website as a joke, and it went viral.

I recalled that cover after finishing Andrew Ehrenberg's 1971 book *Repeat-Buying*, and Byron Sharp's more recent *How Brands Grow*. The financial crisis might be behind us, but for the marketing industry the effluent is probably only starting to hit the fan.

Not only have we, for several decades, mostly ignored valuable knowledge about how to sell more effectively to more people, but we are also confronted with a replication crisis. In 2013, *The Economist* put it this way:

> ... *Nowadays, verification (the replication of other people's results) does little to advance a researcher's career. And without verification, dubious findings live on to mislead.*

> *Careerism also encourages exaggeration and the cherry-picking of results. The most striking findings have the greatest chance of making it onto the page.*

This somewhat pungent view is to miss the point of the work done by Andrew Ehrenberg, Byron Sharp, Peter Field and Les Binet, and their many colleagues. Their work has been an effort of continuous testing of the patterns of findings in many categories and brands, goods and services, durables and consumables in markets around the world.

However interesting the findings, I believe the true value lies in the challenge to readers to adopt an evidence-based way of thinking, as championed by Ben Goldacre, Hans Rosling, Phil Rosenzweig, Nate Silver and Duncan Watts to name a few. This book demonstrates that there are many people who are found in every corner of the industry who are similarly concerned with evidence. Every contributor was given the freedom to write about how they applied or found inspiration from marketing science, as long as assertions were supported by evidence.

Needless to say, I am extremely grateful to all the contributors, some of whom were kind enough to think along the way with me during the process. Thank you for your time and effort. The idea for this book started several years ago after many early morning and late night Twitter discussions with Eaon Pritchard, who almost literally lives on the other side of the world. We both felt that there was room for a book that contained 'a view from the trenches', which was the working title of this project (and Eaon's idea). I would also like to single out my good friend Shann Biglione for his continuous involvement, thoughts and comments in reviewing the papers and ideas for this book. I am also very grateful to the APG for publishing this book, and especially Sarah Newman, Sophie Fairfield and Susannah Lear for their time and effort in making it happen. Finally, I'd like to thank my colleague Henry Coates for helping me keep things simple, and Byron Sharp who taught me to always ask myself the question 'Can you really tell that from the data?'

Nonetheless, the proof is in the eating. In the end, the objective of his book is to stimulate you, the reader, to look for – even demand – evidence, using advances in marketing science to become more effective in what you do. So, thank you for picking up this book, and eating your greens. I hope you benefit from it!

Wiemer Snijders

ABOUT THE CONTRIBUTORS

Tess Alps is the chair of Thinkbox, the body owned by the UK broadcasters, whose role is to help advertisers get the best out of today's diverse, multi-platform TV. Tess set up the company in 2006, and was its first CEO. In 2007, Tess won the Outstanding Achievement award from Women in Film and Television, and in 2013 was voted Media Industry Leader of the Decade by readers of Haymarket's brand titles. In 2018, she was awarded the Mackintosh Medal by the Advertising Association.

Mark Barden can be challenging to work with. Some of the world's best organisations pay him to be this way in his role as partner at the consulting firm eatbigfish, which coined the term, and created all the fuss about, 'challenger brands'.

Phil Barden has over 25 years' client-side brand management experience. After 16 years with Unilever, rising to marketing VP, he worked at Diageo and T-Mobile. Whilst responsible for T-Mobile's brand positioning and development around Europe, he became a client of decode marketing consultancy and first encountered 'decision science'. Decode's work on the successful relaunch led Phil to set up decode marketing in the UK. Phil's first book, *Decoded: The science behind why we buy*, was published in 2013.

Shann Biglione is head of strategy for Zenith Media in New York, overseeing media and comms strategies for the media agency's global clients. Prior to that he served as chief strategy officer for Publicis Media in China, strategy director for Digital Outlook in London and Los Angeles, and digital marketing manager for Walt Disney Studios in Paris. Shann holds a Master's degree in marketing from Aix en Provence's Institut des Adminstrations et des Entreprises.

Julian Cole led the comms planning department at BBDO. In this role, he oversaw a team of 15 comms planners working on Footlocker, AT&T, Mars Chocolate and Petcare, Bacardi, Visa, J&J and American Red Cross. Previously he was head of comms planning at BBH New York, where he launched PlayStation 4, which became the fastest selling platform in video games history. He maintains his *Planning Dirty* newsletter, which goes out to 8,000+ planners monthly.

Jerry Daykin globally leads digital strategy and media partnerships at Diageo. As well as helping brands including Smirnoff, Johnnie Walker and Guinness tap into the growth potential that media channels provide, he has also been instrumental in helping the business tackle some of the challenges currently facing the digital media supply chain. The output of that, Diageo's 'Trusted Marketplace' approach, has gone on to form the basis of the new World Federation of Advertisers' Media Charter.

Mark Earls is a recovering planner who now writes, consults, talks and teaches on mass behaviour, and how to change it. His work reaches parts that others' doesn't, and has been adopted in surprising places such as animal welfare, public policy, psych ops as well as by the usual business suspects.

Helen Edwards has an MBA from London Business School and a PhD in marketing. She is co-author of *Creating Passion Brands: How to build emotional brand connection with customers*, and an award-winning business columnist. She is a partner at Passionbrand strategic brand consultancy.

Paul Feldwick was an account planner for over 30 years at Boase Massimi Pollitt, which later became DDB London. He is now a consultant, coach and author – his book *The Anatomy of Humbug: How to think differently about advertising* was published in 2015.

Adam Ferrier is a consumer psychologist and the co-founder of Thinkerbell, an agency that fuses marketing sciences and hardcore creativity – or as they like to put it – 'Measured Magic'. Adam is also author of the 2014 book *The Advertising Effect: How to change behaviour*, co-founder of MSIX (Marketing Sciences Ideas Xchange), and sits on the boards of Tribe (social influence) and Good Thnx (social giving). Adam is a weekly guest on Australian national TV show *Sunrise*, and a regular panellist on others. He was also state under-12 Chess Champion of Western Australia.

Peter Field spent 15 years as a strategic planner in advertising and has been a marketing consultant for the last 20 years. Effectiveness case study analysis underpins much of his work, which includes his pioneering work on the link between creativity and effectiveness. His latest work (with Les Binet), *Media in Focus*, examines the media myths and truths of the digital era. Peter has a global reputation as an effectiveness expert and communicator, and speaks and consults on this topic regularly around the world. He is a contributor to the 'Wharton Future of Advertising' project.

Tom Fishburne (the Marketoonist™) started cartooning on the backs of business cases as a student at Harvard Business School. From an email to 35 co-workers in 2002, his cartoons have grown by word of mouth to reach several hundred thousand readers each week and have been featured by *The Wall Street Journal, Fast Company, Forbes,* and *The New York Times*. Tom is a frequent keynote speaker on innovation, marketing and creativity, using cartoons, case studies, and his marketing career to tell the story visually. The Huffington Post ranked his South by Southwest (SXSW) talk the third best of the conference out of 500.

Tom Goodwin is the EVP, head of innovation for Zenith USA. Tom's role is to understand new technology, behaviours and platforms, and ideate and implement solutions for clients that take advantage of the opportunities they present. An industry provocateur and commentator, Tom has been voted the number one voice in marketing by LinkedIn, his followership encouraged by Business Insider and *Fast Company*. Tom is a columnist for *The Guardian*, *Marketing Week* and *The Drum*, and frequent contributor to *GQ* and *Ad Age*, among other titles. He is a regular guest on i24News' 'Cutting Edge' section. Tom is the author of the recently published *Digital Darwinism: Survival of the fittest in the age of business disruption*.

Charles Graham is a senior lecturer in marketing at London South Bank University, with interests in long-term behavioural brand loyalty, competitive market structure modelling and effective brand portfolio management. After graduating from Cambridge, Charles spent nearly 15 years in industry before becoming an academic. During that time he gained national and international experience in brand management, NPD and franchising, working with start-ups and international businesses. He became an Associate of the Ehrenberg Centre for Research in Marketing in 2007, and is an adjunct research fellow at the Ehrenberg-Bass Institute.

Philip Graves has been described as one of the world's leading experts in consumer behaviour. In addition to running his own consumer insight company, Shift Consultancy, he is an associate at Frontier Economics, where his work is at the forefront of aligning commercial market research practice with insights from behavioural economics. His first book, *Consumer.ology*, was named one of Amazon's top 10 best business books in its year of publication (2010).

Bob Hoffman is an author and speaker. He has written several successful books including *BadMen: How advertising went from a minor annoyance to a major menace*, and is creator of the popular *The Ad Contrarian* blog. Bob has been the CEO of two independent agencies and the US operation of an international agency. Bob's commentary has appeared on the BBC World Service, *The Wall Street Journal*, MSNBC, *The Financial Times*, *The Australian*, New Zealand Public

Broadcasting, Fox News, Sky News, *Forbes*, Canadian Public Broadcasting, and many other news outlets throughout the world.

Patricia McDonald is an award-winning strategist with over 20 years' experience at the UK's leading agencies, from BBH to The&Partnership. She is the former CSO of Denstu Aegis's Isobar. She combines a passion for creativity (helping return Levi's to Cannes Gold-winning highs) with a commitment to effectiveness, having won numerous IPA Effectiveness Awards.

Becky McOwen-Banks is an award-winning creative director, speaker and judge with over 17 years' Adland experience in Australia and the UK. An active member of the creative community, Becky works with many initiatives for change: 'SheSays' (London and Sydney), 'The Girlhood', IPA Talent & Leadership committee, 'The Girl Effect' (Rwanda), partnering the founding of Creative Equals – as well as being the only female CD on the IPA Council in its 100-year history. And she's not done yet!

Costas Papaikonomou is one of the founding partners of the Happen Group, and since 1996 has worked across the globe in many areas of innovation – from strategy to design, from commercialisation to manufacturing. He pursues the balance between technology, consumer need and business relevance, driving for the innovative leap to achieve this. Costas has led insight-led projects across cultures and categories on all continents (including the Antarctic), for over 100 major FMCG corporations – helping them create evolutionary and revolutionary breakthroughs that grow revenue through smart execution. He is an acclaimed satirist and author on the topic of business and innovation.

Gareth Price is a global planner at J. Walter Thompson London, working on Bayer and Shell. He won the 2017 IPA President's Prize for his essay, 'Thinklong', which outlined a seven-point plan to tackle short-termism in marketing. He has been published in *Admap*, *Campaign*, the *International Journal of Market Research* and WARC. A former England international at 1500m, Gareth has also run a 2:24 marathon.

Eaon Pritchard is head of strategy at UM in Melbourne. Following an unsuccessful attempt at pop and DJ stardom (although he did achieve one global techno-house hit in the mid-1990s), Eaon turned to advertising – first (and equally unsuccessfully) as a creative director before discovering account planning and strategy. His subsequent career includes multi-award-winning spells at Weapon7 in London and Clemenger BBDO in Melbourne. Eaon writes regularly for WARC and other industry titles, as well as his own blog *Never Get Out Of The Boat*. Eaon's first book, *Where Did It All Go Wrong? Adventures at the Dunning Kruger peak of advertising*, is fast becoming a cult classic among discerning advertising types... and there's a second one on the way.

Anjali Ramachandran is director at Storythings, a content studio that helps clients such as Pearson Education, Omidyar Network and the Gates Foundation tell complex stories. With a background in digital product and technology innovation at PHD Media, Made by Many and Nike, Anjali believes in the power of strong narratives and impact-driven media. Anjali is also the co-founder of global network for women in tech, Ada's List, with over 5,000 members.

Kate Richardson is a consultant, marketing strategist and digital thinker with almost 20 years' experience helping people join the dots between brands, communications, content, digital, media and technology. She's led both businesses and teams, working in major media companies, global communications and media agencies, not-for-profits, and most recently, a digital agency start-up. Over the last decade, Kate's helped ambitious local companies and major multinationals like Unilever, Coca-Cola and Microsoft unlock growth through strategy, innovation and creativity.

Mark Ritson has a PhD in marketing and has been a faculty member at London Business School, MIT and Melbourne Business School. A regular commentator on the industry, Mark has worked as a consultant for some of the world's leading brands.

Doc Searls is editor in chief of *Linux Journal*, co-author of *The Cluetrain Manifesto*, and author of *The Intention Economy: When customers take charge*. Doc is also director of ProjectVRM at Harvard's Berkman Klein Center for Internet and Society, co-founder and board member of Customer Commons, and a marketing veteran who co-founded and served as creative director for Hodskins Simone and Searls, which for many years was one of Silicon Valley's leading technology advertising agencies. Doc also co-organises the twice-yearly Internet Identity Workshop at the Computer History Museum in Silicon Valley, and is a frequent speaker at other gatherings under the auspices of his consultancy, The Searls Group.

Byron Sharp is professor of marketing science at the University of South Australia, and director of the University's Ehrenberg-Bass Institute, which is sponsored by many of the world's leading marketing companies (including Coca-Cola, Unilever and Nielsen), and ranked number one in the world for university research on brand management. An acclaimed academic, Byron's research into loyalty and brand performance has been published widely, and he serves on the editorial boards of seven international journals. Byron is author of the bestselling 2010 book *How Brands Grow: What marketers don't know*, and *Marketing: Theory, evidence, practice*. With Professor Jerry Wind at Wharton, he organised two conferences at the Wharton School on empirical laws concerning advertising, both of which resulted in special issues of the *Journal of Advertising Research*.

Richard Shotton is author of the bestselling 2018 book *The Choice Factory: 25 behavioural biases that influence what we buy*. He began his career 18 years ago as a media planner, and now specialises in using behavioural science to make advertising more effective.

Rich Siegel has been a copywriter for longer than he wants to admit. In addition to advertising, he has dipped his toes in movies and television, and authored three distinctly non-bestselling books. He currently blogs/vents at roundseventeen.blogspot.com.

Wiemer Snijders frequently speaks and writes about marketing science and buyer behaviour. He graduated from both university and the Academy of Arts. Wiemer is a partner at The Commercial Works, where he offers research and advisory services centred on using the fundamentals of buyer behaviour to make marketing more effective – and simpler. He works with clients in direct and indirect channel consumer goods and services in a variety of countries.

Rory Sutherland is the vice chairman of Ogilvy, where he has worked since 1988. This attractively vague job title has allowed him to form a behavioural science practice within the agency whose job is to uncover the hidden business and social possibilities which emerge when you apply creative minds to the latest thinking in psychology and behavioural science.

Brandon Towl is CEO and head writer for Words Have Impact, a firm that specialises in content strategy and production, creative copywriting and thought leadership. He earned his PhD in Philosophy-Neuroscience-Psychology from Washington University in St Louis in 2008, and taught courses in cognitive science and neuroscience research methods for many years before moving into the private sector.

Sue Unerman is chief transformation officer at MediaCom, the largest media agency in the UK, where she drives transformation and change for clients. She was included in the inaugural FT Heroes list for women who have championed gender equality at work, and nominated as one of the Female Lead's 20 in data. Sue is the author of two books, *The Glass Wall: success strategies for women at work – and businesses that mean business*, and *Tell the Truth: Honesty is your most powerful marketing tool*. She blogs for *Campaign* magazine and at www.sueunerman.com.

Robert van Ossenbruggen is a partner at The Commercial Works. Robert has a background in psychology, methodology and marketing. After leading the methodology department of a large Dutch research agency, Robert started as an independent marketing intelligence professional in 2004. Today, he supports brands working in an evidence-based way, and teaches at several business schools and industry bodies.

Ryan Wallman is an internationally acclaimed copywriter, and currently associate creative director at Wellmark, an Australian healthcare communications agency. Ryan is probably better known for his satirical work, and has twice been listed in Business Insider's 'Best 30 people in advertising to follow on Twitter'.

Kate Waters is one of the founders and the chief strategy officer of Now Advertising. She has worked in marketing communications for over 20 years, in advertising, direct/digital and PR, and on award-winning campaigns across multiple sectors. Kate is a passionate advocate for effectiveness in the industry.

Amy Wilson is a senior marketing scientist at the Ehrenberg-Bass Institute for Marketing Science, University of South Australia. With a background in psychology and marketing, and a passion for health behaviour change, Amy's research investigates how marketing, particularly advertising and communications, can be used to facilitate healthier decision making and behaviour. Amy works on cross-disciplinary industry and academic projects, has published in various high quality marketing and health journals, and co-authored the social marketing chapter in *Marketing: theory, evidence, practice.*

Faris and **Rosie Yakob** are co-founders of Genius Steals, the nomadic strategy and innovation consultancy. Faris is the author of the 2015 book *Paid Attention: Innovative advertising for a digital world.* Faris and Rosie write, speak and consult for companies all over the world. Their newsletter, *Strands of (Stolen) Genius,* was named one of seven must-read emails 'for the curious creative'.